MW01200894

Modifying and Scratch-Building O-Gauge 'Streets Vehicles

Improving and Building SuperStreets and E-Z Street Cars, Buses, and Trucks

H. Lee Willis

Printed by CreateSpace

H. Lee Willis
Cary, NC

ISBN-13: 978-1502390417
ISBN-10: 1502390418

Preface

'Streets – Williams By Bachmann's E-Z Street and its progenitor, K-Line's SuperStreets – are delightful systems of operating roadway that perfectly fit into the spirit of O-gauge model railroading. But only three different trucks, a single style of bus, and one car are available to run on these roads. Each is sold in many colors and trim variations, but that does not change the fact that there are only five basic types of vehicles to run on 'Streets roadways.

In late 2005 I began converting 1:50, 1:48, and 1:43-scale die-cast model cars, buses, and trucks to operate on 'Streets roads, in order to get a wider range and more realistic model cars, trucks and buses to run alongside my toy trains. Most of the cars worked well. A few did not. But none of the buses and large trucks I attempted to make ran well. Some didn't work at all. I began what can only be described as a research and development program to discover why what worked worked, why what didn't didn't, and how I could improve my conversions to get what I wanted. Over time I learned how to improve designs until I had a very wide range of realistic model cars, buses, trucks and tractor trailers driving around my layout. This book explains what I learned and how I build these models.

An earlier book, *'Streets for O-Gauge Model Railroads,* covered the basics of roadway and vehicles and how to use and care for them. Its final chapter presented a number of projects that readers could do that would change the look of 'Streets vehicles, broadening the range of vehicle types and looks that they could run on their layout. But I set down three criteria for projects in that earlier book: no disassembly of vehicles could be needed, no power tools could be required, and "advanced modeling skills" could not be necessary. While some of those projects produced very different-looking vehicles, those criteria severely limited what could be done.

There are no such limits here. Every project in this book requires disassembly of 'Streets and die-cast vehicles; one cannot do a conversion without that. And while strictly speaking no projects *require* power tools, when used correctly they reduce the time required and result in better work. Opinions will vary on what "advanced modeling skills" are, but most readers will likely agree they are needed for some of the more involved projects in Chapters 7, 8, and 9.

The chapters in this book fall into two categories. Chapters 1, 2, 5 and 6 present information and "theory" about 'Streets vehicle design and construction needed to understand why some methods work and some do not. They are positioned within the book where their information is first needed. For example, Chapter 1 discusses how to disassemble 'Streets vehicles. That is necessary for every project, so it leads off the book. All projects also require that flanged metal wheels be added to the diecast model being converted, so Chapter 2 discusses a number of issues that that revolve, so to speak, around 'Streets wheels. Chapters 5 and 6 discuss problems one encounters only with longer and larger vehicles, such as flange binding, wheel friction, working with multiple axles, how to assure adequate power and traction, and control of weight distribution in larger vehicles. Therefore, those two chapters are located in the middle of the book, just before the chapters on long, large, and heavy vehicles.

Chapters 3, 4, 7, 8, and 9 present projects organized as much as possible in order of vehicle size and project complexity. Cars, pickups and smaller vehicles are covered in Chapters 3 and 4. Large trucks, buses, and tractor trailers are covered in Chapters 7, 8, and 9 respectively. Each chapter gives at least one and usually several step-by-step project descriptions, along with summaries of additional projects to illustrate important concepts and alternative possibilities.

Safety is a concern every reader is urged to keep in mind. Something as innocuous as a pin vise drill may look harmless, but it can inflict a nasty, deep cut if misused. Care – beginning with just thinking ahead at each step and asking "What could do wrong? – is perhaps the most important thing when working with both small and large tools, including particularly power tools. Safety goggles or glasses are recommended when working with files and power tools (including the Dremel rotary tool) which have unpredictable ways of scattering small metal particles at high speeds in odd directions, including right back at a person who is often trying to eyeball a particular operation from only a few inches away. A disposable dust mask is a good idea when working with sanders or grinders that may create dust, too.

Cost will also be a concern to many readers, and to the extent possible this book includes projects for every budget. Projects in Chapter 3 in particular are designed for economy; the Brinks armored car presented there requires only a 'Streets bus, a third of a six-dollar sheet of thin styrene, and some shop materials. Chapter 9's lead project – the Easy & Inexpensive Tractor Trailer – requires only a 'Streets panel van, a fifteen dollar die-cast toy, some discarded scrap, and glue and paint.

At the opposite end of the cost spectrum, conversions of scale buses and tractor trailers often start with a die-cast model costing over $100 and require up to $180 in additional parts, so a few models in this book will cost over $300 to complete. Readers must judge for themselves which models are worth the cost and the time. Cost can be reduced by foraging for free materials to use, and shopping for bargains. Frankly that is part of the fun, too.

Finally, while readers certainly can follow the book's step-by-step projects to complete exact duplicates of the models converted here, my intention is for this book to inspire readers to apply their creativity and imagination to "departing from the script." Many model tractor trailers, cars and buses other than those covered here can be converted using the same techniques interpreted and adjusted for the unique dimensions and features of those models – readers can pick what *they* want on *their* layout. And while one can copy exactly the Brinks armored car in Chapter 2, with some changes it could be made into an awesome SWAT team truck or an army field reconnaissance car, and the basic idea behind its construction could be applied to the panel van, too. Readers are encouraged to build on what is presented here, to branch out as they want. That is the real message of this book: If no one has ever done if before, it might be fun to try.

H. Lee Willis
November 2014

Table of Contents

Introduction and Basic Reference Information

1

This book covers modification and scratch-building of vehicles for ‘O-gauge model roadways made with the K-Line and Lionel SuperStreets and Williams by Bachmann E-Z Street product lines – what the author refers to simply as ’Streets. Since this model roadway system was first put on the market, a number of different toy buses, trucks, and cars have been produced to run on it. They provide a lot of fun and have made ’Streets very popular.

But despite more than a decade of growing ’Streets popularity, there are only five basic types of vehicles available, many looking more like toys than models. Techniques and projects presented in this book can help model railroaders increase both the variety of vehicle types running on their layouts, and the realism of traffic on their roadways. The projects are fun, too, and produce great results as can be seen in Figure 1.

The modification and scratch-building techniques covered here were developed by the author, who is entirely self-taught as far as ’Streets is concerned. In many cases the methods presented were conceived after a good deal of experimentation and trial and error. Where possible an explanation is given as to why a particular method is used and what potential mistakes it is trying to avoid, but readers should understand that what is presented will sometimes not be the only way, and perhaps not even the best way, possible. But in every case what is shown does work, and was the method used to produce the models shown.

Figure 1: Only a few of the ‘Streets vehicles covered in this book.

This is a companion volume to 'Streets *for O-Gauge Model Railroads* which covers the set-up and use of 'Streets roadway pieces and power supplies, and the operation, servicing and repair of 'Streets vehicles. In its final chapter that book presents a series of easy-to-do customization projects aimed at changing the appearance of standard 'Streets vehicles in order to help create a wider range of "looks" to the vehicles running on a layout. But those projects were deliberately limited to those that could be done without dis-assembly and with only modest modeling skills.

This book picks up where that earlier book left off. Projects covered here *do* require disassembly and some degree of model-making skill. Descriptions and step-by-step outlines of projects assume basic workshop and model-making skills. For example, readers are expected to know how to cut metal, plastic, and wood safely and cleanly, how to prepare metal and plastic for repainting, and how to use various glues, cements, and epoxies; how to cut, how to paint, and how to glue are not explained.

Similarly, while step-by-step project discussions explain what and how power tools were used, they assumed the reader understands these tools, and knows how to operate them effectively – and safely. *If in doubt: read the instructions!*

Gradually Increasing Complexity: Projects in the final chapters of this book require far more work and more modeling skills than those in earlier chapters. Also, later chapters assume familiarity with techniques and methods described in step-by-step detail earlier and do not go over those details again. For these reasons, readers should read or at least scan the book through before jumping into projects in the final two or three chapters.

Cost of Completed Models: Projects covered here will cost from about $60 to nearly $300 to complete. Many require a die-cast, tinplate, or plastic model – the vehicle to be converted to 'Streets – and many need one or more standard 'Streets vehicles to provide a "donor chassis." Larger vehicles require parts from additional 'Streets vehicles. An eighteen-wheeler requires five axle-wheel sets and perhaps heavy-duty motors to handle its size and weight. Cost breakdowns for selected projects covered in this book are shown in Table 1.

Table 1: Cost of Some Projects

Item	Cost
Armored Bank Delivery Car (Chapter 2)	
K-Line Shorty-Bus NIB + shipping	$54
Plastic sheet, glue, paint	~$6
Total	$60
1950 Ford sedan scale model (Chapter 3)	
American Heritage model, '50 Ford	$25
WBB E-Z Street sedan	$53
Shipping for both	$8
Total	$86
Greyhound Scenicruiser (Chapter 6)	
Corgi model, Scenicruiser	$89
WBB panel van (1.5 required)*	$95
Upgraded motor	$24
Shipping for all	$15
Total	$216
Union Pacific Eighteen-Wheeler (Chapter 7)	
SpecCast Model, UP tractor trailer	$54
WBB panel van (2.5 required)*	$157
Upgraded motor	$24
Shipping for all	$10
Total	$245

*The three-axle bus and the five-axle tractor trailer share the parts of one sixty-three dollar panel van: needing a total of eight axles between them.

Tools Used

A variety of standard shop tools are used including various types of pliers and cutters, wire-insulation strippers, small hand files, drill bits, and so on. (Figure 2).

An X-Acto knife, particularly with a #11 blade for cutting and scoring sheet styrene, is perhaps the author's most often-used tool (Figure 3). Quality varies greatly among available blade holders and it is worth paying a bit more for one that locks securely and does not allow the blade to gradually work loose.

Pin-vise mini drill (Figure 3) and bits of 1/32 up to 3/32 inch are needed to start holes (later enlarged with other drills) at just the right location, and for drilling holes as small as .03 inches. Nearly all drilling is done manually.

Screwdrivers warrant special mention. Figure 4 shows several used frequently in projects covered here. Phillips head sizes: #1, 0, 00, 000 and others may be needed. In a few cases, such as in the interior of the WBB sedan or on the motor-gear-sub-frame of any plastic 'Streets chassis, the screws are not much larger than those found on eyeglasses and require a 000 driver. A small slot-type screwdriver is also used, sometimes to unfasten screws, but more often as a small lever to pry tight-fitting parts from one another, as well as for other purposes.

Larger screws are encountered when disassembling 'Streets vehicles and die-cast model cars and trucks prior to conversion. They usually have heads of 3/16 or 1/8 diameter (#0 or #1 screwdriver), and some are often made of softer metal than might be desired. It is easy to knobble the screw slots if one does not both use the correct-size screwdriver and apply plenty of downward pressure on the screw when first breaking it loose.

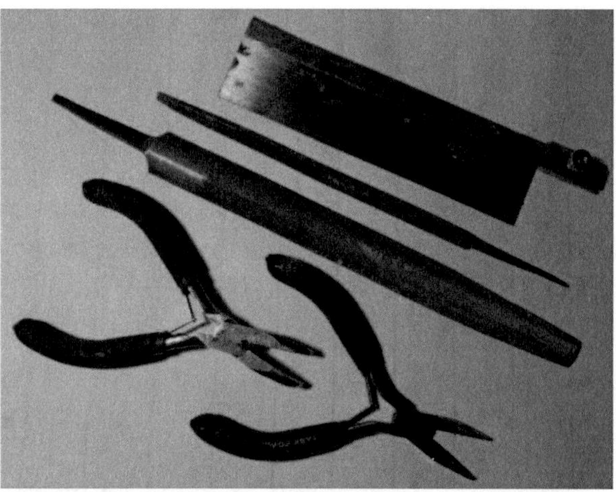

Figure 2: Standard shop tools like these and others are useful for the projects discussed in this book.

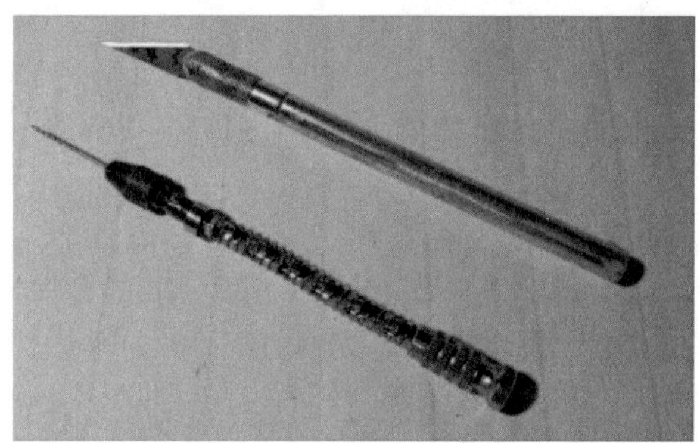

Figure 3: Pin vise drill and X-Acto knife with a #11 blade are both just about indispensable for many projects.

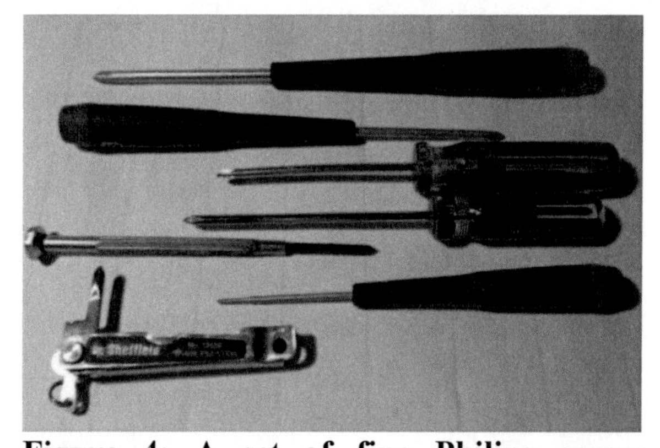

Figure 4: A set of fine Philips screw drivers is a necessity. Some projects require three or four sizes from 0000 to 1. Other drivers including flat and triangle-heads may be needed for die-cast models.

Glues and Cements (Figure 5) include Duco General Purpose Cement (green tube) and Plastruk General Purpose Plastic Welder (orange label, not white), as well as white general purpose or yellow wood glue. Duco and Plastruk are applied where and as experienced modelers would expect. The white or yellow glue is used only as gap filler in some projects, as will be described later in the book.

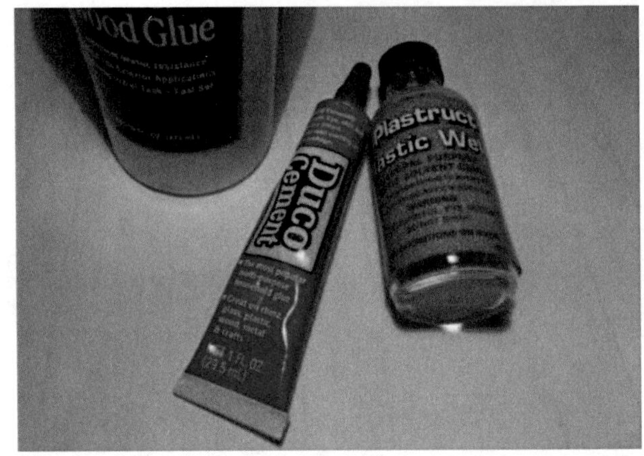

Figure 5: Duco general-purpose cement and Plastruk Plastic Welder.

Loctite Epoxy Repair Putty (Figure 6) is used extensively to bond parts together, mold new mounting towers and tabs, and so on. Some projects require nearly a full tube. Chapters 3 and 4 will explain both why and how it is used. There are other options that might work as well, such as JB Weld, but the author has not used them and cannot verify that they work similarly.

Body Filler. Roughly a third of the projects in this book will require "body work" on metal or plastic models. The *non-mixable* type of Bondo glazing putty (Figure 6) works very well for these purposes and is used in all cases.

Figure 6: Bondo non-mixable filler spot putty and Loctite Repair Putty.

Sandpaper is used for both rough work, such as shaving down the dimensions of cut plastic or metal pieces, and for smoothing edges and finishing "bodywork" on model vehicles. The author prefers wet-dry paper, in a variety of grits from #80 to #800 (Figure 7).

Paint and primer. Rust-Oleum Gray Auto Primer (Figure 7) and Rustoleum paints in "rattle cans," are most often used in those projects where models have to be repainted. Testors brush-on enamels are used exclusively for trim and small parts.

Painters tape (Figure 7) is used for more than just painting. It is often applied to the entire outside of a model during conversion in order to protect it from scratches and abrasions it might receive during handling and modification.

Figure 7: Sandpaper, painters tape, and Rust-Oleum Gray Auto Primer.

Bench Power Tools

All projects in this book can be completed with manual handheld tools. However, the following tools reduce the time required, produce cleaner, more precise work, and are potentially safer to use if handled properly.

Dremel rotary tool and solder gun (Weller 260/200-watt) are the only handheld power tools the author uses (Figure 8). Dremel high-speed cutters # 115 and 99 (Figure 9) are indispensable for cutting out interior obstructions in die-cast bodies, and other purposes.

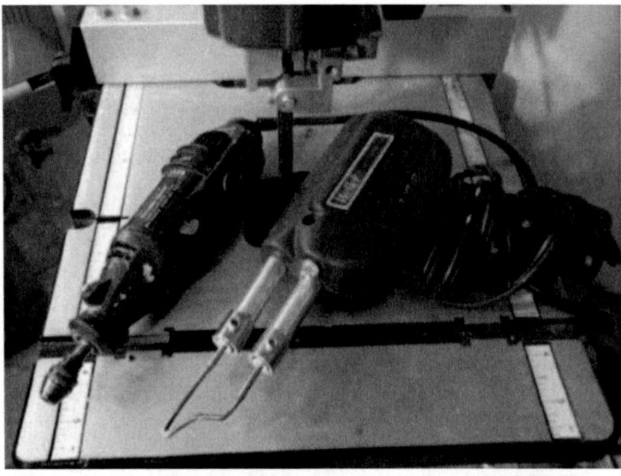

Figure 8: Dremel rotary tool and Weller 260/200-watt solder gun are power tools used quite often in projects covered here.

Band-saw (Figure 8). The 59.5-inch bench blade band-saw shown is fitted with a 24-tooth-per-inch blade that cuts most die-cast metal bodies easily, and slices through plastic cleanly.

Figure 9: Dremel high-speed cutters # 115 (left) and #199 (right).

Bench belt sander (Figure 10). Heavy-handed use can ruin a model quickly. But when used with forethought and a light touch, it can trim pieces to precise lines, smooth edges, and square pieces to the dimensions needed, etc.

Drill press (Figure 10) makes drilling more precise. However, a hand pin-vise is used to start all holes that are drilled, without exception.

Figure 10: Bench band saw, belt sander, and drill press together cost less than two 'Streets RTR sets but are so very useful. While it is possible to do all projects in this book with handheld tools, these three make work faster and more precise. The author thinks that when these tools are used safely, there is slightly less risk of injury and damage to models than would be the case if he were using only manual tools.

Summary: Types of Vehicles

Only five types of vehicles have been made for 'Streets, most in many different colors and trim variations.

Generic Panel Van (Figure 11) is a 1:48 model of a mid-nineties panel van with a mixture of Dodge, Ford, and Chevy features. It was made as a track-inspection vehicle prior to 2004 with an extremely heavy metal chassis and in slight variations from 2005 onward with a lighter plastic chassis. Lionel produced a TMCC version in 2010. All versions have the same die-cast metal one-piece body and an opaque plastic window insert: these are the only 'Streets vehicles without an interior. All also have a cast-in tab on the rear bumper for a trailer hook and wheels oversized for them from a model standpoint. The WBB version produced since 2012 has improved center pick-sups and is arguably the most dependable 'Streets vehicle ever made.

Its wheels have a diameter of 18.5 millimeters: a scale 31 (1:43) or 35 inches (1:48) – suitable for medium or small heavy trucks.

Delivery Step-Van (Figure 12) is a 1:48 model of a Morgan Olson P-1000 delivery step van body as used by Federal Express, UPS, and so on. The best version of this model was produced from 2005-2006. It had larger wheels and lever-action center pickups. From 2007 slightly smaller wheels and the somewhat more delicate spring-arm center pickups were used. Lionel produced a TMCC version in 2010.

All versions have a plastic chassis. It is the longest and the heaviest standard 'Streets vehicle. At its widest – across its side-view mirrors – the step-van is wider than a 'Streets roadway lane. It cannot pass itself or the school bus in an immediately adjacent lane without knocking off its mirrors.

The step van has a full interior including driver and rear cab wall, but the rear "box" is empty.

Early versions had 21.5 millimeter diameter wheels, a scale 36 (1:43) or 40 (1:48) inches (buses, large trucks). Versions after 2006 had the same wheels as the panel van.

Figure 11: The panel van is 110 mm long by 45 mm wide by 47 mm high. It has a 67 mm wheelbase and weighs from 7 to 13 oz. depending on the version.

Figure 12: The step van is 131mm long by 51 mm wide by 65 mm high. It has an 80 mm wheelbase and weighs 13 oz. It is the largest 'Streets vehicle ever made.

Vintage Truck (Figure 13), produced from 2005 to 2010, is representative of a 1934 Ford medium truck. It has a two-piece die-cast body with an interior with driver and a plastic stake-bed mounted on its metal body. The vintage truck has the smallest wheels, but the longest wheelbase of all 'Streets vehicles, yet it is by far the lightest 'Streets vehicle. It can be challenged for traction and benefits from an ounce or two of weight placed in its load bed.

Its wheels have a diameter of 15.25 mm: a scale twenty-six (1:43) or twenty-nine inches (1:48) – as for automobiles and small pickup trucks.

School Bus, produced from 2005 to 2010, is a 1:48 scale model of a traditional American school bus as made by Bluebird or IC Bus, except it is very short (Figure 14). It has a plastic chassis and a full interior with driver and two rows of seats. It has by far the largest wheels of any 'Streets vehicles, but the shortest wheelbase, which makes it a good runner through curves.

Its outer wheels have a diameter of 23 mm: a scale 36 (1:43) or 40 inches (1:48) – suitable for very large buses and trucks.

Sedan (Figure 15) is a 1:48-scale four-door automobile that has styling features reminiscent of cars produced from 1950 to 1980. It was introduced in late 2012 and is offered in police and taxi versions with blackwall "tires" and in civilian versions in several colors with whitewall tires. Unlike previous 'Streets vehicles, it has a heavy metal chassis (with an adjustable wheelbase) and uses a lightweight plastic body. The car has an interior with steering wheel and dashboard but no driver (the author added that in the photo) but only for the front seat. It has frosted windows in the rear.

Figure 13: The vintage truck is 127 mm long by 45 mm wide by 47 mm high. It has a 80 mm wheelbase and weighs just 5.5 oz.

Figure 14: Shorty school bus is 102 mm long by 50 mm wide by 63 mm high. It has a 63 mm wheelbase and weighs 9.7 oz.

Figure 15: The sedan is 117 mm long by 43 mm wide by 37 mm high. The wheelbase is 69 mm, adjustable by +/- 10 mm. It weighs just 7 oz. Author added driver figure.

Removing the Bodies

Depending on the vehicle type, the body and chassis are held together by between one and three screws that fasten through the underside of the chassis. These screws are located near the front and rear of the vehicle (red arrows in Figures 16-19). ***Do not loosen the two screws near the center of vehicles with a plastic chassis (yellow arrows in Figures).*** They hold the motor-frame to the chassis and it is difficult to re-align them once loosened. On the school bus, step van, and sedan, between one and six screws must be loosened in order to remove the interior, which is necessary to gain access to rectifier, wiring, motor, and pickup leads underneath. The panel van has no interior, and that in the vintage truck is press-fit into the upper body and comes off with it. It can be pried out if needed.

Figure 16: School bus body is held to the chassis by two screws mounted just ahead of the front axle. Once they are removed, the front of the chassis can be pulled up and forward a bit, pulling a tab loose at the rear (green arrow) and, freeing the chassis. Interior removes from chassis with one screw, located in the interior floor near the back.

Figure 17: Panel van is the most difficult to dis-assemble. The two rear screws on the panel van remove easily, but the front screw is is located *under* the front center-rail roller pickup. Car must be taken since that pickup is both delicate and has a wire attached. On the WBB versions, a small screw in the base of the lever-arm pickup assembly unfastens, and the base pulls off a small locator peg that fits in a hole in that base. The whole assembly can then be pushed aside enough to get at the front mounting screw. On earlier versions (photos above) two tiny screws (white arrows) must be removed from the end of the spring arm and mounting tower and pushed aside: the screw is in a well behind the mounted tower. Once that screw is removed the body simply "falls off."

Figure 18: Step-van and Sedan are the similar: three screws are removed and the body can be pulled straight up and away from the chassis.

The interior in each must be removed once the body has been taken off in order to get at the machinery and wiring. Interior in the sedan is two pieces held on by six screws (Figure 28, in a few pages, gives details). The interior in the van is one-piece and has a single screw.

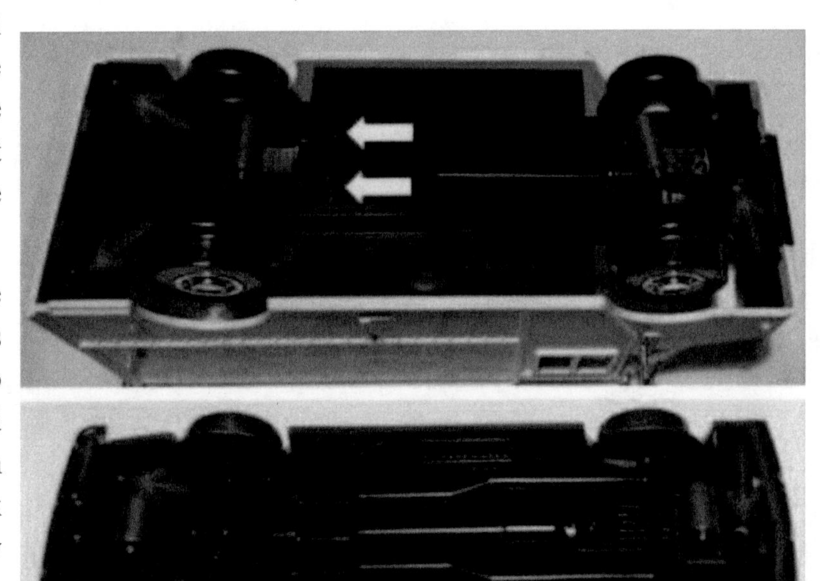

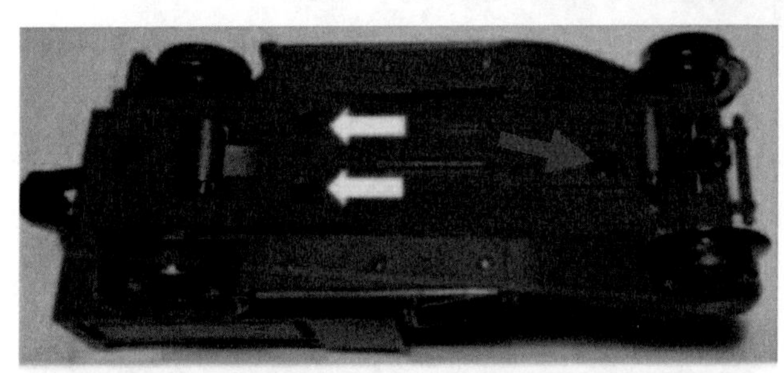

Figure 19: Vintage truck has only one screw (red arrow) that must be removed in order to separate the truck's body from its chassis. Once that is done the lower portion of the body (fenders and running boards) and the chassis are removed from the upper body as a unit, by pulling them up at the front and then forward, freeing a tab from the lower body that fits into a slot in the back of the upper body piece (white arrow). The chassis is then removed from the lower body in the same fashion (yellow arrow points to that tab and slot).

.

Interior is press-fit into the upper body and can just be left in it until re-assembly

Two Types of Chassis

Two types of chassis are used for 'Streets vehicles the *plastic chassis* which always has a metal body, and the *metal chassis,* which to date has always had a plastic body attached.

The Plastic Chassis: Details

The plastic chassis is the original SuperStreets chassis and was the only type used for the first decade of production. It is still in use by WBB, in the generic panel van. Manufactured in slightly different lengths and with different sizes of wheels, it was used for four vehicle types: the generic panel van, the '34 Ford medium truck, the postal/delivery step van, and the short school bus. Although of different lengths and appearance, etc., all of these vehicles basically have the same chassis and interior layout.

Figure 20 shows a typical plastic chassis, this taken from the delivery step-van truck. The chassis itself is one piece, made out of a flexible hard plastic or rubber-like material which does not meld well with most plastic cements and adhesives but bonds well but not exceptionally to epoxies and with ccyanoacrylate. In all plastic chassis, the rear axle is powered by a small motor mounted longitudinally (Figure 21).

Figure 20: The plastic chassis and the various components mounted on and in it.

Electrical pickup on the plastic chassis is made from all four wheels and two center-rail roller pickups mounted underneath the body. Power from the track is fed to a bridge (full-wave) rectifier and from there to the DC motor: the positive terminal is on the vehicle's left (passenger's) side and the negative on the right (driver's side.)

Electrical contact at the front axle on all plastic chassis is made with the front-axle contact brush (Figure 22) which fits under a small plastic retainer plate that holds the front axle and that brush in place. The retainer is held to the chassis by two screws.

Figure 22: Front-axle contact brush and the plate that holds it and the front axle in place.

The motor-gearbox-rear axle is held in a plastic sub-frame mounted to the chassis by two screws from underneath (Figure 21) and a small tab in the back end of the gearbox that fits into a slot in the chassis. Removing the screws releases the assembly. There are six screws on the underside of the sub-frame that cannot be reached until it is removed from the chassis. Two hold the motor (Figure 23) and four the gearbox. The motor's screws can be removed and the motor worked out of the gearbox. If the four screws for the gearbox are removed the gearbox will release and free the rear axle.

Figure 21: The motor-gearbox-axle assembly releases with the removal of two screws (see Figure 2). On its underside are screws that hold the motor (yellow arrows) and gearbox (red arrows) to the assembly frame.

Figure 23: The vintage truck uses the motor on the left; all others use the motor on the right. Both types have a press-fit brass worm gear on the front shaft, no flywheel, and a mounting plate held to the front face by two machine screws. The larger one has a motor body exactly 1 inch long.

Figure 24 shows the two axles. Each has two thin nylon washers that fit between wheel and chassis to reduce friction. The rear axle has sintered metal bearings that fit into recesses in the chassis made to hold them. This particular chassis had one traction tire. Some 'Streets vehicles have none, and a very small number had two. There seems to be no pattern to which vehicles have them and which don't: the author has otherwise identical vehicles with one, two, and no traction tires. Generally 'Streets vehicles don't need traction tires in order to run well unless pulling a trailer. Those with none have noticeably better electrical connectivity that contributes to smoother running but don't climb quite as well.

The two center-rail electrical pickups are mounted under the axles. Most plastic-chassis vehicles use the spring-arm type rollers shown in Figure 25. The front and rear are similar, but *not* the same part. They have slightly different mounting hole locations, as shown. The rear pickup mounts from the top of the chassis, the front to a small tower that projects down from the chassis, and in front of the front axle. WBB panel vans use lever-arm pickups (Figure 26) instead.

Figure 24: The axles all have metal wheels press-fit onto them. Plastic hubcaps are fit into recesses in the wheels. Both axles have nylon washer/spacers that fit between chassis edge and wheels (red arrow). The rear axle has a gear to engage the motor's worm gear (green arrows), and two sintered metal bearings that fit into slots in the chassis and to carry the axle (yellow arrow points to one).

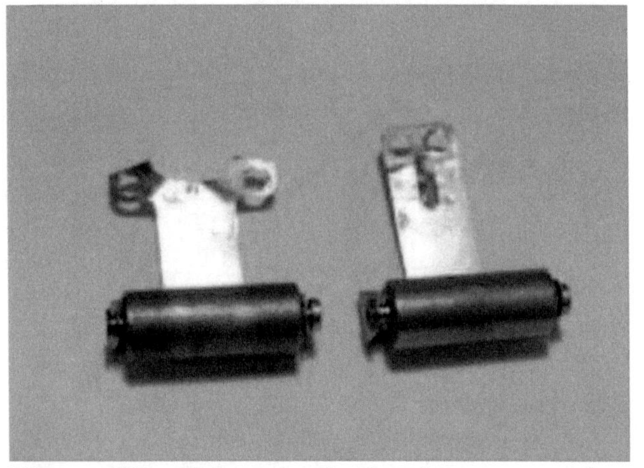

Figure 25: Although similar in construction the front and rear rollers on plastic chassis are of two types, as shown.

Figure 26: When it began producing the new E-Z Street product line, Williams by Bachman replaced the spring-arm rollers (Figure 7) on the plastic chassis with small lever action rollers shown here. They work much better, in the author's opinion justifying the slightly higher price Bachman charges for their versions.

The Metal Chassis: Details

The metal chassis (Figure 27) was first used by Williams by Bachmann (WBB) for its sedan which debuted in late 2013. The layout of major parts is identical to that of the plastic chassis. The rear axle is powered by the same longitudinal motor as in the generic panel van, located in the same place. There are center pickups front and rear. There is the same rectifier, mounted in a circular recess in the same location, and wired in exactly the same way. But there are differences, the biggest being that the chassis is metal, weighing 6.0 ounces.

The chassis is disassembled in the same way as the plastic chassis is, the only differences being:

- The interior (Figure 28) consists of two plastic pieces - a dashboard and a front seat - that are held to the chassis by six small screws.
- The two gearbox mounting screws are mounted on the top, not accessed from underneath.
- The wires to the motor fit into recesses in the metal chassis.

Figure 27: The metal chassis and the various components mounted on and in it.

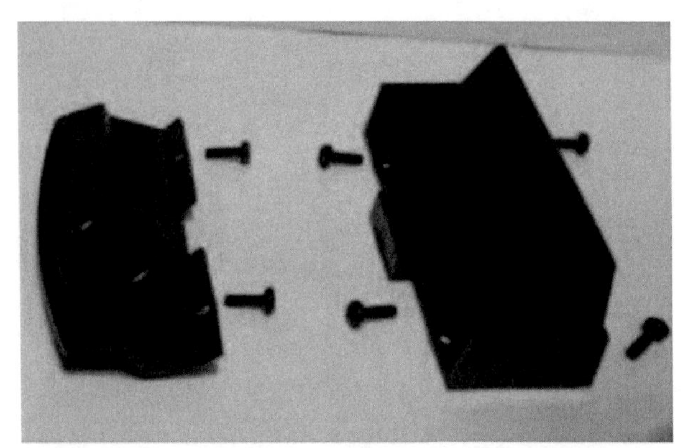

Figure 28: The dashboard and bench seat are mounted to the rear part of the chassis with two and four screws respectively.

A unique feature of the metal chassis is its adjustability. It is cast in two parts that can be moved back and forth to adjust the wheelbase to between 2 11/32 inches and 3 5/32 inches. As delivered with the sedan it is set to 2 11/32 inches. A series of teeth molded into the two parts locks them in place with two machine screws (Figure 29).

Chassis connected to outer rails. The metal chassis holds both axles, which are also made of metal. This means that all - chassis, axles and wheels - are electrically connected to the outer rails when the vehicle is running. So there is no need for the front axle brush as in the plastic chassis. But both center pickups have to be electrically insulated from the chassis. The pickups are telescoping types that move straight up and down with a small spring to provide pressure to keep them in contact with the rail. They are mounted inside insulating plastic boxes that fit through the chassis (Figure 30). The roller projects out the bottom to make contact with the center rail and the frame sticks out on the top where a red wire is attached to route power to the rectifier (see Figure 27).

One Traction Tire. All metal-chassis vehicles the author has seen have a single traction tire on the right (passenger's) side of the rear axle, as can be seen in Figure 30.

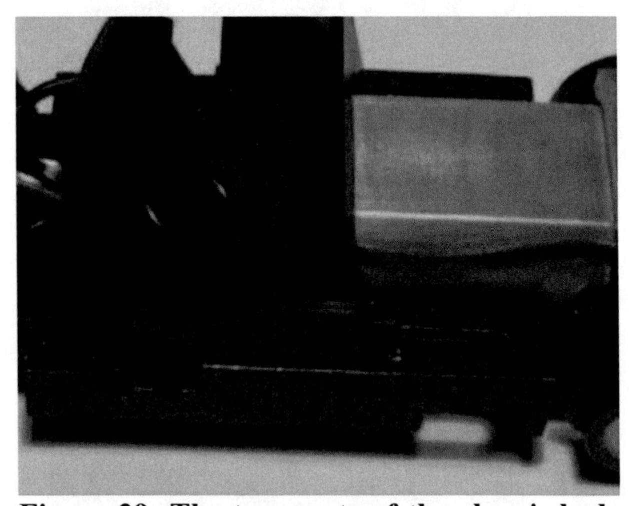

Figure 29: The two parts of the chassis lock into place with a set of teeth on each side as seen in the photo above, and are held in place by a machine screw on each side. Note the interior mounted in this photo.

Figure 30: The center pickups telescope within a plastic box mounted through square holes in the chassis – at the rear located just behind the gears, and in front just ahead of the front axle.

Removing the Rectifier

'Streets vehicles come with a rectifier installed:

- They run on AC or DC power (0-18 volts).
- They run only forward, regardless if AC or the polarity of the DC power fed them.

Many owners remove the rectifier and wire the motor directly to the power leads from the rails. The vehicles will then run only on DC but they will run backwards if polarity is reversed. The ability to put the cars into reverse adds a new operating dimension.

The rectifier is in the same location and wired identically in all 'Streets vehicles, regardless of what type, when built, or who built them. It is recessed in a cup molded into the middle of the chassis (Figure 32). Power from the track, whether AC or DC, flows into the rectifier from a red wire (front and rear center pickups) and a black wire connecting it to the axles/wheels/outer rails. DC power leaves the rectifier on a red wire (positive, on the left – passenger – side). See Figure 31.

Figure 31: Rectifier has four leads. Front and rear wires are respectively the red outer- and black inner-rail inputs feeds from the road. Upper (red, positive DC) and lower (black, negative) are DC output.

Figure 32: The WBB sedan chassis is laid out like all 'Streets vehicles. Regardless of type, the rectifier always sits in a small cup-like depression molded into the chassis in the center near the front. The major difference among chassis is that on the sedan chassis, which is metal, the chassis, gearbox and motor case are "grounded" – electrically connected – to its wheels and axles and thus to the outer rails. All other vehicles types have a plastic insulating chassis.

Step 1: Remove the body, and if necessary the interior from the vehicle to get at the rectifier.

Step 2: Cut all four wires attached to rectifier as close as possible to the rectifier (Figure 33).

Step 3: Remove the rectifier. Usually it pops right out but on some old K-Line models it has to be pried out.

Step 4: Strip away the shrink-fit insulating sheath from each of the three leads that had it (the double red does not on most models).

Step 5: Connect and solder the red leads that went to the rectifier together, Connect and solder the black wires that ran to it together.

Step 6: Test the new connections by holding the vehicle down on a powered (DC) track, pushing lightly to establish contact. Make sure everything works well. Apply electrical tape to insulate all exposed wires (Figure 34).

Step 7: Reassemble the vehicle.

The vehicle will now run only on DC power but will back up if DC polarity is reversed.

Figure 33. All four leads have been cut flush at the rectifier, leaving as much of the wires as possible. No harm comes from leaving the rectifier in its place, but the author removes it anyway.

Figure 34: WBB sedan with the re-wiring completed. The rectifier has been removed, the wires soldered as indicated in the text, and the junctions taped. The vehicle will now go forward when positive DC polarity (positive on the middle rail) is fed to it, and backwards when that polarity is reversed.

Wheels and Rollers

2

A die-cast model converted to 'Streets must lose its original wheels and tires and be fitted with flanged metal wheels, otherwise it will not run on 'Streets roadway. The wheels fitted to it must be the right size. A die-cast car will need "car-size" wheels while a big rig will need much larger wheels. The "look" must be right, too. A car's tires need a "street" look if the model is to look realistic. Truck and buses tires must look like truck and bus tires. Heavy construction vehicles need "off-road" tires. This chapter looks at wheels as well as the other "road contact" equipment, the center pickups, and discusses their use in converted die-cast and scratch-built 'Streets models.

Appearance is Important and Easiest To Get Right By Using 'Streets Wheels. Wheels taken from 'Streets vehicles – whether because a 'Streets chassis is used for the conversion of a model, or because the axles are removed from that chassis and put in a scratch-built chassis – look fairly authentic, like they belong on a car, truck, or bus. They are the easiest wheels to use in a conversion.

Wheels of the right size taken from toy locomotives and rolling stock will function as well as 'Streets wheels, and can often be found by sorting through spare parts bins or buying broken locos at TCA and other swap meets. Taking that route is usually cheaper than buying new 'Streets vehicles just to take their chassis and axles. A section later in this chapter will show how to modify them so they look less train-like and more like wheels with tires – for an appearance nearly as good as 'Streets wheels.

Five different sizes of wheel have been used on 'Streets vehicles (Table 1, Figure 1). Each is unique to one type of 'Streets vehicle, except those called "panel-van wheels." While step-vans made in the first two years of production (by K-Line rather than KlbL) had larger "truck" wheels unique to those vehicles, those made after 2007 had the slightly smaller panel van-size wheels instead.

These five wheels vary in diameter from 15.25 mm (29 scale inches at 1:48 to 26 at 1:43) to 23 mm (43 and 40 inches respectively). Flanges vary slightly in both depth and angle, but not significantly. All have the same gauge, but the width from side to side varies substantially, from 38.5 mm (scale 72 or 65 inches) for the vintage truck to 46.5 mm (scale 89 or 80 inches) for the school bus. Wheels from toy trains come in just about any diameter but are usually no wider than the narrowest 'Streets axle.

Table 1: Dimensions of 'Streets Wheels

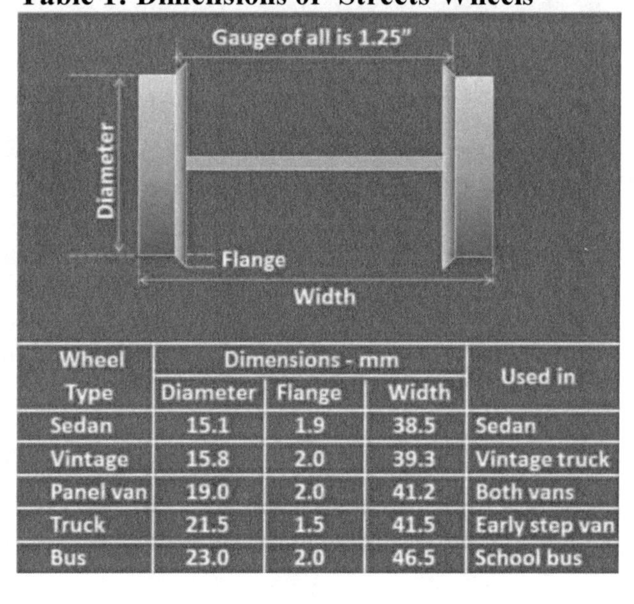

Wheel Type	Dimensions - mm			Used in
	Diameter	Flange	Width	
Sedan	15.1	1.9	38.5	Sedan
Vintage	15.8	2.0	39.3	Vintage truck
Panel van	19.0	2.0	41.2	Both vans
Truck	21.5	1.5	41.5	Early step van
Bus	23.0	2.0	46.5	School bus

Figure 1: Wheels from the five types of 'Streets chassis. They vary in diameter by nearly two to one and vary in width across the wheel outer edges by a scale eighteen inches.

Figure 2: Left: Bus wheels match the width of this New Ray 1953 Mack B-61; right, step-van wheels don't: they leave an unrealistic scale one-foot gap between tire and fender edge.

Width Matters, Too

Figure 2 shows two New Ray 1:43 Mack B-61 cabs poised above wheels taken from the K-Line/Lionel school bus (left truck) and the K-Line step-van (right truck). Either of those wheel sets has enough diameter to look good on a big-rig, but note how the bus's wheels nicely fill out the Mack's fenders out to just inside the fender, so they look quite realistic while, on the right side, the step van wheels don't. They leave an unsightly gap inside the fender – the track is far too narrow to look realistic. Readers should keep in mind that the gauge – distance between the flanges – is the same for both, as it is for all O-gauge wheel sets, at 1 ¼ inch. It is the thickness of the actual wheel, from flange to outside edge, that varies in these cases.

Figure 3: Locomotive axle originally far too narrow and too train-like in appearance, has had fiber washers glued to the sides of its metal wheels, adding a scale eight inches to its width so that it does an adequate job of "filling out" the Mack's fenders. How this was done will be shown later. A second washer could have been glued to either side to add a bit more width. That was not done here, and the hub is painted red, because this axle is destined for another project, and was used here only as an example.

Figure 3 shows a B-61 cab with a locomotive axle that has wheels about the same diameter as the school bus wheels. The axle has been widened by gluing fiber washers that are 1/16 inch thick onto its wheels, then creating a new hub, and painting it appropriately. While the look is not as authentic, it is acceptable – and this axle cost only 65 cents at a swap meet.

Width is a consideration at the other end of the vehicle-size scale, too. Sometimes with smaller or narrower cars, even if the wheels are the right size, a 'Streets or other axle is too wide, particularly if wheels have to fit inside fender skirts in a thick die-cast body. If it is a matter of only a millimeter or so, the outer edge of the wheels can be ground away so the axle will fit. However, some times there is no way to convert a small car (Figure 4). The author actually found a set of flanged wheels with a tiny enough diameter for this Mini (at a TCA show) but there is still no hope to convert it.

Figure 4: Not going to happen. This 1:43 Mini's tires fit *into* the flange grooves! Any O-gauge axle is wider than the car is!

Big Wheels Help Make a Big Truck

Figure 5 shows a Gearbox 1:43 Chevy pickup cab with different combinations of wheel size and ride height. The top two images have it atop wheels from the WBB sedan (a scale 29 inches at 1:48 or 26 inches, typical large car size, at 1:43).

The look of the cab changes depending on ride height – the space between the top of the wheel well and the top of the tire. With the chassis mounted so the wheels are far up into the wheel wells and the gap is small, the cab looks like it is on a light pickup. If the gap is made just a bit more, as in the second image, the same wheels contribute to the look of a heavy pickup or light truck.

Larger wheels makes the cab look like it belongs on a larger truck, but this "trick" of adjusting wheel-well gap works with those, too. The bottom two images in Figure 6 show how. Depending on the fender well gap, the cab looks like it is on a medium or heavy truck.

Buses and big rigs usually need the largest wheels. Generally, cross country buses have larger wheels than city buses, and a greater wheel-well gap: city buses use smaller wheels and ride as low as practicable to reduce the step-up height for passengers who are frequently embarking and disembarking. Big rigs vary and one has to experiment with wheel size and gap size to find the best combination to give the desired look.

Figure 5: Wheels make the truck.

Use Wheels a Bit Smaller than the Model's

The eye plays tricks when looking at the wheels on 'Streets vehicles: it regards them as slightly bigger than they are. Wheels with a flange, even though it is in the back of the fender well, look a tiny bit bigger to the eye than they otherwise would. For the best look, whenever possible, modelers should pick a 'Streets wheel that is very slightly smaller than the model's original tires. A model might have tires 21 mm in diameter. The panel van's wheels (19 mm) would very likely look best on it. *Rule of thumb: when possible pick a wheel by about two to three scale inches less in diameter for the conversion.*

Center Pickups

While five different sizes of wheel have been used on 'Street vehicles, only three *types* of center pickups have been used (Figure 6): the spring-arm type (most K-line vehicles), a small lever-action one similar to those on locos and cabooses (WBB Van and all TMCC vehicles), and a telescoping model on the WBB sedans and some very early panel vans. Each type was produced is several slight variations. As examples, there are two types of spring-arm pickups (see Chapter 1, Figure 21), and the lever-action pickups on the WBB panel van are not exactly the same as the lever action rollers on Lionel TMCC vans.

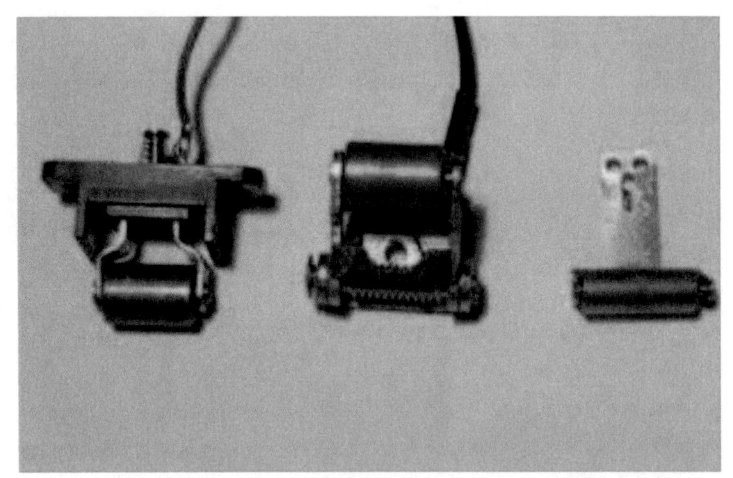

Figure 6: Left, the telescoping center pickup from the sedan. Very early (2004) metal-chassis panel vans had similar pickups. Middle, a lever-action pickup from the WBB van, early step-vans, and Lionel TMCC vehicles is like those on modern O-gauge locomotives. Right, a spring-arm roller pickup from K-Line and K-Line by Lionel non-TMCC models works well if correctly adjusted but is much more delicate than the others.

When scratch building a chassis, any O-gauge center rollers can potentially be fitted, although spring-pressure must be checked. Rollers taken from a ten-pound loco may have too much spring tension to be held down firmly by a nine ounce bus. Their spring pressure may push the bus's wheels right up off the roadway's rails.

A useful trick when working with either the early K-line step van or the WBB panel van is shown in Figure 7. While both have very good lever-action rollers installed at the factory, both chassis have the clearance hole and mounting screw holes cast into them for the original spring-arm-type rollers, too – all are left empty as delivered by the manufacturers. Whether on a conversion or on a stock vehicle, one can add a spring-arm pickup in its original position just ahead of the rear axle. A third roller noticeably improves the electrical connectivity at low voltages and thus slow-speed smoothness when running.

Figure 7: Salvatore Manella's Fish Co. delivery truck from Chapter 3 is built on a stock step-van chassis, but with a third center roller added to improve low-speed smoothness.

Widening Axles and Changing the Look of Train Wheels

It is possible to mount the 'Street's bus's tires outside of the rim lip that normally holds them in place, attached only to the outer part of the wheel (Figure 8). They have to be glued to the rim but they will stay put if glued well. This adds a scale fourteen inches – well over half a foot on each side – to the width of the axle, so it will now fit the very largest 1:43 truck models, such as the New Ray 1:43 Kenworth w900 – a monstrous tractor that is a scale twelve inches wider than the Mack B-61 shown earlier.

Figure 8: Bus tires have to be glued in place, and new wheel hubs made inside each tire, as shown later, so the bus axle gains width to match larger 1:43 model truck widths.

Wheels from any 'Streets vehcile other than the bus are all metal. Those, and wheels taken from locomotives or rolling stock, can be widened by gluing any of the following onto each wheel's outer side:

- Metal, fiber, or rubber washers
- Tires and wheels taken from the model or another model with the right-size tires

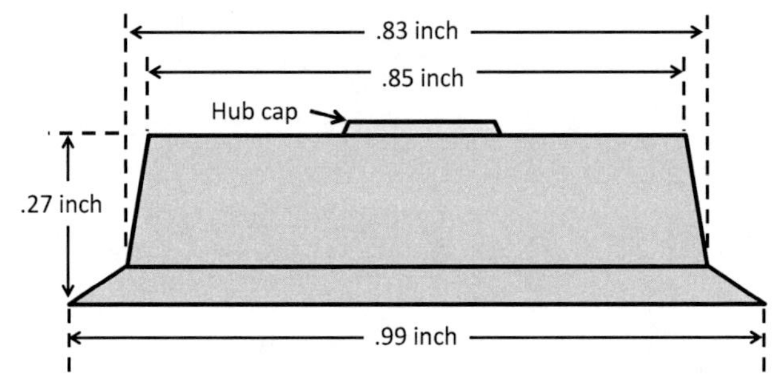

Figure 9: Dimensions of the step-van's wheels. Other 'Streets wheels, and most locomotive and rolling stock flanged wheels, are made similarly, with a noticeable taper from near the flange, where the wheel actually rolls on the rail, to the outside edge of the wheel.

'Streets wheels are tapered toward their outer edge - on the order of about 1/50 inch (½ millimeter) toward the outside as compared to near the flange (Figure 9). Further, they ride on rails raised about two one-hundredths of an inch = ½ mm, above the road surface. Therefore, a modeler adding wheel width in this way has a tolerance of about 4/100ths inch – one mm – a for the diameter that she or he must match. The washer or tire or whatever is glued on could actually be slightly wider than the wheel at its outer edge. Still, it is best from both a functional and appearance standpoints to make its diameter slightly less than the wheel. "Three-quarter inch" metal inch washers the author bought are actual .74 inch in diameter and fit the panel van wheels (.75 inch at the outside edge) quite well. It is quite easy to glue metal and fiber washers onto wheels: 3M metal adhesive works well for metal washiers, and Duco Cement works well for fiber washers. Paint thinner cleans up any excess glue for either. It can be very difficult to glue anything round so it is centered so perfectly that there is not a perceptable wobble to them as they rotate. For this reason alone, the author prefers metal washers to full disks: one can see through the washer's hole to align it with the center of the wheel to much more accurately center it.

Washers glued onto the sides of wheels will widen the wheel-axle set so it better fits a wide vehicle like a bus or big rig tractor. In cases where wheels and axles from a locomotive, toy train rolling stock, or caboose are being used, the washers may also make the wheels look much more tire-like.

Figure 10a shows a wheel and axle from a K-Line locomotive bought as spare parts at a swap meet. The inner edge, where wheels ride the rails, is slightly larger than the school bus wheels (.91 compared to .89 inch) and thus a good fit for really large trucks, but it is not nearly wide enough, and does not look particulary roadlike. In Figure 10b, a 7/8 inch fiber washer has been glued to it with Duco Cement. The cement was applied liberally to the wheel near its outer edge alongside and inside its lip. The washer was put on and centered exactly, using the hole in the washer and the axle center to align it correctly. Once the cement started to harden, any excess was carefully loosened and whiped off with paint thinner.

The center "hub area" was then gradually filled with more Duco – it was dripped a bit at a time, very carefully, and allowed to spread out into the empty space under the washer (capillary action seems to draw it in – see Figure 10c). As it draws itself inside more was added until after several of these steps the glue grabbed the inside edge of the washer's hole all around. It can be helped to cling to the washer hole's inner edge with a knife point if needed. Surface tension will then smooth out the glue's surface across "the hub" into a circularly symmetrical but slightly concave profile. It is best to do each side separately a day apart, letting the axle stay overnight with the freshly-done side upward until it hardens well.

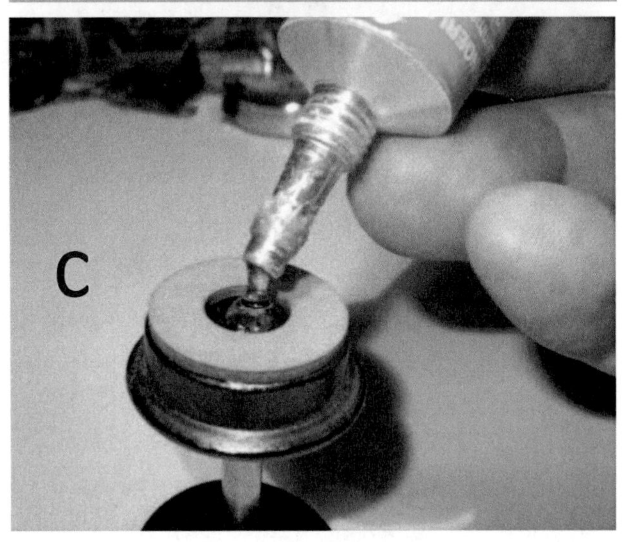

Figure 10: Washer is glued onto a locomotive wheel. See text for explanation.

Painting is best done with a wheel turning so that the paint is spread circularly. The rig shown in Figure 11 helps do this. The larger of the two parts is a wooden frame that holds seven D cells. A copper paddle connector can be inserted at the front of any battery, so as to give between 1.5 to 10.5 volts DC as needed. The switch shown on the battery frame is used to turn power flow on and off: it is not essential but nice to have.

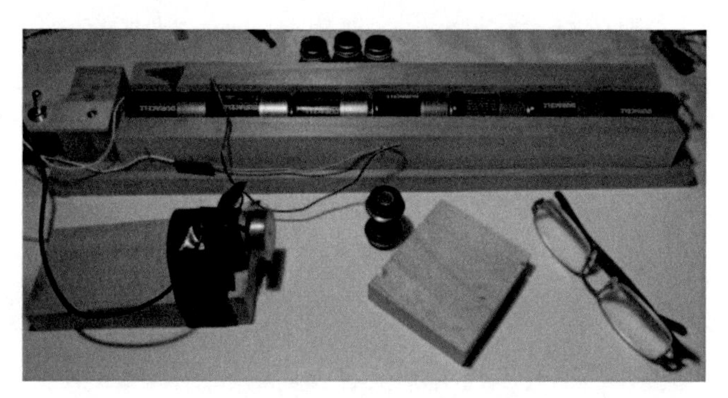

Figure 11: Machinery made to help paint wheels well. See text for explanation.

Powered axles are painted while on the vehicle by using alligator clips to connect the batteries in Figure 11 to the center pickup and a front wheel. About 4.5 to 6.0 volts works best to turn the wheels at the right speed for painting. The vehicle is held in one hand and a brush with paint on it in the other, with the brush then lightly held against the spinning wheel.

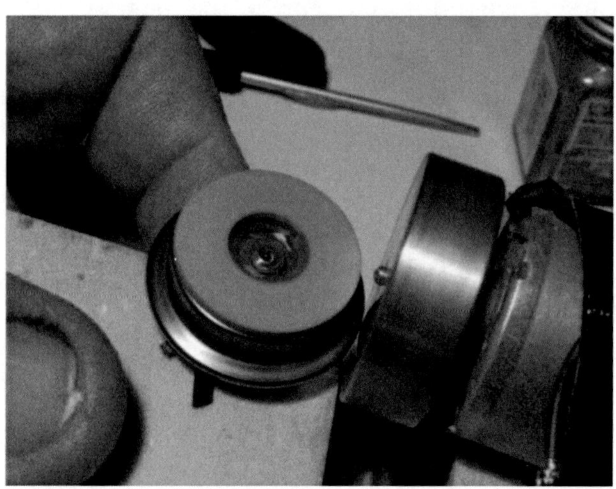

Figure 12: Unpowered axles or loose axles are pressed against the spinning flywheel to spin them. While they spin, a paintbrush is then held against them spread paint circularly.

The second device shown in Figure 11 is a large flywheel motor attached to a heavy wooden block. To paint a wheel on an unpowered axle, the motor is connected to the power (about 1.5 to 3.0 volts is all that is needed) and the opposite wheel on the axle held against the flywheel, causing the axle to spin as a brush is held to it. Wheels can be painted prior to mounting or while on the car. The wheel-axle from Figure 10 is shown being spun in Figure 12: the wooden block shown in Figure 11 has slots cut into it so axles can be held in it.

Generally it is best to paint a wheel from the inside out, a color at a time, letting each color dry before doing the next. The completed wheel from Figure 10 is shown in Figure 13. It was painted red in the center hub (covering the dried glue dripped into it in Figure 10c), silver on the inner edge of the fiber washer to simulate the steel wheel's outer trim ring, and flat black where the tire would be.

Figure 13: Completed wheel from Figure 12.

Tips on painting wheels. Painting the wheels on vehicles can contribute a lot to a realistic look (Figures 14-17). Particularly when painting the sedan wheels, note that "doggie bowl" hubcaps have a smaller diameter than the stock silver hub, and that the tire should be wider than the wheel's thin outer cast rim.

- Taxis, pickup trucks and police cars look more realistic with body-colored wheels (Figures 15 and 17).
- Light delivery trucks can have body-colored or contrasting wheels (Figure 14).
- Painting the outer wheel glossy black or body color, the center "doggie-bowl" hub-cap silver, and the "tire" portion of a wheel flat black, makes a car look like a base, economy model. Police cars also have this basic look to their wheels (Figure 15).
- A more premium look is created by painting white walls and full width silver wheel covers (Figure 16).
- Some big trucks and buses have chrome wheels: 'Streets wheels, with their shiny chrome hubs can be left as is (Figure 18).
- But many trucks have black or colored central hubs, with a silver of contrasting color rim and perhaps an inner hub painted a contrasting color (Figure 18).

Figure 14: Converted Divco milk truck looks very incomplete without these red wheels.

Figure 15: This '50 Ford unmarked police car has silver "doggie bowl" hub caps, gloss black wheels, and tires painted flat black.

Figure 16: This premium WBB sedan (see Chapter 2) has wide silver "wheel covers."

Figure 17: This Ford taxi has its wheels painted on one side and not on the other, demonstrating the very real difference painted wheels can make to a realistic look.

Figure 18: Texaco tanker version of the Easy and Inexpensive Tractor-Trailer from Chapter 8 would not have that "Texaco" look without its red wheels and silver rims. Scenicruiser would be more authentic with blue centers on the wheels but the author liked the all-chrome look. De Camp Bus Lines GM 4515, and the Volkswagen bus to the right, both look good with painted wheels.

Body-Off Vehicle Customizing Projects

3

The projects described in this chapter involve removing the stock body from a 'Streets vehicle, modifying it so it has a new look, and then re-installing it on its original chassis. They are among the least expensive projects to do in this book, because they do not require an additional die-cast model for conversion. They are also among the easiest to do because no modification of chassis is required. In spite of this they produce a wide variety of different-looking vehicles to run on a layout (Figure 1). In addition, they are a lot of fun to do and help develop skills that will be needed for more complicated projects.

This chapter is a series of overview discussions of individual projects, of from one-half to two pages in length. Most are more detailed than a quick summary but less than a full step-by-step guide. The goal is to explain what each new vehicle project is, and how it was built, and to show any important concepts or lessons learned that are associated with that particular project. Most involve some cutting of the body, along with fabrication of new parts, the use of body filler, and repainting.

These projects have been selected to show the range of different projects and approaches that a modeler can take – and to inspire readers to be creative and try new ideas. Readers can follow along and re-create what is explained here, but can also use these just for inspiration and come up with their own unique projects.

Figure 1: Some of the vehicles made in this chapter.

Bank-Delivery Armored Car

Figure 2: The roof of the school bus is cut off just above the windshield and a thick styrene sheet attached using Loctite repair putty. After the epoxy hardens any putty sticking out the sides, blocking windows, etc., is cut out, and the metal sides and epoxy are sanded flush, as shown.

This bank-delivery armored car (Figures 2 – is made from the shorty bus. The body removed from the chassis. The roof is cut of it just above the level of the top windshi frame (a band saw makes this easy but it can done manually with care). A piece of 0.10 0.12 thick styrene sheet, too large by 1/16 to inches on both sides and at the rear, is bon on in place as a new roof, using Loctite Rep Putty. It is applied liberally (see Figure 2) a pressed into every nock and cranny. While s soft, it can be cut out where windows will be on the completed model – but the more left, the stronger the model is. After the putty hardens, a belt sander is used to grind the two sides and rear side of it flat, making the body, roof, and repair putty that flowed through the windows smooth and flush (Figure 2).

Thin (.02 in) styrene sheet is measured and cut for the sides and rear walls, and cut out for windows. Left and right side pieces are trimmed a bit too large in back and at the bottom - a margin to eventually be cut away flush when it is all assembled. Each side is positioned exactly in place with its windows in the correct location and its top flush with the top of the roofline, and then glued to the body with Duco cement and clamped (Figure 3). At the top the styrene is then bonded to the styrene roof piece with Plastruk plastic weld. When the glue and cement have hardened, a rear panel is cut to fit between the two sides and fitted-glued-clamped-bonded in place, with plastic weld being used again to bond the rear panel to the side panels and roof. When all glue is dry, scissors are used to cut the excess of the side panel margins flush with the roofline, and sides. All seams are then sanded and filled.

Figure 3: Styrene sheet is cut for both sides and glued on with Duco (to the metal sides) and Plastruk (to the styrene roof).

Next, the body is sanded with # 320 wet-dry sandpaper, and then primed and painted (using Rust-Oleum rattle cans).

The original windshield is reinserted and lightly tack-glued at edges that won't show. Clear plastic, as once protected and displayed some product recently bought, can be rescued from the trash and the flat portions cut to form the windows, which are taped in using Gorilla Tape. (Note: Gorilla Tape looks like black duct tape but holds better and seems to last forever, not dry out and lose hold.) The back and rear side windows are painted black on the inside.

Figure 4: After priming the body was painted glossy gray and remounted.

The front of the original interior with driver is trimmed to fit and mounted to the chassis. Brinks logos were printed on thin paper and glued to the sides and rear. Owners can add miniature license plates, mirrors, etc., for detail if desired, as they choose (Figure 5).

Figure 5: Completed armored car has a very different look and purpose than the school bus from which it was built. This model lacks some details that it is best to avoid unless one can do them very well. Rivets, hinges, door handles and so forth are best "left to the imagination" unless they can be done very well, but rear view mirrors, a hood ornament and other details can be added if desired.

Figure 6: The body is cut as shown. Horizontal cut must be above the base of the front chassis mounting tower so it is retained.

Heavy Duty Delivery Truck

Among 'Streets vehicles, the step van is the least amenable to *body-on* conversions: It is already a box and about as wide as a vehicle should be, so not the best platform on which to mount additional "stuff." But those features make it perhaps the most suitable for *body-off* conversions that involve cutting, several of which are covered in the next few pages.

The stock step-van was converted to the heavy delivery truck in Figure 7. A notch was cut out of the step-van's body (red lines in Figure 6) with just two straight cuts into the body using a band-saw. Plastic styrene sheet (1/8 inch) was cut and mounted to cover both open faces of the notch, using repair putty mushed around on the junction between plastic and metal on the inside of the die-cast body. When the epoxy had hardened the plastic was trimmed flush with the step-van body on the outside.

In this case, the author had bought a toy truck at a garage sale which had a body the same width as the step-van's body (many 1/43 trucks do – or are so close it does not matter). The top portion of that cab was cut off and windows inside painted black, and when the paint was dry, repair putty was used to fill the inside of that cab. A screw from underneath through the styrene mounted earlier was put it into that putty to attach it in place). Filler was applied, sanded, and the new body primed and painted, and several signs attached. Mirrors, exhausts, license plates, logos, etc. can be attached as

Figure 7: The completed heavy duty delivery truck looks quite good and is close to scale. Owners can attach details like mirrors, exhaust, license plates and so forth as they wish.

Utility Bucket Truck

The toy utility truck shown in Figure 8 can be found in toy and variety stores and on just about every mass market, die-cast, and toy-train web site. It has a die-cast metal cab and a plastic body with bucket mechanism and is nearly the perfect size and shape for a conversion onto the step-van body. For a low-cost toy, it is surprisingly complicated to take apart: a dozen screws must be unfastened from underneath as it is disassembled in three distinct "layers," but at every stage it is straightforward and there are no surprises when taking it apart.

Figure 8: This toy utility truck with a die-cast cab and plastic chassis and utility body, is widely available for around fifteen dollars.

Figure 9 shows the step-van body and the utility truck's cab after being cut with a band-saw. There are several important points here:

- Inside the step-van body, the rear mounting towers project from the roof of the van and thus would be cut off when it is. Repair putty was first squeezed in and around them, lower down below the layer of the cut, as shown in Figure 9's inset, to hold them in their original place when the cut is made. It is allowed to harden before the cut is made.
- After that epoxy has hardened,the cut is made low enough that the plastic utility truck rear body will slip right over the motor and internal parts (see cut line shape in Figure 9).
- At the front, the cut in the step van has been made higher (see Figure 9) than in the back, both to properly position the cab, and so that it is above the height of the front chassis mounting tower base.

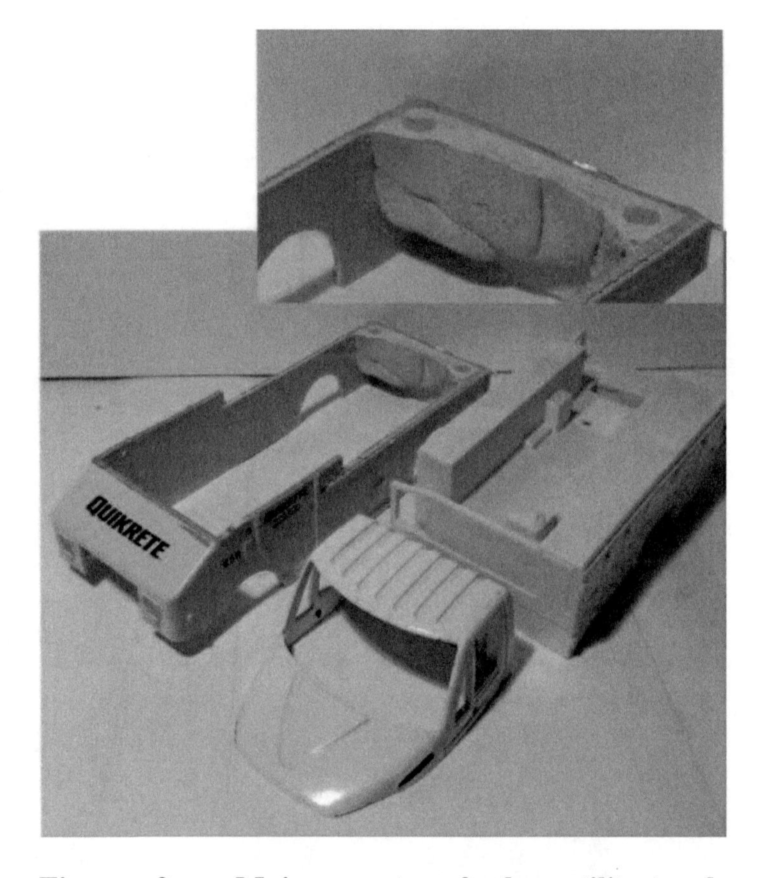

Figure 9: Major parts of the utility-truck conversion. Include the step-van body and the top half of the utility truck cab, both shown here after cutting with a band saw. See text for details on what was done.

The cab, which is just wide enough to match the width of the front of the step-van body, was attached with repair-putty. While holding the cab and step-van body in one hand so they were well aligned, the author rolled repair putty on the inside over the seam where the two met and spread it out about 1/4 inch thick for at least 1/ 2 inch on both sides of the seam. When it hardens it grasps both sides of the seam and holds them together.

The sloping nose of the step van, and the horizontal cut of the cab, left a monstrous gap at the front of the truck. This was filled entirely with repair putty, pushed in fully so it filled all the space available and grasped every bit of surface of both metal bodies.

After that repair putty had hardened it was sanded to the shape seen in Figure 10. Bondo glazing putty was applied and when dried, sanded. The body was primed and painted.

The rear utility body on the toy is plastic and easy to cut. It had to be shortened about one quarter inch (sliced off at the front) and various projections underneath cut away with a Dremel. But with that and a little bit of further trimming – all obvious when one tries to fit it to the truck body – it slipped over the rear of the truck body just tightly enough: a perfect fit. The arm and bucket assembly and other equipment and details taken from the toy truck were then glued onto the utility body. Mirrors and other details complete the truck shown in Figure 10.

Figure 10: The completed utility bucket truck – perhaps not the most aesthetically pleasing of vehicles to ever grace the road, but it is definitely a truck with a very different look

Bartoletti 642 Transporter

The Fiat-Bartoletti race car team transporter (Figure 11) was a fixture at European auto races throughout the 1950s and 1960s, used by Gran Prix and LeMans racing teams including Ferrari, Maserati and Cobra. The model shown in Figure 11 was made from the step-van. The body was notched at the rear for the transporter framework (all scratchbuilt) at a level just above the motor and extended an inch further back with styrene sheet. The front had a piece of fine-grain wood bonded and screwed to square off the nose, which was then carved, filled, and sanded to shape. This "semi-scale" model looks great carrying a couple of race cars.

Figure 11: The author's favorite conversion of the step-van is this Fiat-Bartoletti transporter.

Figure 12: The first two body-off conversions the author did were these two military field vehicles, made from the step-van (foreground) and the shorty school bus (back).

Two Military Vehicles

The field patrol car at the back of Figure 16 was made by cutting the roof and sides off the short bus, installing a sheet-styrene roof and interior, and mounting a model machine gun and various other military fittings in back. Body modification done was much like that done to the Brinks armored car.

The armored car was made from a delivery step-van by making a single cut to remove about 3/8 inch at the top, then installing a plastic roof. Various fittings and guns were applied, and its body, like the patrol car's, painted and re-installed. Anyone deciding to make a vehicle anywhere like these needs to be aware of the "using repair putty to retain the original mounting holes" technique discussed in the utility bucket truck earlier in this chapter (Figure 9).

MODIFYING THE WBB SEDAN

The various cars on this and the next page were made from the stock WBB sedan by removing the body from its chassis and doing "bodywork" on it. Many bear a family resemblance to the stock sedan, as if they were different models from the same manufacturer. The plastic is easy to work. Almost all were repainted.

Figure 13: B-pillar was snipped out. Door seams except the front-most were filled, and a longer two-door line scribed. Porthole window was drilled. Rear bumper cut for continental kit was added. Not that different, but different.

Figure 14: Limosine was made from two bodies. Adjustable chassis was lengthened one notch. First body was cut at B pillar, other body was cut "one notch length" ahead of B-pillar. When glued together they made a body about a scale nine inches longer.

Figure 15: Business-man's coupe – a "notch" shorter – was made from the two body sections left over from the limosine.

Figure 16: Sport coupe. B pillar was removed, door seams were filled and scribed for a two-door. The A pillers were removed and replaced with new pillars farther back and slanted to form a wrap-around windshield (stock clear front windows are still used). Rear 3/8 inch of roof were removed, trimmed, and glued back in at a sloping angle. Gaps and scratches were filled and sanded, and the body repainted, etc.

Figure 17: Horizontal cut was made through entire truck 3/16 inch above top of wheel wells, and a 1/8 inch thick styrene sheet inserted and body glued together (raises body height by a scale 6 inches, and forms pickup bed "floor"). Windshield was repositioned more vertically. Scratches were filled, sanded, and truck painted.

Figure 18: Light pickup. The rear half of the roof was cut off. Rear door seams in sides were filled. Pickup bed and back of cab were made with thin sheet styrene. Barrel halves were glued in bed. It was repainted.

Figure 19: Station wagon. The trunklid was cut out all the way to the pack. A station wagon rear was built from styrene sheet glued to the roof just above the rear seat and extended back, thin sections used as windows at rear. The body was filled, sanded and painted. Most difficult was cutting and fitting clear plastic as rear windows.

Figure 20: This "premium" WBB sedan shows that small changes can make a big difference. The front windshield posts were snipped out and the windshield's area opened up by carefully filing away 1/32 inch and nearly 1/16th inch of plastic at the top and bottom of the windshield frame respectively. New A pillars were installed a bit farther back on the car than the originals. A center pillar was painted on the windshield. In the back of the car the rear window was similarly cut to a wider area so it was larger. Original "window glass" is used, unmodified. Grill, bumpers, and hood trim were cannibalized from a discarded die-cast New Ray 1950s car and grafted on.

A good deal of chrome trim was painted on, and the wheels were painted with "full wheel covers" for a premium, upscale look. The result is much more realistic but still very generic look – people are sure they have seen a real car like this but can't quite place what make and model it is.

This is among the author's favorites, both for the good look, and the subtlety and simplicity or how it was obtained.

Mack Delivery Truck

The final project in this chapter stretches the chapter's theme, perhaps to the breaking point; just half the original body is remounted on the chassis. The other half is replaced with a cab from a die-cast model. But no modification of the chassis is made beyond snipping a few pieces of plastic off and drilling four holes; so this project makes a good transition to the next chapter's project which requires more work.

Parts needed include a New Ray 1:43 model of a 1953 Mack B-61 tractor with any of several different trailers, sold for around twenty-two dollars including shipping from many internet retailers. The trailer is not important to this project. The step-van is ideally an early K-line version with the slightly larger wheels, but later K-Line by Lionel versions with panel-van size wheels work well enough.

Step 1: Remove the body from the chassis (three screws, see Chapter 1). Remove the interior from the chassis (two screws). Remove the driver (onc screw underneath the seat). Save it for later use.

Step 2: Cut the four posts off the body as indicated in Figure 21. Slice the front off at the red line along the front – this cut goes right through the front mounting hole and its post. Trim the remainder of that post off and file the front edge of the chassis where it was cut smooth and flat (Figure 22). Trim the front wheel well space further towards the rear by cutting out the chassis plastic indicated by the yellow lines. Figure 23 shows completed chassis.

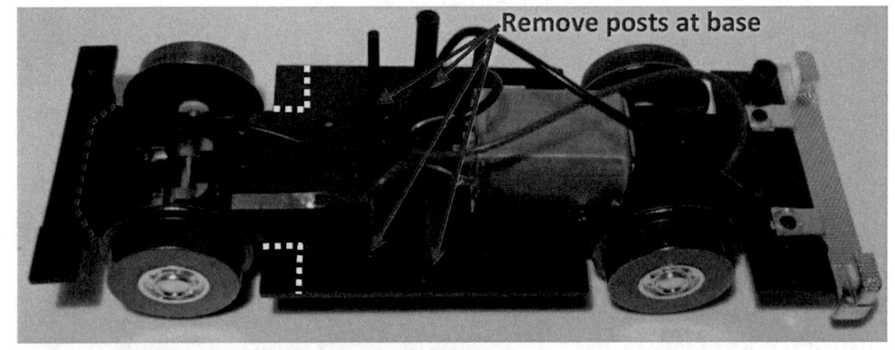

Figure 21: Bare chassis of the step-van.

Figure 22: Front post removed and edge trimmed flat.

Figure 23: Step-van chassis completed.

Step 3. Disassemble the Mack B-61 model tractor by removing every screw seen from underneath. Some loosen minor parts like the fuel tanks, but by removing all of them and all other screws exposed as those minor parts are removed, eventually the entire model comes apart. Set everything but the cab aside. Pull out the interior – it slips out from underneath. Glue the driver from the step van into the driver's seat and replace the interior (Figure 24).

Figure 24: New Ray 1:43 Mack tractor just out of the box.

Step 4: Wrap the cab in painter's tape to protect it from the residue that will get on hands when repair putty is used. (Handling the putty – which is unavoidable – leaves an invisible residue on hands that *will* mar glossy paint and more with permanent fingerprints.)

Step 5: Fill the cab with repair putty from the underside, pushing it into every nook and cranny around the interior from door to door, filling the area under the hood, all to the level of the lower edge of the back of the cab (the bottom floor of the interior is at that same height. Leave the wheel wells empty of putty (to provide room for the wheels, as shown. Trim bottom 3/16 inch off the lower end of exhaust stack so it will clear later on, as shown.

Figure 25: Cab is covered with painter's tape. Loctite repair putty is pushed into every nook and around the interior, filling the cab flat to the level of the lower edge of the cab: note the 1/16-inch high lip left at the front by doing this. Wheel wells are left empty so there is room for wheels.

Step 6 The cab is intended to fit with the bottom of its radiator cover resting on the front of the chassis (Figure 30), and will be held to the chassis by two screws. Drill the two 1/8-inch screw mounting holes in the chassis as shown in Figure 31 – they are each 5/16 inch in from the outer edge of the chassis and about 7/16 inch ahead of the motor well in the chassis front edge (Figure 26).

Figure 26: Front of cab will rest on edge of chassis.

Step 6: Drill two holes in the chassis 5/16 inch in from the outer edge of the chassis and 7/16 inch ahead of the motor well in the chassis front edge (Figure 27). These are for screws that will be inserted from the underside to hold the chassis in place.

Step 7: Make two spacers as shown in Figure 28. The ones shown were made from 5/16 plastic tube but anything about that diameter – such as a used Bic pen, etc. – that will let a screw through it will do. They will go under the cab, with the screws passing through them, to position it at the right height above the chassis floor.

Step 8: Holding the cab in place on the chassis with its front edge positioned as in Figure 26 and aligned straight side to side with the chassis, start two holes in the repair putty/interior floor for the screws by lightly drilling through the holes from underneath the chassis into the cab floor, using a pin vise with a narrow bit. Then drill these out to a depth sufficient for the screws that will be used.

Step 9: Mount the cab on the chassis by again positioning the cab on the chassis, inserting the positioning spacers (Figure 28) between cab and chassis and screwing the chassis to the cab. Figure 29 shows the result: the cab mounted on the chassis.

Step 10: Position the original body alongside the completed cab and chassis so that its rear mounting posts line up with the mounting holes in the chassis. Mark where to cut it so it will fit just up to the Mack's cab (blue tape in Figure 30. Cut the body evenly at that line – a band saw is the preferred tool to do this cleanly.

Figure 27: Two mounting holes (Step 6).

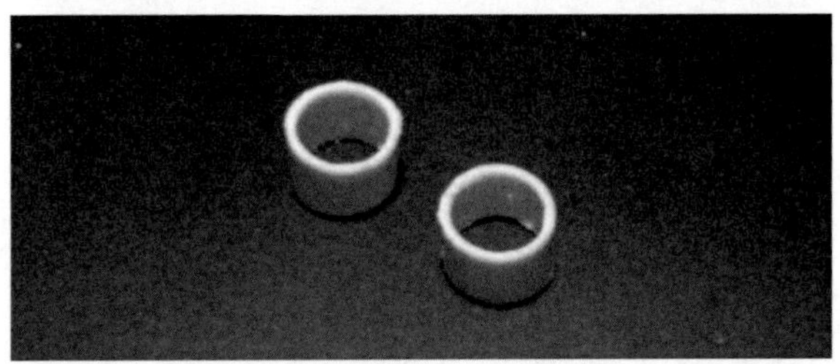

Figure 28: Spacers are made to position back of cab level with front.

Figure 29: Cab mounted on chassis. The spacers have been put in place and a screw inserted through each into the bottom of the cab putty/interior floor.

Figure 30: Original body is positioned in and marked for cutting.

Figure 31: Front panel will have a gap with the bottom edge (right, red arrow).

Step 11: Mount the rear portion of the body on the chassis using its two original mounting screws (Figure 31). Note the distance that a front panel will have to leave from the chassis in order for it to sit down on the chassis floor (red arrow in image).

Step 12: Make a front panel of 0.12 inch thick styrene (Figure 32). The step-van's rear body is not absolutely square, so the panel will need to be a bit wider at the bottom than at the top. Bond it to the rear body (Figure 33).

Figure 32: Front panel for rear body.

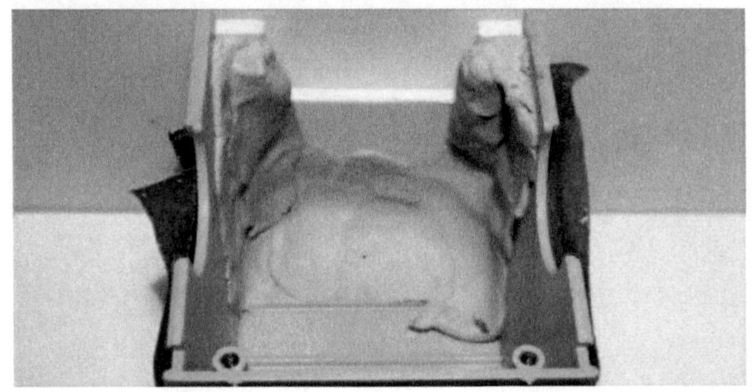

Figure 33: Repair putty is mushed around the junction of panel and body to hold it in place. It is made thick near the sides to provide room for mounting screws.

Step 13: The rear body is mounted to the chassis using screws from underneath the chassis up into the repair putty of the rear body. (holes are drilled in the chassis for them as for the two for the cab, explained earlier).

Figure 34: The model, completed. A very different look would b obtained if one were to paint the wheels green and white, but the author prefers them chrome.

Step 14: The conversion is done. At this point the model can be finished by painting (including the cab, or justthe rear body as the author has done. Details can be added: bumpers, rocker panels or step-tanks, mirrors and other equipment as the modeler wishes (Figure 34). An electronic flywheel will fit easily inside the rear box and improve slow speed running, if the owner wants to add it as explained in Chapter 6.

Variations on This Theme

Although it takes the project completely away from the "no chassis mods required" concept, the chassis in the preceding Mack truck example could have been lengthened 11/16 inch and the original body cut just behind the cab doors, making for a longer and bigger-looking truck, yet no so long that the original motor won't push it through curves (it will slow quite a bit more than the stock version, going through those curves, though).

Panel Van variation. The same approach as used on the step-van above can be used on the panel van chassis, mounting a Road Signatures Ford F-1 cab or any number of other model pickup cabs instead (see Chapter 4 for how to mount most pickup cabs in an *extremely* easy and quick way).

The panel-van body's rear section can be cut and installed in a way basically identical to that used on the preceding step-van example, giving a somewhat smaller truck since the panel van itself is smaller. And of course, one could lengthen the chassis to make a longer truck, too (Figure 36).

Figure 35: These "photoshopped" images show how the same basic idea as that used in the Mack cab example earlier could be applied to the panel van instead using a Ford F-1 pickup cab. Top: at the van's chassis and wheelbase left stock it looks very much like an ice-crean truck from the 1950s. Bottom: stretched to the longest the van body can be cut, it looks just like the oil-field exploration electronics trucks the author's father used in the 1950s.

Converting Die-Cast Cars and Pickup Trucks

4

Many die-cast 1:43, 1:48, and 1:50 models of cars and light trucks can be converted to run on 'Streets roadways using the sedan, panel van, or the older vintage truck chassis, with little modification. There are situations where the panel van or vintage truck chassis must be used, but when possible the sedan chassis is the easiest to use.

The WBB sedan is the chassis of first choice for body-conversion projects, particularly for model cars, for three reasons:

a) It has car-sized wheels.

b) It is easy to find and inexpensive to buy.

c) It has an adjustable wheelbase, so it can accommodate different vehicle needs.

In addition, if one intends to mount a plastic or resin – that is, lightweight - body on a 'Streets chassis, then only the sedan's metal chassis will do for the conversion. Only the sedan's metal chassis has enough weight on its own to hold rollers and wheels down on the road by itself. Any plastic chassis is light to the point that it requires the weight of a die-cast metal body to hold it down on the rails. Unless one is prepared to glue a great deal of lead shot into a completed model, the metal chassis is the only choice for converting plastic models.

This chapter begins by going through a representative 'Streets-to-die-cast conversion step-by-step, showing what must be done and the way the author has learned to handle the different aspects of that conversion. It then discusses a number of other considerations that modelers will run into when doing conversions, stressing each with capsule summaries of other projects to illustrate issues that might come up and show how to handle them.

Figure 1: All die-cast or plastic scale models. All run on 'Streets.

1950 Ford

This conversion is straightforward and yet it touches all the bases, making it a good example to begin this chapter. This die-cast model is sold under several brand names: White Rose, American Heritage, and when police or fire, First Response Replicas. This particular model is intended to be an unmarked police car once completed, and will be given blackwall tires (the WBB police and taxi chassis have blackwalls; the other sedans have white walls). It will be converted to a police sedan chassis.

Figure 2: The die-cast model dis-assembles with just two small screws and comes apart with no problems. Body, bumpers and grill, and windshield are kept for when the conversion is reassembled.

Step-0: Compare the die-cast model and a WBB sedan to make sure the conversion is feasible. In this case it is, but sometimes it is clear the no amount of work will fit the chassis to the model's body. Check the die-cast model to make sure it is complete and in good shape. Check that the sedan's chassis runs well.

Step 1: Disassemble the model (Figure 2). Parts needed are the body with its antenna, grill, bumpers and mirrors, and the windshield. Set aside the windshield in a protected place. Interior, wheels and chassis are not needed.

Step 2: Remove the body from the WBB sedan chassis (Chapter 1 discusses how), then remove the interior and set that aside (Figure 3). Body, bumpers and windows are no longer needed.

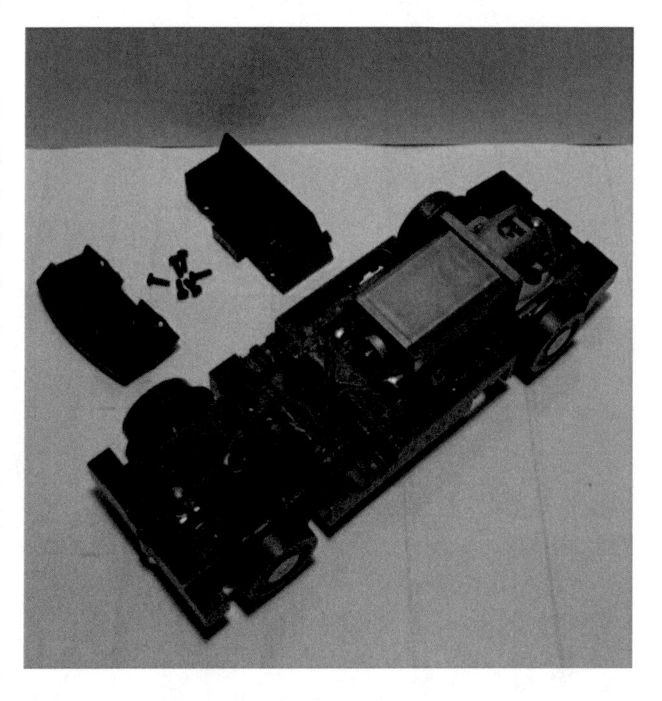

Figure 3: The base WBB chassis. Interior is set aside for a while but will be used eventually.

Step 3: Compare wheelbases of the die-cast body and the chassis to see if the wheelbase on the chassis has to be adjusted. In this case the answer is no, but in many cases it is yes. If that is the case, the adjustment is done at this time.

Step 4: Trial fit the body and chassis to make sure that they can be made to fit together, and to identify the work that will need to be done to make them fit. Figures 5 and 6 show some of the points one checks at this time.

In this case, the Ford body looks almost as if it were designed to fit this chassis (Figure 5). In a few cases, this is not the way it works out, and one has to spend time deciding if the chassis can be made to fit inside the body (sometimes the answer is no) and if so, if the amount of work required is worth spending on the model (again, sometimes the answer is no).

Anyway, there are two issues (Figures 6-7):

1) At the front the chassis is slightly longer than the die-cast body.
2) The chassis will not slip far enough into the body so the wheels ride at their right height. See also Figure 7.

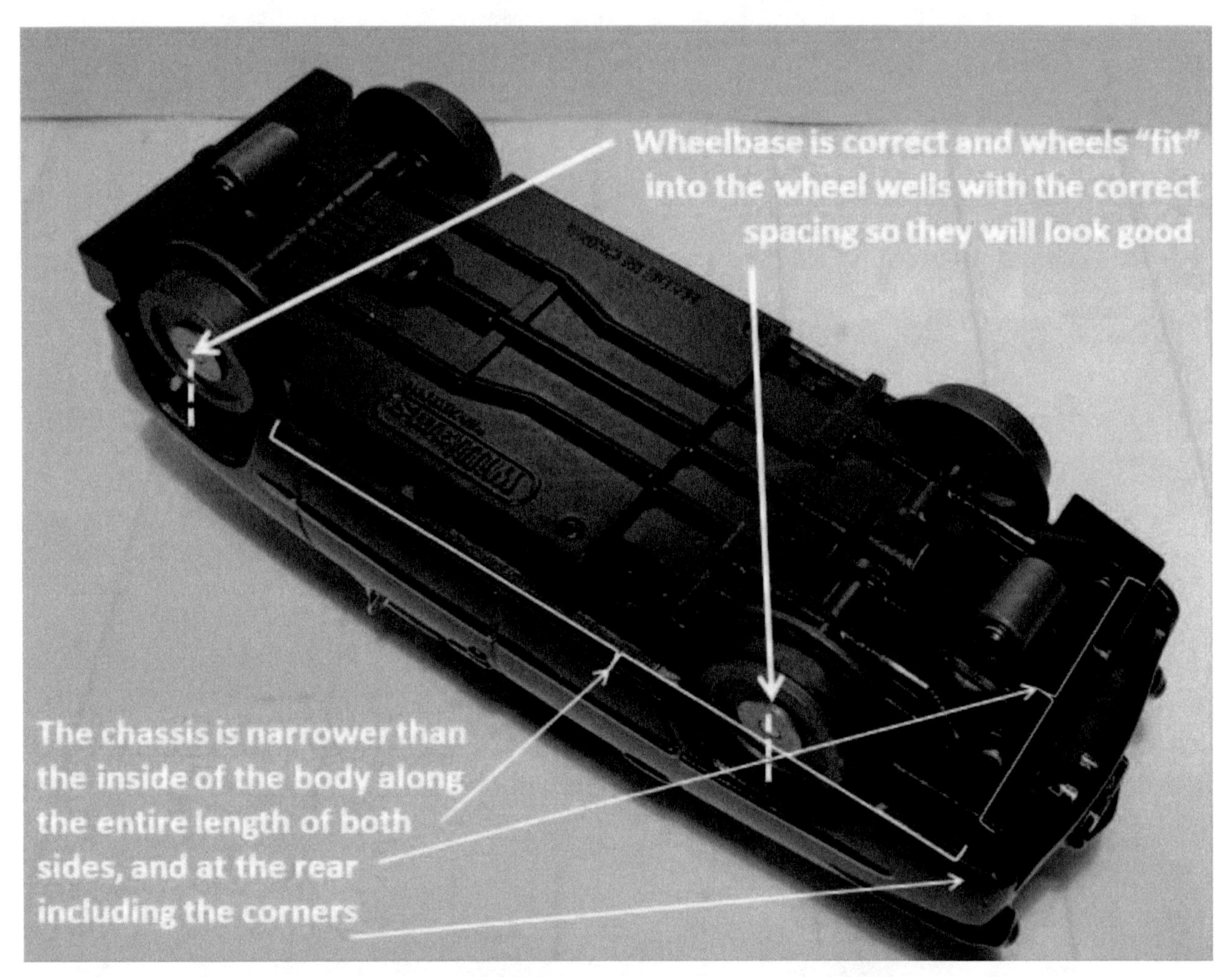

Figure 4: A trial fit and study of the body and chassis is *the* important step. It is all good news here. The chassis is narrower along the sides than the body, so it will fit *in* the body, particularly at the rear corners. In addition, note that there is room for the wheels to fit up inside the body with plenty of clearance. That is not always the case.

Figure 5: Issues that have to be dealt with to make a good fit. See text for details.

Figure 6: The plan will be to cut away the body along the red dotted line so the front of the chassis can fit up into the front. Leave the chassis unmodified for now.

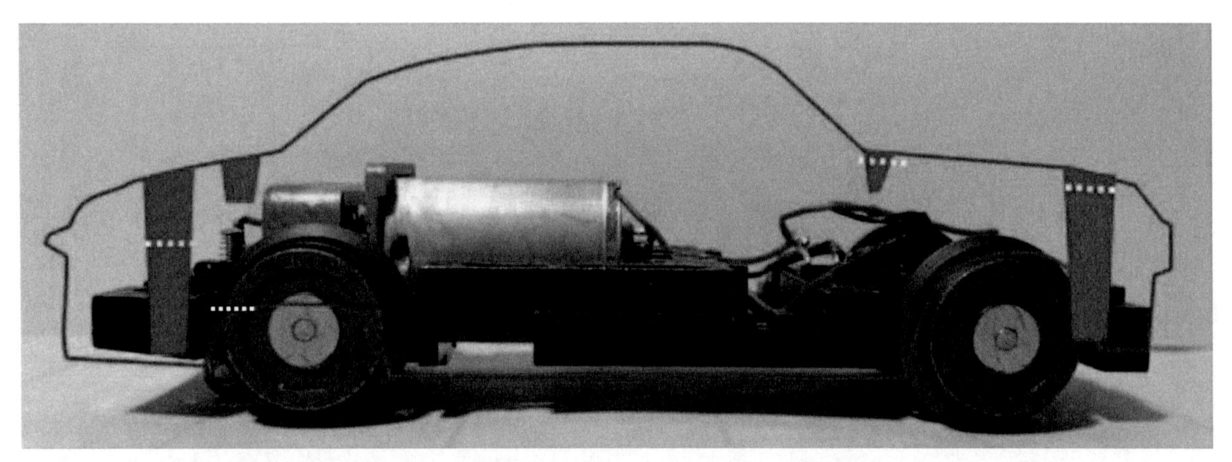

Figure 7: While there is a slight mismatch at the front, the major reasons the chassis will not fit up into the body as it should (shown by the red profile, which is where the body *should* sit relative to the chassis) are the two mounting towers cast into the body (to which the original chassis was attached) shown by solid red areas. They are blocking the chassis from moving farther up. They, and two smaller projections, are out cut at the white lines.

Step 5: Wrap the body with painters tape before moving on to heavy-duty work that might accidently mar its paint finish (Figure 8).

Figure 8: Blue painters tape protects the body during cutting and other operations.

Step 6: Remove the two mounting towers and the other small projections shown in Figure 7. Cut metal off the nose of the car as in Figure 6. The author used a Dremel rotary tool with the high speed cutter, at speed "1" – slow, and just took his time. It required all of eleven minutes.

Figure 9: Normally the author does not remove the protective tape at this point, but he did so for this photo. With the towers and the metal at the front removed, the chassis fits nicely, and naturally, into the body at what looks like a good height. The author re-taped the car before proceeding.

Step 7: Measure and study for new mounting towers. The body with chassis is turned over and the locations of its three mounting holes in the chassis checked (arrows, Figure 10). Towers to attach it at these points must be installed in the body in the next step. T*he point of this step is to study if and how to do it, make note of where in the body the towers must be, and verify that they will not interfere with any pickup wiring or whatever else inside the car.*

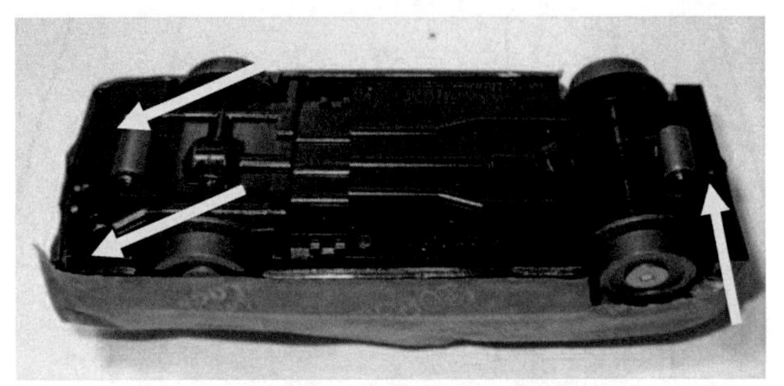

Figure 10: Blue painters tape protects the body during cutting and other operations.

Step 8: Make the towers with repair putty. At the front, the tower is in the middle and just ahead of the front pickup spring assembly. (There is barely enough clearance for it, but there is enough. At the rear, the towers must leave room for the rear pickup between them. Nothing helps as much as experience here, at installing the putty, and at eyeballing just how high and where the towers need to be. (It helps to practice on an old model first, if available.)

Figure 11: The author deliberately touched the bottom of the chassis here to demonstrate. Nothing but sandpaper is going to remove this epoxy fingerprint. Wash hands after using the putty!

Step 9: Wash hands with soap and hot water before removing the tape. Working with the putty leaves an invisible film on fingers and hands that will leave permanent fingerprints on glossy surfaces: they will not wash off with anything weaker than painter remover! Wait fifteen to twenty minutes, then use soap, hot water, and lots of scrubbing to remove the film from hands and fingers. (Figure 11).

Step 10: Test fit the chassis and body. Cut and file the towers until the chassis and body fit correctly. *Test run the car with the body just resting on the chassis* (Figure 12 – the windshield is not even installed yet. Make sure nothing is binding on the center pickup springs and machinery inside, and that the rear wheels don't bind against the body (it's close). If they do, insert small spacer shims at the rear to raise the body slightly.

Figure 12: It's alive! Maybe it's not done or pretty yet, but it runs.

Step 11: Drill holes in the epoxy and test fit the chassis to the body with screws. Once it fits well, remove screws and body from chassis.

Step 12: Touch up the wheels with paint. On this, a police car, one wants wheels as in chapter 2, Figure 15. On most other cars, one often wants to paint wider "hubcaps" or whitewalls and so on (Figure 13).

Step 13: Build a rear interior. The WBB sedan had frosted rear windows so that one can not see the motor and gearbox. This model has clear rear windows. Make a cardboard piece as shown in Figure 14 by tracing the edge of the window piece from the B-pillar location back around, cutting it out, gluing a small "rear seat back" onto it, and painting it black.

Figure 13: Wheels give off subtle clues the eye picks up that one may not even consciously recognize yet convey a lot of meaning as to the purpose and type of vehicle, so don't dismiss the idea that painting the wheels can change the "appearance" of a car, as was covered in Chapter 2. "Doggy bowl" hubcaps are appropriate for the police car in this example. More generally fit the wheels to the car: white walls and big wheel covers contribute a lot to the look of the modified "premium" WBB sedan in the photo above, while blackwalls and painted wheels to base models or "working" vehicles.

Step 14. Install the original interior back on the chassis (it will fit into this body). Note, in this conversion, that one could have left the interior on the chassis the whole time. More generally it must be removed to adjust wheelbase or if really heavy work and cutting of the chassis is done.

On some conversions, particularly those where the wheelbase length is changed, the interior will not fit at all or at least not without trimming and modification, but here it fits perfectly.

Paint interior details, and install a driver and passenger figures if desired. The author always does – a moving vehicle looks silly without a driver!

Step 15: Assemble the model. Turn the body upside down, place a bit of glue (Duco works well) in the middle of the inside roof, and drop the windshield piece in. Position the rear interior made in Step 12 so that it rests on the edges of the windows piece; then put the chassis with interior in on top. Screw the chassis down.

Figure 14 Trace the window piece from the B pillar location back to make the rear interior cover.

Step 16: Glue on bumpers and grill. The rear bumper must have part of its original mounting tab cut away, and the front must have its entire mounting tab removed, so before they can be fit tight against body. The author glued them to the body with Duco cement, which dries in about four hours (Figure 15).

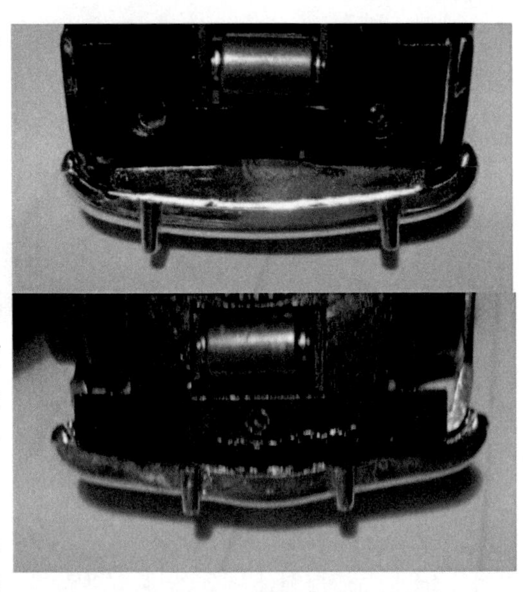

Figure 15: The bumpers have to be trimmed as shown here, and then glued onto the body. Compare to Figure 3.

The vehicle is complete. The author removed the radio antenna, since this is a police car and pictures of unmarked cars in 1950s TV shows like Dragnet don't show any radio antenna on Joe Friday's and other unmarked Ford police cars.

Figure 16 shows the completed car running down Main Street or the author's ayout. Figure 1 at the start of this chapter shows two other 1950s Ford models converted just like this: the marked police cruiser on the left rear, and the taxi in front on the middle right side.

Figure 16: The unmarked police car passes as Joe Friday (no hat) and Frank Smith (hat) discuss a case. When not running, this cars stays parked at the curb there. The author cut small slots in the parking lane for its wheel flanges so it looks natural parked there.

Considerations for Conversions

The 1950 Ford converted in the previous section is not a simple conversion: nothing involving sixteen steps should be considered simple. But it was a straightforward conversion without a number of complicating factors that sometimes make a project lengthier or risker. Some of these are covered below.

Figure 17: This lovely series-two Triumph Spitfire by Spark would look good running on 'Streets, but its too narrow by a scale tire width, at least: at its extreme width it can't bridge the 1 ¼-inch gauge.

Can you even make it work? Sometimes the answers is no. The 1:43 Triumph Spitfire in Figure 17 shows one reason. At its widest the car is 1/8 inches narrower than O-gauge's 1 ¼ inch rail-to-rail width – there is just no reasonable way to make it work. Beyond that, it would be a difficult conversion, requiring a scratch-built narrow chassis with a very small motor. The author is not sure the body (it's die-cast but very light) would even hold down the two center rollers against their springs.

Figure 18: Some early-era model profiles conflict with chassis running gear..

Internal interference. The author has encountered several models of pre-war coupes that had trunks that were too low as shown in Figure 18. The body interfers with the gearbox and rear pickup assembly. Some modern sports cars that are otherwise wide enough (i.e. 2002 Corvette) to fit O-gauge and to contain the 'Streets axles, have a hood so low near the front that it will not clear the front wheel flanges or front pickup assembly.

Remember it is the internal profile that matters. On some die-cast models the metal is only about 1/20 to 1/16 inch thick and it is easy to judge if and where interference might be a problem. On others, noteably Brooklin, and on resin models, the material is quick thick.

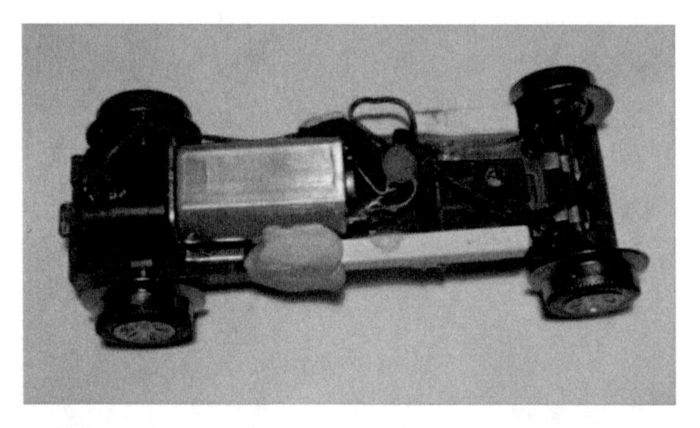

Figure 19: This narrow vintage truck chassis was shortened to fit the '48 Chrysler discussed later in this Chapter.

The vintage truck chassis is narrower than any other chassis and is the chassis of choice when a car has running boards (Figure 19).

Police Cars & Metal Chassis

Police cars are usually fairly boxy and, if not always large, definitely not small, so many are easy to convert. The three shown here were all rather easy. The Ford police cruiser in Figure 20 was converted exactly as was the 1950 Ford sedan discussed earlier. Like the sedan, it is a First Reponse brand model, but a coupe rather than the sedan version. This model has no interior because it is fitted with a larger, slower-turning flywheel motor (which can barely be seen in the photo) as will be described in Chapter 6, to make it a smoother slow-speed runner. Other than that its conversion was as straightforward as the sedan shown earlier.

Figure 20: The Ford Patrol Coupe was converted exactly like the sedan in the earlier section. The Dodge was easier still.

The Motormax NYPD Dodge Diplomat shown required the WBB adjustable chassis be shortened one notch, otherwise everything fit perfectly. The only cutting required was removal of the two original mounting towers inside the body. The body did not have to be cut or altered in any other way.

Figure 21: Repair putty at both ends of the Dodge body forms attachments for the shortened but unmodified chassis.

The 1950 whaleback Nash Police cruiser shown in Figure 22 is typical of many sedan conversions: all four corners of the chassis had to be trimmed and rounded a bit in order for it to fit. This is *very* common. Also about 3/16 inches of the front was cut off – a job for which a bandsaw was almost indispensable. So much of the front chassis had to be removed, right up the front of the pickup assembly, that a custom mounting hole to the side had to be made for attaching to the car body. Finally, the adjustable wheelbase was increased by a notch for this car, to fit the long body.

Figure 22: 1950 Nash required chassis corners be rounded and that it be shortened by 3/16 inch up front.

Mustang GT – Problems with Size

The Yat Ming die-cast 1968 Mustang GT shown in Figure 23 was just wide enough, just tall enough, and just long enough to squeeze a WBB sedan chassis into it. The wheels barely fit within the fenders – exact positioning was key!

Figure 23: While difficult, this '68 Mustang is a very good-looking, good-running model.

It was not clear that this car could be converted to the WBB chassis – the author considered using the narrower vintage truck chassis. But this was done in 2013, at a time when the Vintage truck was getting hard to find and the author's stock of them limited. Also it was not obvious the small, thin-cast body would weigh enough to hold a plastic chassis on the road.

Figure 24

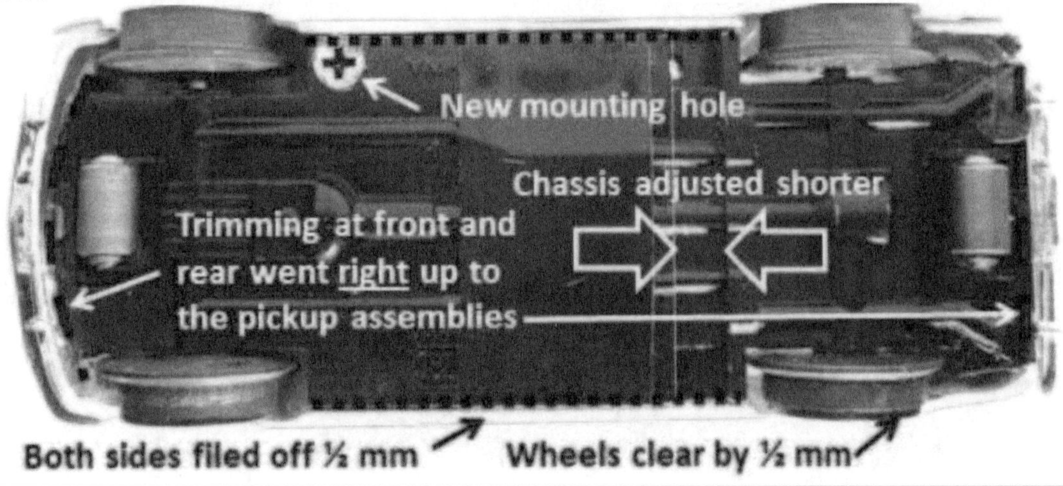

Length: The sedan chassis was adjusted to its shortest position and the wheelbase exactly matched. The body's short front overhang meant the chassis had to be trimmed in front, leaving barely enough structure around the front pickup assembly to contain it and none at all for mounting holes up front (it is off to the side behind a front wheel). At the rear, the situation was nearly as tight, the chassis cut line passed through the back of the two mounting holes there, making them notches, which were filled with repair putty and drilled from the back to make holes into which the dual exhausts fit.

Width: Measurement and study made it clear from the beginning there was barely room, if that. In fact, it proved necessary to grind about 1/2 mm off each side along most of the length of the chassis. This proved a lengthy job - done by hand, checking frequently, with a file.

Height: There is not a lot of room left inside the car with all the sedan chassis machinery there. Mustang's slopping back leaves very little room over the rear center pickup assembly, and actually touches the very back upper edge of the gearbox, but it fits.

VW Bus – Too Small by Half

Yat Ming presented another challenge with the VW van shown in Figure 25. Like the Mustang, it was too short and too narrow, but at least height was not a problem!

Width was a bigger challenge than in the Mustang. The VW is actually wider than the Mustang by about a millimeter: the WBB chassis will slip into the VW body snuggly without filing any metal off its sides, etc. In fact, this vehicle has no mounting screws: the body grasps the sides of the chassis and holds it firmly with tension alone.

Figure 25: VW van required extensive work – more than any other car in this book.

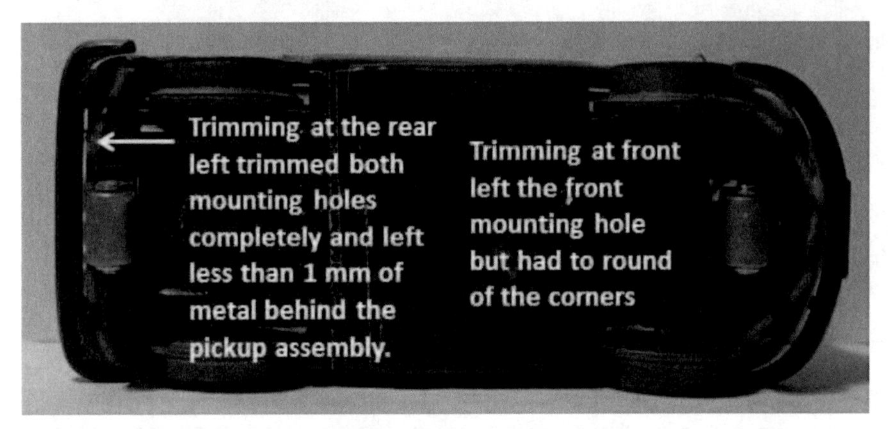

Figure 26: VW with WBB sedan chassis from underneath.

The problem with width was at the top of the rear wheels. The stock body had fender skirts cast into it and the rear wheels had to fit up inside the body. The streets axle was too wide by about 1.5 mm. The author considered grinding a millimeter off the outside of each wheel but rejected that as unfeasible: it would have removed the rim holding the traction tire on the one side, and made the wheels awfully thin. Instead, the wheel wells were cut away (see photos) so the wheels did not contact the body.

Length: The VW's wheelbase was shorter than the shortest length of the adjustable sedan chassis by about one and one half extra notches.

The author added another notch of adjustment to by trimming a "notch-length" off the front end of the rear section and filing the front section

Anyone attempting this will quickly see what to do, but some study to determine how to do the cuts most easily pays off. When shortened that one extra notch, the chassis wheelbase was still about three millimeters too long. The rear fender openings, which had to be cut away be cut out anyway to provide side-to-side clearance for the wheels, were cut farther back.

Height: Readers may have noticed that the body does not fit all the way down on the chassis so the rocker panels are even with the bottom of the chassis. This is deliberate, both for appearance – the van looks good at this ride height - and because the front wheels would rub against the top of the wheel well (neither the front axle nor the rear will fit inside the body). The van's height provided a lot of room inside, which was put to good use: this vehicle has a very large electronic flywheel (covered in Chapter 6). As a result it runs very smoothly slowly - at just eighteen scale miles per hour.

Something Different

The Crown Victoria Yellow Cab in Figure 27 certainly is not different; it is ubiquitous in cities and at airports throughout the United States. But this model is quite different: it is a *very* light plastic body from a broken 1:43 Carrera GO! slot car the author bought at a garage sale for a dollar. The two mounting towers inside were removed with a Dremel tool.

Figure 27: This Carrera GO! body fits an unmodified WBB sedan chassis perfectly, and was very easy to convert.

The author took a WBB sedan chassis and built three new half inch mounting towers out of plastic tube of a diameter that would just grasp the original mounting screws and attached them. The body was then placed over the chassis and the towers trimmed in height a bit at a time until the body had the right ride height. Plastruk cement was them used to glue them to the body.

All WBB, But...

Mounting the body of the WBB panel van on the chassis of the WBB sedan might seem bizarre (Figure 28), but it results in a panel van with correctly sized wheels: it looks realistic now, *a scale model.* And it was simple: the wheelbase fits without adjusting the chassis length. Some trimming of the chassis front and rear has to be done, but nothing extreme.

The result is a more accurate looking model of a van, with the properly sized wheels, a subtle difference but one that counts if it is to be mixed in with scale models a good deal. The model is quite heavy (metal body *and* metal chassis) so it is smooth running, first because that road-hugging weight conveys smoothness by itself, and also because the interior room permitted an electronic flywheel to be fitted (see Chapter 6).

Figure 28: Mounting the WBB panel-van body on the WBB sedan chassis makes for a much more realistic model of the generic white panel van that is the preferred vehicle of serial killers, rapists, and perverts on TV detective shows.

Divco Milk Truck

One of the most distinctive trucks of the 1950s was the Divco milk delivery truck, which the operator could drive while standing. American Heritage's 1:43 model is nicely detailed and available in a number of different corporate liveries, including Borden's (Figure 29). It is a good candidate for a fairly easy conversion. Among 'Streets chassis the sedan has wheels closest to the Divco's tire size, so the sedan chassis will be used for this conversion.

Step 1: Close all six doors of the Divco and use masking tape to firmly attach them to the body, pressing the tape firmly against outer door surfaces and on the body around the doorways– otherwise the doors will fall loose upon removing the interior for the body as the truck is disassembled. Once this is done disassemble the die-cast model (Figure 30).

Step 2: Test a WBB sedan to make sure it runs well. Remove its body and interior from the chassis. Body, bumpers and both parts of the interior are not needed. Adjust wheelbase to the shortest possible.

Step 3: The chassis is trimmed 1/16th inch straight across the back and 3/16inch across the front, as shown in Figure 31. Again, a band-saw is recommended to make clean cuts.

Figure 31: Chassis is trimmed at the ends. Red lines indicate original extent of chassis.

Figure 29: American Heritage 1:43 die-cast model of a Divco Borden's Milk Truck.

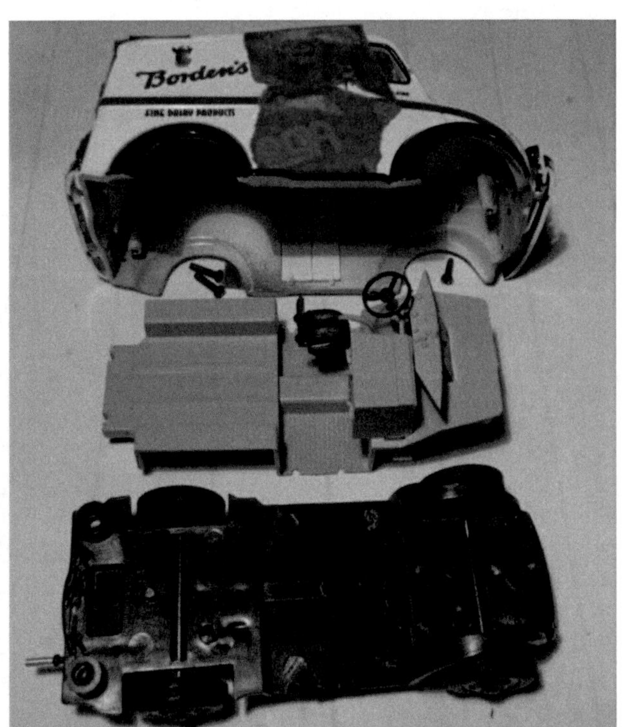

Figure 30: Divco truck disassembled, with doors taped beforehand so they don't come loose from their mounting when the interior is removed from the body.

Figure 32: Four mounting-positioning towers were made from Repair Putty. Gorilla Tape was used to fasten doors somewhat better during modification (the 'Streets chassis will secure them firmly in place once inserted in the body). Dashboard is just taped in place.

Step 4: Protection. As discussed earlier in this chapter, the repair putty to be used in Step 5 leaves an invisible film on fingers that will mar glossy surfaces. Cover the entire outside of the die-cast model with blue painters tape to prevent damage to paint and logos.

Step 5: Mounting/positioning posts for the 'Streets chassis are made using Loctite Repair Putty as shown in Figure 32. The two in the corners at the rear must clear the rear center pickup assembly at the center and the rear wheels in front of them, but are otherwise easy to make. These are made to a height about 1/8 inches above the original tower height

The two narrow positioning posts at the front must bracket the front pickup assembly without interfering with it, and are made to merely position the chassis at the right height: The front will be fastened using a method covered later. They are made to the same height as at the rear.

Step 6: Wait fifteen or more minutes. Wash hands well with soap to remove epoxy film. Remove tape from body or leave it for now.

Figure 33: New dashboard is made of cardboard marked with ballpoint pen. Divco model's steering wheel is attached.

Step 7: The dashboard is made as shown in Figure 33 and taped into place in body.

Step 8: Trial fit the body. Trim posts, and so forth to alleviate any clearance issues (there were none with the posts shown in Figures 32 and chassis shown in Figure 31). With the chassis in place drill through the chassis mounting holes at the rear to position the mounting holes correctly. Drill them about ¼ inch deep.

Step 9: Paint the wheels red to match the original wheels on the Divco model.

Step 10: Mount body on chassis, screwing it down at the rear with the original WBB screws. At the front use repair putty to fashion two hold-down tabs (Figure 34).

The conversion is complete (Figure 35).

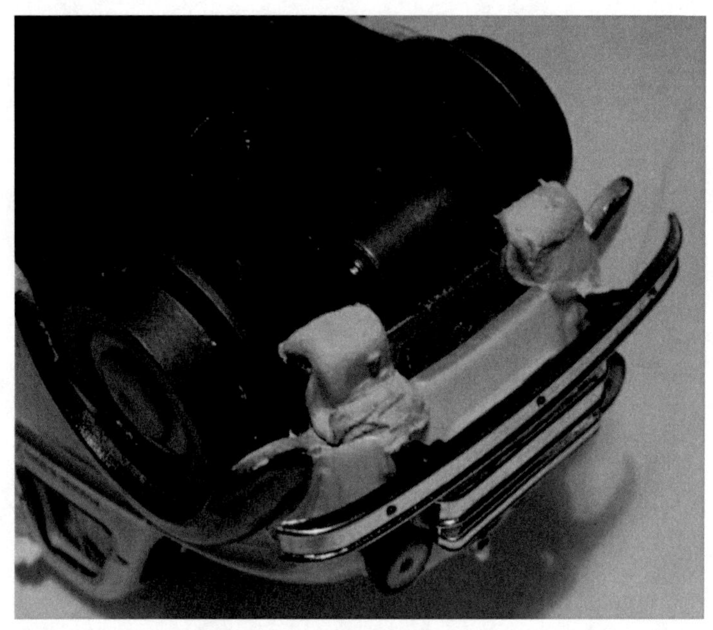

Figure 34: Once the chassis is mounted and the screws in the rear are screwed down, repair putty is used at the front to make these two small hook-tabs that hold the front in place.

Figure 35: Divco truck looks good, and natural, cruising Main Street on this 1950s layout. The author added a driver, barely visible in this photo.

1954 De Soto Four-Door Sedan

Some Brooklin models are cast so thick that the model's interior does not have enough room for a conversion, but the 1954 DeSoto in Figure 35 was not one of them. As in most big sedan conversions nothing but the mounting towers inside had to be cut away. Brooklin metal is particularly soft, and cutting the towers away presented no problems. The WBB chassis was adjusted one notch longer in wheelbase. About 3/16 inch of the chassis had to be cut at the front just barely preserving the chassis's front mounting tower (Figure 37).

This car is the heaviest automobile the author has, at fifteen ounces it is twice the weight of a stock WBB sedan. The original motor seems to handle the added burden with no sign of being especially overtaxed. The added weight and an electronic flywheel make it a smooth runner.

Figure 36: Brooklin DeSoto body on a WBB sedan chassis weighs nearly one pound.

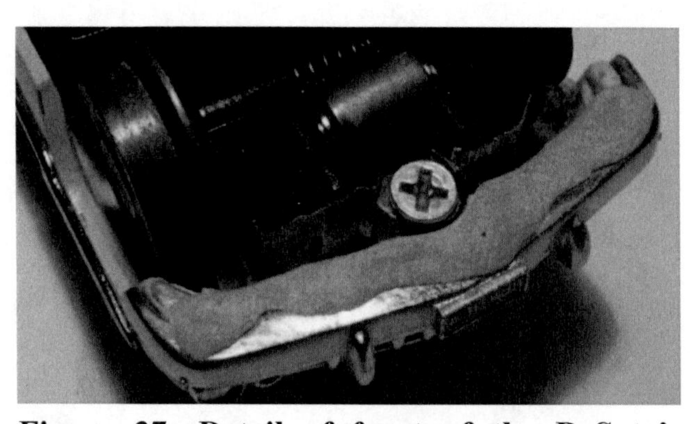

Figure 37: Detail of front of the DeSoto's chassis shows a type of trimming necessary with many models that have a short front overhang. The front of the chassis is trimmed off but a small tube of metal about 2 mm thick is retained around the mounting hole.

1956 Ford Fairlane IXO

The IXO 1956 Ford Fairlane sedan (Figure 38) is a very good-looking conversion. The original chassis mounting towers were cut out of the body with a Dremel, and no other work to the body was required except addition of new mounting towers. The WBB sedan chassis was adjusted one notch shorter and ground slightly narrower along the sides behind the rear wheels. About 3/16 inches was cut off the front of the chassis. Since the model has Thunderbrid emblems on the front fenders, two holes were drilled in the chassis at the rear and wires glued in for dual exhausts. This car has an electronic flywheel (Chapter 6) that fills the entire inside of the body, so there is no interior or driver.

Figure 38: This IXO '56 Ford Fairlane is the author's favorite converted car.

Cars on Plastic Chassis

The metal sedan chassis is almost always easier to use for car conversions than a plastic chassis. However, it is the only chassis narrow enough to fit inside a car body with running boards on the sides, like the Solido 1948 Chrysler sedan shown in Figure 39. It is the only chassis that has "wire wheels" which are necessary for the right look for some older cars.

Figure 39: Solido 1948 Chrysler sedan uses the narrow vintage truck chassis.

As shown in Figure 40, the vintage-truck chassis was shortened only 1/8 inch just in front of the rectifier. Beams and epoxy were used to bond-reinforcce it (Figure 40). While definitely not pretty from underneath, the chassis is strong and durable: it was completed in 2008 and has operated for over one thousand hours. The author also uses this chassis for the New Ray Chysler 300 shown in Figure 41: he has more converted car bodies than chassis.

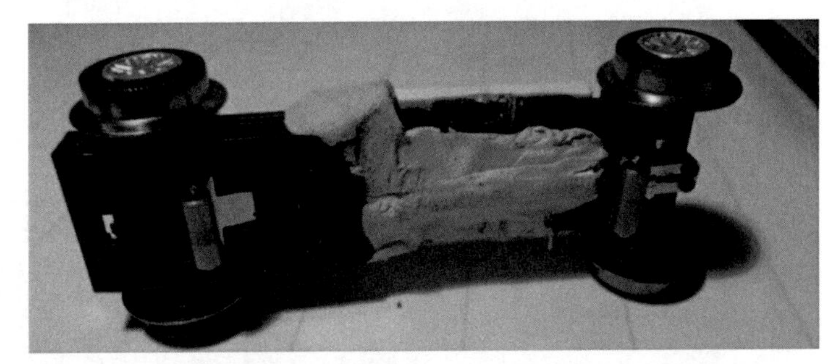

Figure 40: Chassis looks ugly but has about 1,000 operating hours on it.

Figure 42 shows a '54 Cadillac convertible converted at about the same time as the Chryslers. It looks particularly good with wire wheels – enough of a reason to pick the vintage truck chassis over the WBB sedan.

Figure 41: New Ray '55 Chrysler 300 on the same chassis.

These conversions were all very straightforward. Modelers who wish to put a car body on a plastic chassis must remember that the plastic chassis needs the weight of a *heavy* die-cast body in order to push its pickup springs firmly down on the roadway. A lightweight body, even if die-cast, will create problems (usually whenever the total vehicle weight is less than 4.5 oz.). The vintage truck weighs 5.1 oz, the Cadillac convertible when converted weighed only 4.3 oz. elven pennies (1.0 oz) were squeezed into all the empty space inside the body to bring it up to a weight roughly equal to what it was originally.

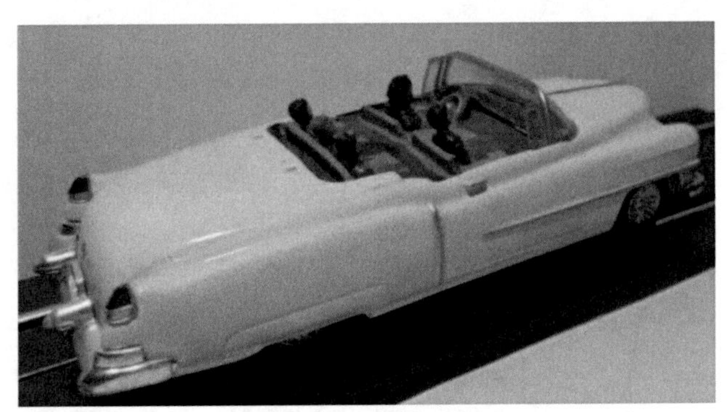

Figure 42: 1954 Cadillac convertible on another vintage truck chassis

Easy Conversion: Postwar Pickups

These are among the easiest plastic-chassis conversions possible, and yield really nice looking models.

Many 1:43 models of *modern* pickup trucks – those with full width cabs and wide load beds – will fit nicely on the sedan chassis. The floor of the pickup bed has to be cut out completely – the motor must to go up and into that space. A bed cover or simulated load can be made to hide the motor. Other than that, such conversions are often no more involved than for NYPD Dodge Diplomat in Chapter 3, that is, as easy as a conversion ever gets.

Unfortunately, it is just about impossible to fit the WBB sedan chassis into a pickup like either of those in Figure 43 – postwar or other pickup trucks that have a narrow cab because they have running boards, and/or have narrow between-the-wheels step-side pickup beds: Remove metal from the sides of the metal chassis until it is narrow enough to fit, and the "notch arms" that hold the chassis together will have been cut away completely: the chassis will fall apart.

Figure 43: Road Signature Ford F-1 (left) and Matchbox '56 Chevy pickup (right) on mounted on the panel van's plastic chassis.

However, the WBB panel van chassis makes for a *very* easy conversion for either of those two trucks. It does have wheels that are too large to be realistic for a *light* pickup, but is otherwise a near-ideal platform. Most notably, the wheelbases match very well.

While a good deal of trimming and cutting must be done to both chassis and body, every cut is simple – there are seven of them to make, as Figures 46 shows. Figure 45 details all the cuts that need to be made to the die-cast body.

Figure 44: A sedan chassis will not fit in the Road Signature Ford F-1, but a plastic panel van chassis has just the right wheelbase and plastic is easy to work.

Figure 45: Bed floor is cut out along with spaces for the motor (back of the cab) and wheels (sides of bed), too. That is all the cutting of metal that must be done, period.

Figure 46: Six cuts were made to the panel van chassis, all shown in red here, and the front mounting tower is cut off flush at its base. With these modifications the pickup body, cut as in Figure 45, fits as shown there.

The cuts are done from the back of the one-piece metal body. The entire floor of the pickup must be cut out. The lower back metal of the cab similarly is cut out so its back wall is notched in order to fit over the motor. The cuts shown were made with a band saw. Finally, the inside of pickup bed sides were cut out to give clearance for the rear wheels (and their flanges) using a Dremel and a high-speed cutter bit.

The plastic chassis requires seven cuts, only one of which is difficult: removing the chassis's front mounting tower so as to leave the chassis floor flush, or nearly flush. That is not difficult, except that the feed wire from the center pickup emerges through a hole in the body right in front of the tower, and one has to be careful not to nip it in the process.

The other six cuts to the chassis are all simple cuts that make room for fender edges, etc., to slip in and around the chassis. They can be made with a band-saw or a hand saw, or just snipped away with a diagonal cutter and filed smooth, as author did in this case.

Once the cuts are done on both the die-cast body and the chassis, they fit together as if designed to do so. Incredibly, the front bumper can stay attached to the model as it was originally mounted.

be screwed onto the chassis through the original mounting hole in the chassis into the original mounting tower on the truck body.

Imagination and preference determine what to do with the pickup's bed. Figure 47 shows the author's solution for the Ford F-1. Two pieces of cardboard were cut, one that would just cover the motor and a second representing the rear of the pickup bed and an open tailgate. The author's spare parts box was scrounged for two loads that would that were trimmed as shown to fit, then glued on with Duco Cement. Figures 49 and 50 shows the very nice end results.

Figure 47: A rear bumper is attached. Cardboard "floor" is placed atop motor with short bed/tailgate farther back, and a load, cut as shown, glued into the truck.

Figure 48: It looks like it belongs in the country. Big wheels are explained by the "Oil Field Equipment Corp." logo decals the author made: such vehicles run with large off-road tires.

Figure 49: This Matchbox Chevy pickup was converted in exactly the same manner as the F-1, and similarly mounted at the front with the original chassis mounting hole and body towers and screw. Lumber load was installed over a cardboard bed floor atop the motor.

The three models shown on this page are all early conversions done before the WBB sedan chassis was available. The Yat Ming '57 Chevy in Figure 50 was the author's first conversion and a near disaster. When shortening a vintage truck chassis for the car, the author inadvertently epoxied the front axle solid, so its wheels would not turn. In spite of that the Chevy runs superbly, with the non-turning wheels not noticeable. It has close to one thousand operating hours on it since 2006 with only minor maintenance. The Schuco '50 Chevy in Figure 51 was done a year later. It is a quintessential 1950s car. An electronic flywheel was installed in 2012, making it a superb runner.

Figure 52 shows the first truck the author attempted. A vintage truck chassis was lengthened by 5/16 inches and fitted with a Ford F-1 cab and the stake-bed taken from the vintage truck. Even that slight increase in wheelbase revealed potential problems with longer vehicles going through curves; this truck lacks enough weight to have good traction and spins its wheels badly in D-16 curves. Although the problem would be easy to fix with the addition of an ounce to the load area, the author has left the truck too light as a memento of those very early experiments in wheelbase and traction, and it is seldom run now.

Figure 50: Yat Ming '57 Chevy was the author's first conversion, and despite some problems during that first conversion runs fine to this day.

Figure 51: Schuco's '50 Chevy cab was a near-routine conversion when done, and resulted in a nice-looking model that runs a lot on the layout.

Figure 52: This first truck conversion revealed a lot of problems to be overcome in truck projects, but it was clear that pickup trucks could be easy conversions if done right.

Considerations for and Problems with Larger Vehicles

5

Chapters 3 and 4 dealt with cars and small trucks being converted to standard or lightly modified 'Streets chassis. Vehicles that are heavier or longer than those – large trucks, buses, trolleys and tractor-trailer rigs – with their stretched wheelbases and greater weight, will invariably run into several problems that must be addressed during conversion if they are to run well.

Many readers will want to jump right into the large-vehicle projects covered in Chapters 7-9. As much as possible, that has been anticipated in those chapters, and the relevant details are included in examples and projects presented there. But it has often been said that the devil is in the details, and that is definitely true when it comes to large 'Streets vehicles. Readers will find it pays to understand *why* the techniques need to be used – what problems they are trying to fix or avoid. That is covered here.

Rarely is it difficult to convert a die-cast bus or large truck so that it *looks* good. Big models have lots of room inside; as a result there are seldom real difficulties in mating their die-cast bodies to a 'Streets chassis (modified or scratch built). But it can be *very* challenging to make a long-wheelbase 'Streets chassis carry a heavy body well through curves, particularly in a way that looks as natural as possible. This chapter focuses on these troublesome aspects of larger models, and goes over the various work-arounds and construction methods a modeler can use to make a nice-looking, large 'Streets vehicle that also happens to run well.

THIS CHAPTER IN A NUTSHELL

Picking the right-sized wheels and axles is the key to good appearance – but not necessarily to good running.

Long wheelbases create several problems that must be tackled head-on or the vehicle will not run well, if at all.

Details of how and where wheels are attached and what goes where fix many problems.

Weight is seldom a problem, but weight distribution can be.

Traction: whatever the weight, enough of it has to be over the driven axle.

Power – big motors fix many problems encountered with big vehicles.

1:50 is a better scale for big vehicles than 1:43.

Longer Wheelbases

Standard streets vehicles have wheelbases from 2.5 to 3.2 inches long. Longer die-cast models, such as heavy trucks, buses and tractor-trailers, can require wheelbases up to 5.5 or even 6.5 inches long. Those can be made by lengthening a standard chassis, or building an entirely new one. But either way, longer wheelbases create potential problems in running through curves, so much so that some won't run at all.

Even the shortest 'Streets wheelbase, the shorty bus's at 2.48 inches (63 mm), puts its wheels at noticeable angle – about nine degrees – to the rails as it rounds a D-16 curve (Figure 1). This angle creates friction between wheel and rail: the wheel is sliding a tiny bit sideways as it rolls along the rail and its flange is sliding against the side of the rail as it rounds a curve. That friction consumes power. Speed drops compared to went it is on a straight.

If one increases that wheelbase by 50 percent to 3.72 inches, the angle between wheels and rails increases by about half but the friction roughly doubles (Figure 2). Increase it further and friction climbs steeply, consuming more power. Standard 'Streets vehicles are powered and geared for wheelbases of up to 3.2 inches in length – the maximum any of them have (the wheelbases of both the vintage truck and the step-van are that long). Stock vehicles have sufficient power and traction to overcome the friction this wheelbase creates, and so they do well in D-16 and D-21 curves in spite of the friction. Apparently there is a healthy margin built into them, because most will run through D-16 curves even if their wheelbase is stretched by as much as 20 percent (to as long as 3.75 inches). They run slower than normal through curves, but they make it through them.

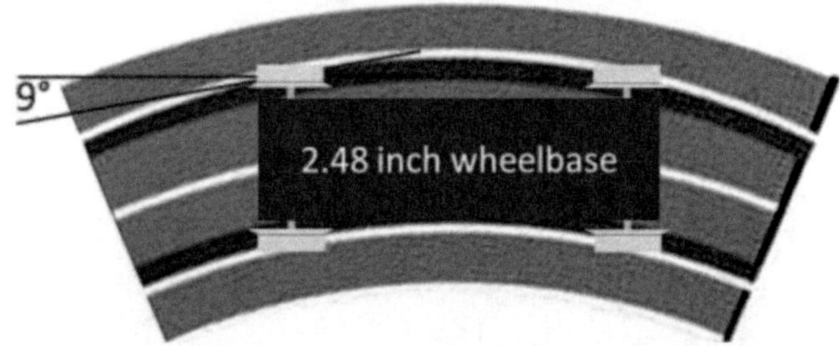

Figure 1: The 'Streets bus's wheelbase of 63 mm (2.48 in.) makes it run at a nine-degree angle to the rails, as shown here.

Figure 2: Angle increases as wheelbase is stretched. Past 3.5 inches a host of problems begin to crop up, making smooth operation more difficult to achieve.

Problems will grow worse as wheelbase is pushed past 3.75 inches. Some of these are manageable, so that wheelbases as great as 4.25 inches can sometimes be accommodated using only the stock motor – if everything else is near-perfect. But friction increases rapidly as wheelbase is lengthned beyond 4 inches, consuming the available power, until there is not enough left to propel the vehicle. Usually, before this point is reached a long-wheelbase vehicle runs out of *traction*: it comes to a stop in a curve, its wheels spinning. Generally, if one adds enough weight to increase traction to where it alleviates the spin, the stock motor will then bog down and stall.

Leaving the rails. With its wheels running at a steeper angle to the rails, the vehicle is directing more of its power to trying to run up over and off the rails. Running off the rails is not

Figure 3: At some point as wheelbase is lengthened, the side of the wheel opposite the rail begins rubbing on the *inner* edge of the roadway's flange-groove (red arrows). This increases friction a great deal. The vehicle may also try to jump the rails.

something that usually happens – other problems occur first – but the vehicle will be *much* more sensitive to rough track, and so on. Less-than-level roadways that seemed perfectly fine before may now create problems.

Decreased contact patch. As the angle between wheels and rails widens, a bit less of the wheel's surface is making contact with the rail. Electrical problems that were not serious enough to inhibit operation may do so now, particularly since the vehicle is more prone to stalling and other problems..

Flange binding. At some point, as wheelbase is lengthened further, a fatal problem is encountered (Figure 3). The wheel flanges begin to touch the edge of the roadway's flange groove on *both* sides of the wheel – that touching the rail (as normal) and the opposite side of the wheel, now rubbing against the inside edge of the flange-groove. The wheel is at such a large angle that its flanges are too wide across the groove.

When this occurs, the amount of friction being created skyrockets and the vehicle is much more likely to stall or to ride up and off the rails. The wheelbase at which this first occurs depends on which wheels are being used: it is somewhat a function of wheel diameter but the depth and angle of the flanges come into play, too. Table 2 gives for each wheel size both the wheelbase the author has determined first cause this problem to surface, and a subjective evaluation of where speed really begins to drop off so seriously that vehicles "don't run right" due to friction alone

Table 1 shows that, rather frustratingly, the larger 'Streets wheels – those that a modeler might wish to use on bigger, *longer* vehicles – are the ones that have the shortest maximum wheelbase limits before flange-binding occurs. Big wheels may look goodl\ on big trucks, but unless some of the "tricks" covered in the next few pages are applied, the big vehicle's wheelbases cannot be much over four and a half inches, which is invariably too short.

Table 1: Wheelbases Where Problems Are Serious, By Type of 'Streets Wheel

Wheel	Wheelbase - inches	
Type	Too Slow	Binding
Bus wheels	-	4.3
Step-van wheels	4.2	5.6
Panel van	4.4	6.0
Sedan	4.0	6.5
Vintage	4.0	6.9

Swivel Trucks Reduce Rail-to-Wheel Friction

If an extra axle can be added to a vehicle, two axles can be made into a swiveling truck (Figure 4). A swiveling truck keeps its wheels parallel to the rails, cutting the amount of friction created in curves. In Figure 4, total rolling friction would be cut nearly in half, despite there being two extra wheels to roll as compared to a two-axle vehicle.

Figure 4 also shows a useful trick: note that the pivot point at which the truck rotates (the white dot) is not at the truck's center but moved forward as much as possible. This reduces the angle of the *front* wheels a tiny bit, further reducing friction and increasing the wheelbase length at which flange-binding first occurs.

A third axle cannot always be added. But when a swivel truck can be used, it is by far the best approach for any wheelbase over four inches.

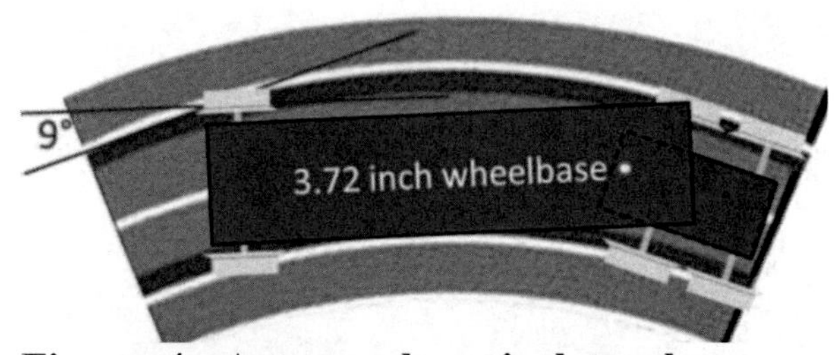

Figure 4: A two-axle swivel truck on a bus (Scenicruiser example in Chapter 8) or truck reduces friction tremendously. In addition, moving the pivot point (white dot) forward reduces the angle of attack for the front axle, further cutting friction and permitting a still-longer wheelbase before flange binding occurs.

Several examples later in the book will use swiveling dual axles, most notably the Greyhound Scenicruiser in Chapter 7, which simply will not work at the wheelbase needed without running into serious flange binding problems unless one is used.

Figure 5: Wheelbase of these two 1:50 Corgi buses was shortened by 1 9/16 inches, so they match the wheelbase of the step-van, on which chassis they are mounted. In many cities, real versions of city bus models were manufactured in shortened versions like this for much the same reason as done here: so they could negotiate tight city corners.

Shorten Wheelbase

Sometimes the best solution to a long-wheelbase problem is to shorten the die-cast model so the required wheelbase is reduced. Figure 5 shows a project from Chapter 7. Two 1:50 Corgi buses have had their bodies shortened 1 9/16 inches so they fit the standard step-van wheelbase. They run very smoothly through D-16 curves. Chapters 7, 8, and 9 will discuss other model conversions where shortening a model's body is an option, and show the advantages and disadvantages of that approach compared to other approaches to getting a good-running model.

Add Power *and* Traction

Often the most workable solution to overcoming the greater friction created by longer wheelbases is to add more power (Figure 6). Some of the motor upgrade projects later in this book are done in order to add a larger, lower RPM motor with a flywheel just to make vehicles run *smoother* at lower speeds. But the author has found that adding a *big* motor to any vehicle with a long wheelbase is a way to "nuke" friction problems. The largest motor shown in Figure 6 is used by Lionel, MTM, and WBB in many mid- and premium-range diesels. It produces more than six times the torque of a standard 'Streets motor. Alone, it will pull a respectably long train, so it is not challenged when fighting the friction of wheels to rails at a twenty-five degree angle as a two-pound vehicle grinds around a D-16 curve, which is the whole idea of using it.

Figure 6: Right, a standard 'Streets motor. Middle, a motor with about twice the power and a flywheel, used in the "Modest Motor Upgrade" in Chapter 6. Left, "Immodest Motor Upgrade" is a motor from MTH and Lionel diesels, which the author uses to repower buses and trucks. Part numbers and details are given in Chapter 6. True?

Reduction gearing adds even more push to the drive wheels. Chapter 6 will show how to build a 2:1 or 3:1 reduction-geared "power unit" for a large vehicle. A reduction gearbox changes the voltage-speed characteristics to improve both slow-speed operation through curves and clear up any marginal electrical connectivity issues (Figure 7). The vehicle will run with exceptional smoothness at very low speeds (down to three scale miles per hour) and push itself through D-16 curves with less drop in speed. But it will also run so slowly that it will be a rolling roadblock to other traffic: it cannot co-exist on a loop with vehicles that do not also have reduction gearing. At any voltage those without will run much faster and quickly catch up to it.

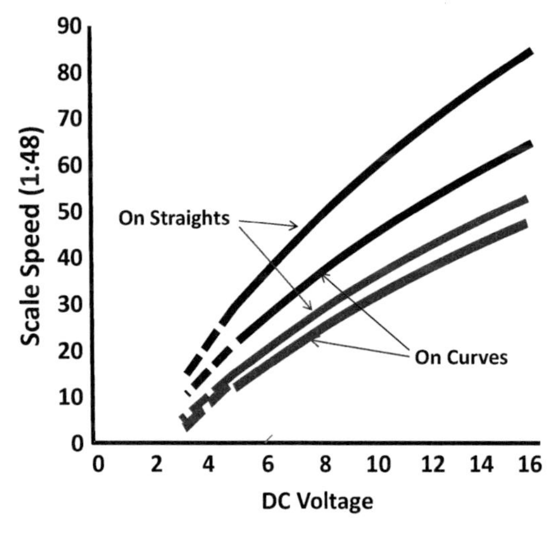

Figure 7: Speed-versus voltage curves as tested for a converted Corgi bus with reduction gearing (red lines) and without (black). With reduction gearing the bus runs much slower at any voltage, but it also slows much less, proportionally, in curves.

Traction is often a more difficult problem to solve than power when building models with longer wheelbases. The powered wheels on a 'Streets vehicle are *always* slipping just a bit in curves The non-traction-tire side slips most, but the traction tire has to slide a tiny bit because it, too, is running at a significant angle to the rail (as was shown in Figure 2).

Figure 8: This rather grainy photo is the only picture the author has of his first converted 'Streets bus. Only on the third attempt, with additional weight added for traction *and* a large motor, would it run decently through D-16 curves, although it slowed quite a bit. This bus was subsequently shortened, re-painted and fitted with a reduction gearbox; it is the rightmost of the two buses shown in Figure 5, and now runs through the author's downtown area nearly every day at scale speeds of ten mph.

The greater resistance that a long-wheelbase vehicle creates can exacerbate that slipping to the point that there is nothing but wheel spin. Adding more power only makes it worse. The author's first attempt at converting a Corgi bus (Figure 8) had only its standard motor which proved insufficient to push its five-inch wheelbase through D-16 curves. The bus would enter a curve and quickly slow to a stop, just spinning its wheels. Traction was increased with a good deal of weight added over the driven axle. The bus would then slow to a stop in a curve with its motor stalled. Only by adding both a large motor (like that on the left in Figure 8) *and* four oz. of additional weight, would the bus run through D-16 curves.

Figure 9: This step-van chassis was lengthened about one inch (see Chapter 7's Corgi Mack fire-truck example). Although the new die-cast body weighed a bit more than the original 'Streets body, a roll of thirty-two pennies (three additional ounces) was mounted atop the motor. This provided sufficient traction without adding so much weight it would overwhelm the stock motor, and while the power is while barely sufficient, in this case it *is* sufficient.

The author adds weight where possible using pennies: eleven weigh roughly one ounce (Figure 9). Pennies are dense and fit well into nooks and crannies, and there always seem to plenty of them available. (They seem more convenient to use than lead shot which is used for an even higher packing density when that is necessary.) A rough rule of thumb is that about two ounces must be added over and above the stock 'Streets weight for each additional half inch of wheelbase added. However, the exact amount that needs to be added, and where it is best located, has to be fine-tuned by trial and error.

Die-cast models of larger vehicles like buses and tractor trailer rigs usually bring some additional weight with them. For example, a typical 1:50 Corgi bus body weighs about 12.5 to 13.2 ounces as opposed to the 8.8 ounces or the step-van body. An upgraded motor, if fitted, adds as much as three ounces more.

But this "natural weight gain" due to body and a big motor is often not enough to provide all the traction the long-wheelbase vehicle needs. Among die-cast buses in Chapter 7 that are not shortened, the Scenicruiser (Figure 10) alone has a swivel truck and it alone required no additional weight be added.

Figure 10: Converted Corgi 1:50 buses from Chapter Seven. Although the Scenicruiser (top) has a wheelbase slightly longer than its sibling, its swivel truck means it runs through curves much easier than the shorter two-axle bus. It needed no additional weight for traction. The lower, two-axle bus, having a smaller body, was about an ounce lighter but required four ounces of additional weight to give it enough traction to run smoothly through curves.

Traction problems can be difficult to foresee. Figure 11 shows the profile of a Corgi 1:48 Birney trolley converted to 'Streets in Chapter 8. The upgraded motor and heavier die-cast body meant the completed model weighed 12.4 ounces as compared to 8.0 for the original van. The author was therefore quite surprised when this trolley spun its wheel badly even on some patches of straight road. A heavier motor placed more toward the center of the chassis in combination with the much heavier body, which despite appearances was much heavier on one end than the other, had shifted weight distribution so much that way too much of the weight was over the un-powered axle. Three ounces of weight added at the extreme end of the trolley, behind the motor so as to give it leverage, solved the problem. The trolley runs very well through D-16 curves.

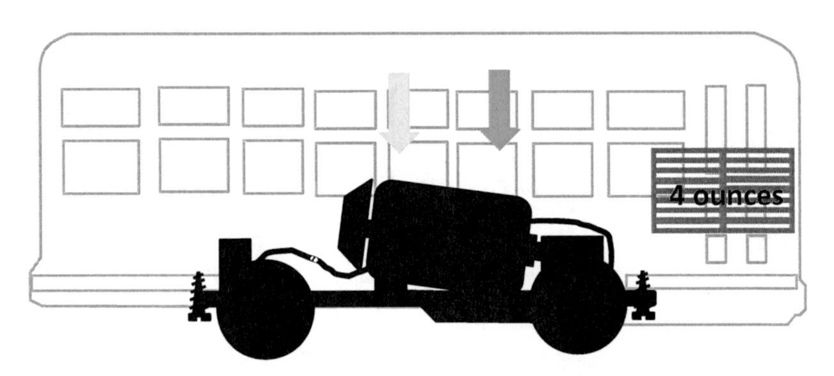

Figure 11: Birney trolley modifications added weight, but shifted center of gravity forward (from green to yellow) so it had insufficient traction. Added weight moved it back.

Front-Wheel Drive Works, But...

Sometimes it is necessary to drive the front wheels rather than the rear. Reasons are:

No room at the rear: This could be a problem with some flatbed trucks, etc.

Need a swiveling truck at the rear: An example is the Scenicruiser in Chapter 7.

It is no more difficult to power the front than the rear axle: just turn the entire chassis around and reverse the leads to the motor.

Front wheel drive should be avoided where possible. It just does not work quite as well as rear wheel drive (Figure 12). After a lot of study, the author gave up trying to determine why: That's just the way it is. Front wheel *will* work well enough: the Scenicruiser and a few others the author has built run well. But either will climb steeper slopes, as well as slow less in curves, when in reverse compared to forward.

Figure 12: This converted Joel 1:50 model of a DAF KF420 tractor has a medium-size motor (middle, Figure 6) mounted vertically and driving the tractor's front axle. It uses a metal track-speeder chassis and lead shot for weight. The tractor weights a full pound with 12 ounces of it on the front axle. The trailer weighs only 6 ounces. Despite this, it will climb no more than a 4% slope, slows very noticeably on D-21 curves, and barely makes it through D-16 curves. It also exhibits just a trace of the shaking discussed at the bottom of this page.

Figure 13: The author was sure this articulated, two-axle drive, tower-mounted large-motor chassis would be the ultimate tractor when he built it in 2011. That was not the case.

A Great but Shaky Idea

The tractor in Figure 13 uses a large motor in a tower position to drive both rear axles (a box freight trailer slips over and pivots around the motor to hide it). The chassis hinges on a pin on the back of the cab so the tractor bends in curves, too. It was a very intricate and involved scratch-building effort. But despite the double-drive axles it pulls no better than single-axle drive, and the tall motor shakes a good deal from side to side – a type of resonance apparently – which usually sets the trailer to shaking and wobbling, too. Tower drive works well in model locomotives, but their chassis and body outweigh their motors by a ratio of about ten to one. Here, the ratio is about one to one, and the tower drive rocks back and forth too much.

1:50 – The Preferred Scale for 'Streets Trucks, Buses and Big Rigs

The author has converted a number of buses, trucks, and tractor trailers in 1:43, 1:48 and 1:50 scales. That has led him to conclude that there is little if any reason to choose one scale over the other on the basis of the work required or project cost. Despite that the author *strongly* recommends 1:50 for buses, trucks, and heavy construction and military vehicles converted to Streets, even though he has settled exclusively on 1:43 for cars and light pickups (whether for 'Streets conversions or for models parked on streets, in driveways and the like on his layout.

The choice of 1:43 scale for *cars* is because there is a bigger selection of cars available in 1:43 than in 1:48 or 1:50, and because a bump in scale helps smaller vehicles be seen against the backdrop of a layout. Still 1:50 is recommended for larger vehicles because of

Selection: A wide range of cars may be available in 1:43, but trucks and buses available in that scale are few and far between. By contrast, a wide range is available in 1:50 scale.

Availability of 'Streets parts that work at that scale: The *only* 'Streets wheels that fit and look good on a majority of 1:43 buses and trucks are those from the short school bus which has been out of production since 2011 and is increasingly hard to find and expensive to purchase. There is no choice if a realistic look is desired but to use wheels that big – none. By contrast, 1:50 trucks and tractor trailers look fine using wheels from the panel van – still in production and easy to find.

Size and "road fit": In either scale, a tractor-trailer rig or bus dominates 1:43 cars, looking as it should: *very big*. The 1950s Corgi 1:50 Mack B-60 tractor trailer at the top of Figure 15 hulks over a 1:43 Pontiac Chieftain station wagon, a big car of that period; it looks impressively big next to cars and pickup trucks. Yet it is far smaller than the New Ray 1:43 model of what is basically the same tractor trailer, shown in the lower image. Either scale works well for conveying to the eye that the big rig is *big*, but

Figure 14: Top, 1:50 Mack B-61 tractor-trailer from Chapter 9 looks big enough with respect to 1:43 Brooklin 1956 Pontiac Chieftain to establish that it is a big, big rig. Bottom, 1:43 Mack B-60 dwarfs it, though, and is so big it creates clearance problems running on a layout.

Figure 15: The Corgi Mack Truck in Figure 14 is itself drafted by a Corgi 1:50 scale Kenworth W925 and low-boy trailer. Despite this road having been widened at the center so the lanes are farther apart than normal, these two trucks barely miss one another.

the 1:50 model fits on 'Streets roadway without creating nearly as many operating problems for its owner. The 1:43 model in Figure 14 has a trailer longer than the 1:50 model (and would ewmain so even if they were the same scale since it is a model of a slightly longer trailer). Both can be converted within wheelbase limits discussed earlier and made so they run well.

What is a problem though is that the 1:43 model's trailer is *wider.* It is just 3/32 inch narrower than a 'Streets roadway lane. That model's greater length *combined* with that width means it is almost certain to knock aside traffic in an adjacent nested lane, and to bump into nearby scenery when going around corners. The 1:50 model, while "big enough to be big," creates fewer and less serious problems, although it may have minor overhang issues, too.

Figure 15 shows that Corgi 1:50 Mack tractor trailer from Figure 14, now converted to 'Streets, passing a Corgi 1:50 model of an even bigger rig. The roadway has been widened by inserting a ¼ inch basswood strip between lanes (see 'Streets *for O-Gauge Model Railroads,* Chapter 7), yet these two trucks miss each other by only 3/16 inch. Were they 1:43, even with added space between lanes, they collide.

While the author much prefers 1:50, the choice of scale to run is to every modeler: Chapter 9 shows how to convert both big rigs shown in Figure 14. Buses and tractor trailers in the larger scale are impressive to watch running. It is best, however, to let a 1:43 big rig have the road to itself, and to anticipate that scenery, figures, parked cars, and buildings alongside or near curves may have to be relocated in order to satisfy the vehicle's appetite for clearance.

Power Modifications

6

This chapter covers adding power and traction to stock, modified, or scratch-built 'Streets chassis. The chapter includes three sections:

Upgrades to larger motors with flywheels for stock and modified chassis.

Electronic flywheels in stock, modified, or scratch-built chassis.

Powerful motor-gearboxes that will drive heavy buses, trucks, and tractor trailers.

It also discusses traction improvements so vehicles can use the power they have well.

Table 1 compares operating problems with potential solutions. A larger X means a project is more likely a good solution to that problem.

Table 1: Problems versus Solutions for Power

Solution → / Problem ↓	Upgraded Flywhl	Electronic Flywheel	Big motor geared unit	Traction addition	Remove rectifier	May Need Repair
Relative Level of Effort Required	4	4	12	3	2	
Want it to be able to back up, too.					X	
Won't run smoothly at high speeds				x		X
Won't stay on the rails well				x		X
Won't run smoothly at low speeds	X	x				
Needs to run at very low speeds		x	X			
Slows too much in curves	x		X			
Heavy vehicle runs & starts poorly			X	x		

Modest Motor Upgrade

This describes a straightforward project that doubles the power in a stock chassis and adds flywheel smoothness. The reader is urged to read through this entire explanation and study it before beginning to work on it.

Figure 1 shows three motors. That at the right is from a WBB sedan, and identical to those in all 'Streets vehicles except the vintage truck, which has a slightly narrower and longer motor. The two other motors are available from Lionel as spare parts for its RTR sets (parts are always available for RTR sets and always relatively inexpensive). These motors are 90% larger by volume than the original motor, run at about a 20% lower RPM at any voltage, and will produce about twice the torque.

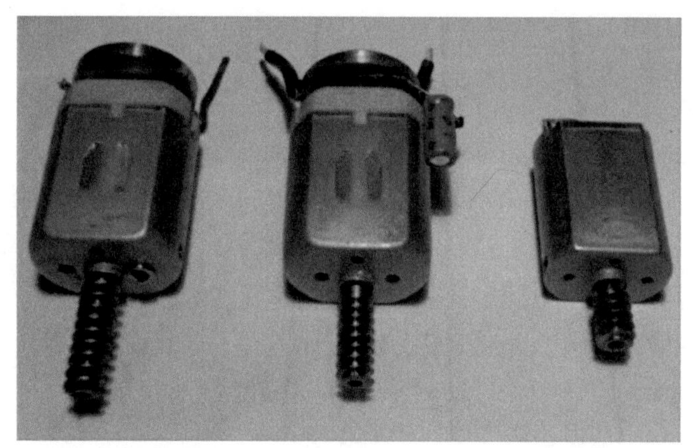

6308661100 710069100 Stock

Figure 1: Three motors. From left to right, motors from Lionel RTR starter locos (0-8-0 on left and Hall class 4-6-0 on the right) and a motor from the WBB sedan. Numbers shown are Lionel replacement parts numbers.

Figure 2: Chassis from a WBB sedan with body, interior, and recifier removed.

Most important, each of the two larger motors is fitted with a flywheel that provides "ride through" – continuation of motor rotation – during momentary lapses in power due to dirty wheels or uneven rails and so on. These are the largest flywheel motors the author has found that will fit into the WBB sedan. They will not fit into the vintage truck (very few other motors will) but will fit into the panel van, the step van and short bus, too

The motor in the middle of Figure 1, Lionel part 710069100, is fitted to the Harry Potter Hall Class loco among other starter-level locos. This motor comes with a worm gear that will mesh well with 'Streets axles. Price is $18.50.

Part number 6308661100, at the left in Figure 1, is from the Lionel 0-8-0 starter locomotive and has a worm gear that looks quite similar, but in fact has a spiral spacing that will not mesh with a standard 'Streets axle. It costs $13.50. Modelers who have a gear puller and know how to use it on small motors can save $5.00 by pulling the worm from this motor's shaft, and then pulling the worm from the stock motor's shaft and mounting it on the new motor. Otherwise, 710069100 must be obtained.

Step 1: The body and interior are removed from a sedan chassis. The wires to the rectifier are cut and it is removed (Figure 2).

Step 2: The two screws holding the adjustable chassis sections together are removed (red arrows in Figure 2) and front and rear chassis pieces are separated.

Step 3: The motor-gearbox is removed by detaching the two screws (Figure 3). Warning: the gearbox holds the motor bearings (red arrows) in their slots. They can easily pop out

Figure 3: The rear part of the WBB adjustable-length chassis sparated from the front. With the motor-gearbox removed, the rear-axle bearings (red arrows) can easily pop out of their slots. It can be difficult to work them back in.

Out of the slots cut for them in the chassis: It requires tedious and frustrating work to coax them back in. The figure shows the chassis resting on a wooden block so as to minimize pressure while completing Step 4.

Step 4: Thin styrene is made into the two pieces shown attached to the chassis in Figure 4. These hold the axle bearings in place. The bottom of the motor gearbox is a good reference for determining the position adn diameter of the four holes needed: one in each piece for the mounting screw, and one for a positioning tab.

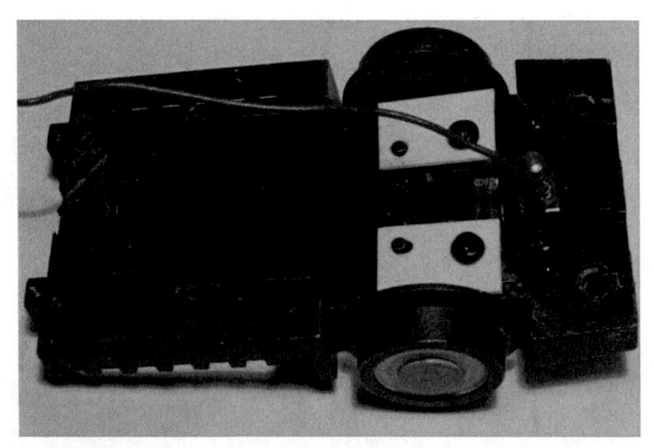

Figure 4: The two fabricated motor-bearing retainer plates installed.

Figure 5 shows an important detail. The bearings are recessed about .025 inch below the level of the chassis deck, so the two tabs shown on the gearbox fit into them. Small thin plastic pieces were cut and placed in those recesses before the two pieces shown in Figure 4 were screwed on top, to fill the space in and hold the bearings firmly. A drop of plastic welder was placed on each, then the other piece was screwed on top of it. When both sides are done the chassis is as in Figure 4. The plastic pieces must not block the top of the rear axle gear.

Note: author is aware that this step requires pieces be cut and drilled to rather close tolerances and assembly that is delicate and tedious to perform. Everything shown here was learned via some frustrating lessons, but the best advice that can be given is to study these photos and the chassis pieces carefully, plan ahead, proceed carefully, and try again until it works.

Figure 5: Plastic spacers must be inserted above bearings. See text for details.

Step 5: The floor of the rear chassis is cut away as shown in the upper image in Figure 6, using a band-saw (or manual handsaw). Then the insides of the adjustment arms are ground at an angle as shown in shown in Figures 6 and 7. There are two key aspects of this. First, the portion of the floor to be cut out is only the front

13/16 inch. This leaves sufficient metal for strength of the chassis. Second, the grinding removes more metal for a deeper cut toward the rear. A cylinder laid so its rested on these two ground edges would slope at an angle toward the rear.

Note: A Dremel rotary tool with a 115 high-speed cutter bit was used to grind the metal away. *Safety goggles or glasses should be used here.* The Dremel tosses small metal particles at high speed in all directions.

Step 7. The two chassis sections are reassembled at the original wheelbase (two notches showing in this case) as shown in Figure 7. The area around the rear of the rectifier cup is ground away (yellow arrows in Figure 7).

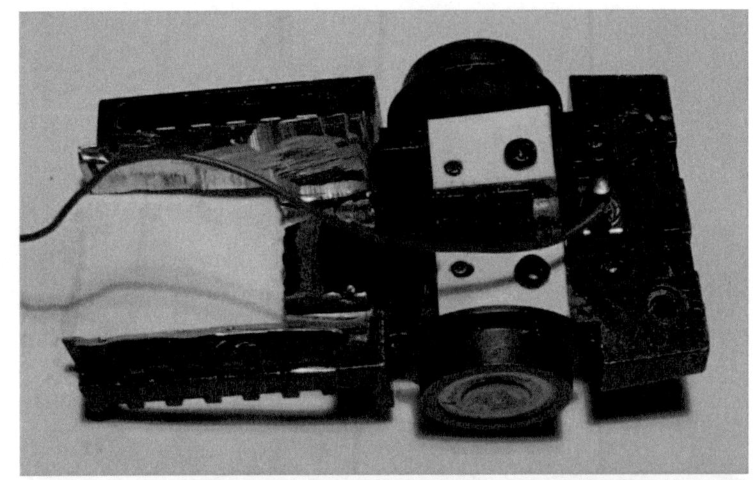

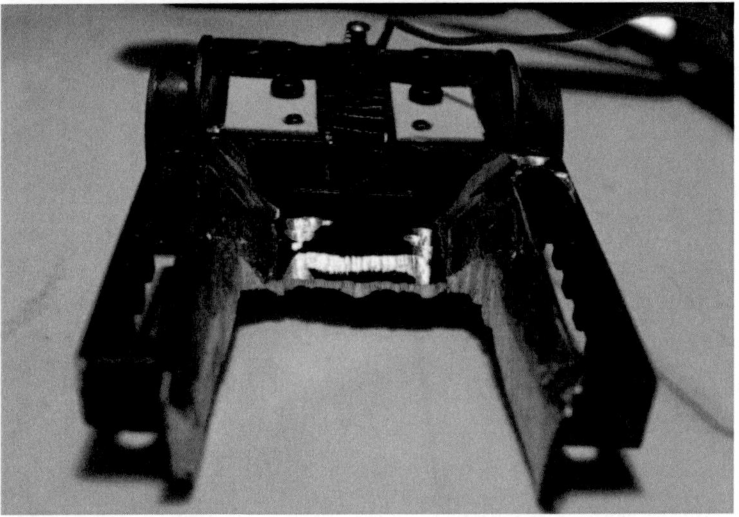

Figure 6:Two views of rear chassis after preparation.

Figure 7: Chassis pieces reassembled at original wheelbase length.

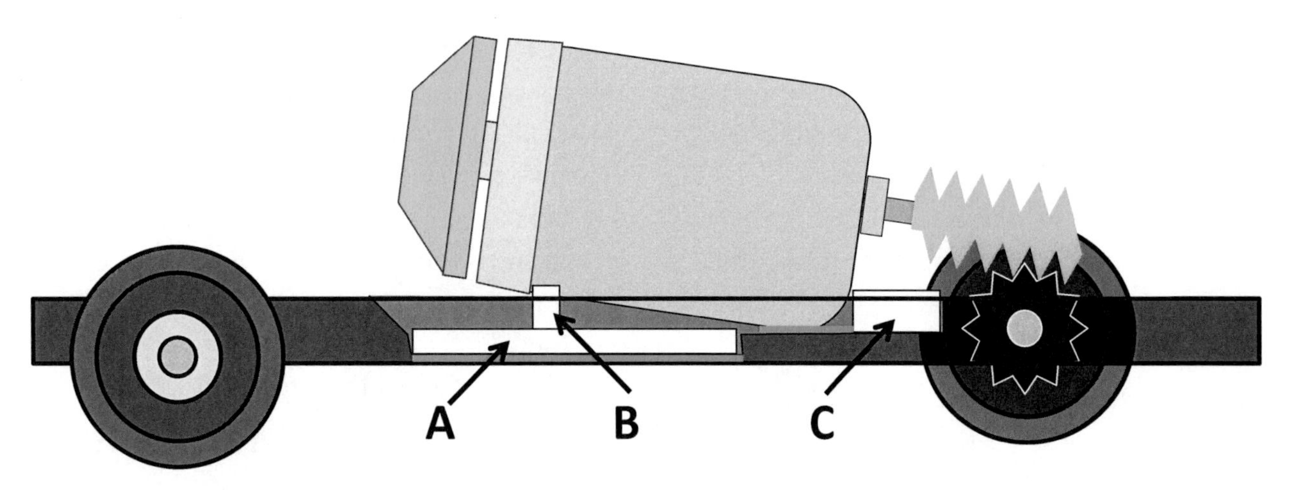

Figure 8: Diagam of motor mounting. See text for details.

Figure 8 shows how the motor will be mounted. There are several goals that must be simultaneously met:

1. The motor should sit as low in the chassis as possible.
2. The worm and gear must engage; but not bind: the worm must not be pressed into the gear so it is pushing down on it.
3. The motor needs to be firmly held in place.

The author's method is to make the two plastic pieces indicated in as white blocks in Figure 9. The leftmost (items A and B in Figure 8) is a mount to go under the motor and hold it up at the rear. Piece A is made of thin styrene, and a thicker plastic piece, a motor support beam, is glued atop it (B). By cutting out the floor at the front of the rear chassis section (as was shown in Figure 6), a recess for this piece to fit in was created: piece A+B cannot move about once clamped in, so the motor will be held firmly.

The front edge of the motor rests against the floor of the chassis. A styrene insert, C (see Figure 9) is cut to size and placed in the chassis well ahead of it to prevent it moving rearward.

By shimming the height of piece B, one can change the angle of the motor and affect how the worm and gear engage. A modeler must work at this by adjusting the height of B until goals two and three are met: the worm and gear engages fully but does not bind, and the motor fits firmly in the chassis. The author does this by first making sure that the motor will sit down all the way on the chassis floor when placed in the chassis: if not more metal is cut away on the inside sides of the rear chassis as was shown in Figure 6. *Then thin shims are fitted as needed.*

Figure 9: The two plastic pieces that must be fabricated. Left, the support that goes under the rear of the motor (piece A+B) ***with one shim the author had to add for proper adjustment in this case.*** **Right, piece C.**

The two thin green lines shown in Figure 8 indicate two layers of electrical tape. These are placed on the bottom of the motor mount piece A+B and on the chassis floor where the front edge of the motor will rest. These provide a very small amount of cushioning for the motor: the vehicle will run smoother and definitely much quieter with this plastic in place.

Step 8: The motor mounts A+B and C are made and placed, with the tape, in the chassis. The motor is positioned so its worm fits onto and meshes with the rear axle's gear, the correct amount of worm-gear engagement being arranged by filing away the top of B or shimming under the piece with cardstock. Patience and care results in the motor sitting with the gears well meshed but not binding, and firmly in place – so it does not rock or flex when held tightly to the chassis by hand.

Step 9: The motor is held in place by hand and electrical tape wrapped twice around motor and chassis. The tape is wound around the chassis just ahead of where the motor sits on motor-mount A+B.

The tape should be wound around the chassis while keeping it under tension. The use of electrical tape to permanently mount the motor may strike readers as a poor-quality short cut, but the author has found no better or more lasting solution. It works well, seems to last a long time, and with a small amount of tension on it holds the motor firmly in place while providing just a bit of vibration absorption.

Step 10: Temporarily wire the chassis power leads to the motor. Test the chassis to see that it runs and goes forward when positive polarity (positive to the center rail) is applied. Reverse the leads and wheels should go backwards. Then solder the leads and apply insulating tape.

The motor upgrade is done. The car now has nearly twice the power and a bit more weight over the rear axle. Despite the greater power, the motor runs at lower RPM, which means the car will run slower at lower voltages, and because of its flywheel, more smoothly.

The larger motor has "eaten" the space originally occupied by the interior: The inside of the windows can be painted to hide the motor.

Figure 10: Completed chassis with the motor mounted.

Doing the Same Upgrade for the Plastic Chassis

Step 1: Cut the wires from the track power feeds to the rectifier, at the rectifier terminals.

Step 2: Remove the two screws that hold the motor to the chassis (underside of the chassis, just ahead of the rear axle.) The motor, still connected to the rectifier, can be removed by working its worm out of the gearbox.

Step 3: Cut off all posts and projections including the lip around the rectifier cup flush.

Step 4: Bend the copper finger with the front and rear axle feeds attached up and to the side.

Step 5: The new motor can be slid down into the chassis and the worm worked into the gearbox. The front of the motor will fit down into chassis well that held the original motor. It will angle up with its back end against the chassis at the front of the well. The flywheel sits just over where the rectifier was, but with it removed and the lip of the rectifier cup razed off, it will face no clearance problems.

One can gradually work the new motor rearward and the worm into the gearbox, engaging the axle gear. The easiest way to do this is to the motor back and the worm into the front of the gearbox until it touches the gear teeth and then push lightly while turning the rear wheels so the axle's gear pulls the worm in.

The proper placement for the motor is with the worm gear almost but *not quite* touching the back wall of the gearbox (about one millimeter clearance – one can look into the gearbox from above to check this). When the motor is positioned correctly, measure the distance from the front of the motor to the gearbox.

Step 6: The rightmost styrene piece in Figure 11 (yellow arrow) was made out of 1/8 inch styrene, long enough to fit between the insides of the rear wheels, and *exactly* the distance measured in the paragraph above. The notch in it is clearance for the worm.

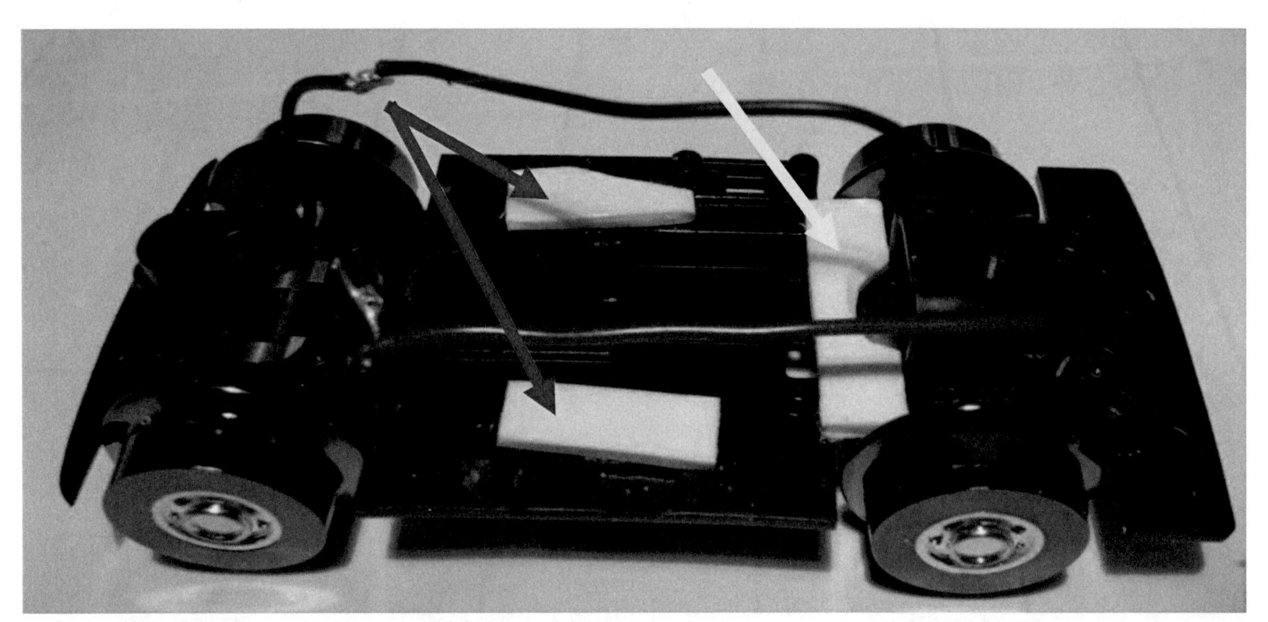

Figure 11: Plastic chassis (WBB panel van). Motor and rectifier have been removed. All posts and projections were razed, and copper tab from axle feed raised up and to the side.

Figure 12: Plastic chassis with the motor installed. It fits perfectly to mesh fully but not too tightly with the axle gear, in the original gearbox, without significant trimming.

Step 7: Once piece C is made, trial fit it in place. Make sure that with the motor pushed all the way to the rear so it is butts up against piece C, the worm-back gearbox wall clearance is correct.

Step 8: Make pieces shown by red arrows in Figure 11 from the same plastic used for piece C, each about 5/8 inch long and 5/16 inch wide.

Place the chassis with motor on a tabletop and check that it is centered side to side. Glue pieces A and B into place one at a time firmly up against each side of the motor using Plastruk Plastic Welder. Plastruck does not hold exceptionally well to the plastic chassis, but it seems sufficient to do the job here if applied well. Once the Plastruk has hardened, the three plastic pieces hold the motor position securely. Tape it in place with plastic electrical tape in an exactly the same way as the upgraded motor was in the sedan chassis conversion described earlier. Solder the feed wires to the motor wires

Step 9: The chassis is complete (Figure 12).

Note: Panel van chassis vary slightly and other plastic chassis, while similar, are slightly different. Sometimes it is necessary to place a shim of up to 1/8 inch under the rear of the motor where it rests on the chassis in order to lift it up and lever it at a greater angle if needed so its worm fully engages the gear. It also may be necessary to cut a bit of clearance at the front of the gearbox cover as shown in Figure 13.

Figure 13: The front edge of some gearbox covers may bind the top of the worm. The front can be cut away with an X-Acto as shown here, without any disassembly.

Electronic Flywheels

Figure 14 shows a 1.5 farad PowerStor brand supercapacitor. It is about the diameter of a nickel. Under the right conditions, this supercapacitor stores enough energy to power a 'Streets vehicle for about four seconds. Installed in the correct way, it acts in much the same way as a flywheel on a motor, but through electronic means. If power from the rails is momentarily interrupted due to a roller hitting a dirty patch of rail or another reason, the supercapacitor will feed what power it has to the motor, keeping it spinning.

Figure 14: PowerStor 1.5 F supercapacitor.

Supercapacitors

For 'Streets purposes, supercapacitors are best thought of as small, fast-charging rechargeable batteries of limited capacity. While they don't store much power compared to a battery, they will fully charge in only a few seconds and discharge just as quickly. They are available in several voltage ratings: 5.5 volts is the highest among affordable small-sized supercapacitors. Exceed the rated voltage for long, and their internal chemistry is destroyed – they cease to function. They are DC devices, too, made to work in only one direction (more on that later). PowerStor and Cornell Dubilier 5.5 V 1.5 farad coin type units cost $5 to $7 each, and are the author's choice for 'Streets applications.

Installing a Supercapacitor Electronic flywheel

Figure 15 shows three PowerStor 5.5 volt, 1.5 F supercapacitors wired in series to the rectifier output terminals of an otherwise unmodified WBB sedan chassis. The units are wired in series so their voltage ratings add: three times 5.5 volts means this string can take 16.5 volts continuously with no problems (it has, too. The vehicle it is installed in has about three hundred operating hours at this time).

As stated above, supercapacitors are DC devices, and they are labeled as such. Note in Figure 14 the top tab has a plus embossed on the terminal. The sides of super-capacitors also have arrows or arrowheads pointing from the positive to the negative side, as can be seen, too.

The capacitors are wired in a string of three, positive to negative terminal, as shown. The positive end of the string is wired to the *negative* DC output terminal of the rectifier, and the negative end of the string to the positive terminal of the rectifier. (On all vehicles the author has examined, the red wire to the motor is the positive lead, and the black wire to the motor from the rectifier, the negative lead).

Why reverse the polarity – negative to positive, etc.? Think of the supercapacitor as a type of electronic spring: the DC voltage is pushed "backwards" – literally electrically shoved -- into the capacitor when power is flowing – "compressing" its field. When the track voltage stops briefly, the spring releases - power flows out of the supercapacitor and to the now-hungry

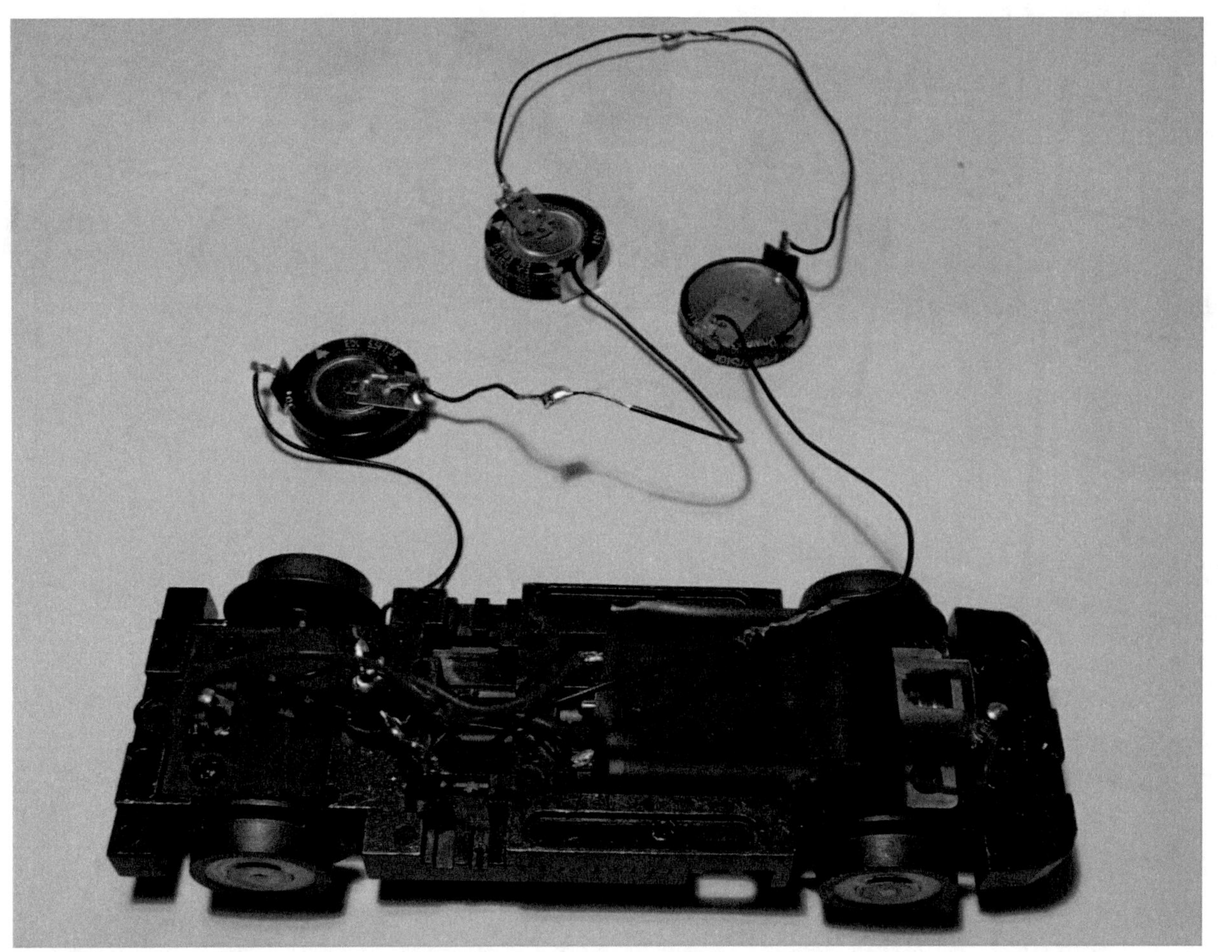

Figure 15: A WBB sedan chassis with three coin-type 1.5 F units wired in series to the rectifier DC terminals – the negative terminal of the supercapacitor string connects to the positive output terminal of the rectifier (red arrow and red wire), and the positive end to the negative rectifier DC terminal (black arrow and black wire).

motor, and in the right direction. Regardless, this is as recommended by the manufacturers, and required for it to work correctly.

The author has wired the supercapacitors together in Figure 15 with lengths of wire sufficient to allow some freedom in how they are positioned inside the car (Figure 16). There is not a lot of room left inside most cars, but usually two fit, one atop the other, above the motor or where the front interior of the WBB sedan goes, and a third slides in just in front of the dashboard area

The author covers both sides of each supercapacitor with electrical tape so that there can be no short-circuits and places them on the body with more tape as shown in Figure 15. In some cases the interior must be removed, in others it can be left intact (Figure 17).

The author leaves the rectifier in place on all vehicles with an electronic flywheel installed. Since reverse polarity voltage can damage the supercapacitor pack, this is done as a protection against inadvertently reversing voltage, etc.

Figure 16: Two supercapacitors are taped in a stack above the motor, and the third above the front axle. The WBB sedan body can accommodate them along with its interior. Some die-cast conversions cannot, and the interior has to be removed to make room for the supercapacitors.

Figure 17: WBB sedan gives no indication it is completely filled inside. This sedan was modified with more realistic grills, bumper, etc., much as was one example in Chapter 3. Author put a driver in the interior before mounting body and screwing the body and chassis together.

Comparison of Performance

Table 2 compares the performance of three WBB sedans: a completely stock one, one fitted with an upgraded motor and flywheel, and one fitting with the electronic flywheel. All but the electronic flywheel have had their rectifiers removed.

Top-speed values are the author's estimates: there is no place on the layout where he can let cars run up to what is truly top speed. Slowest smooth speed is something of a judgment call – it is the lowest speed at which the author sees no variation in or any sign of hesitation. Clean track and wheels means scrupulously and just cleaned. Moderately means after about two hours of running. Dirty means very dirty to the point one can see grime on wheels and rollers.

Ride-through distance is the inches a vehicle will continue to travel when running at seven volts, when power is just shut off. Values are within +/-5% or so.

Table 2: Comparison of WBB Sedans

Vehicle Characteristic	Type of Flywheel		
	None	Mech.	Elec
Top Speed - scale MPH	90	100	88
At voltage of	16	16	16
Power used - watts	3.7	5.1	3.7
Slowest - scale mph			
Clean track, wheels	28	13	9
At voltage of	5+	4-	2+
Moderately dirty	37	25	31
At voltage of	6+	5	5
Very dirty	-	45	30
At voltage of	-	8.9	7
Ride-thru dist. @ 7V	0	2	7
Vehicle can back up?	Yes	Yes	No

Vehicles with flywheels, particularly those with electronic ones, run so well on mildly dirty track, that owners may not notice as the track and wheels becoming dirty. One needs to remember to check every once in a while.

Immodest Motor Upgrade

The "Modest Motor Upgrade" described earlier improves the operation of cars and small- through medium-size trucks, providing roughly twice the power and, due to its flywheel, much smoother operation at lower speeds. But even with that upgrade larges buses and tractor trailers can be underpowered. They require even more power due to their length and weight.

Figure 18 shows a Mabuchi can motor with flywheel that can be found in many locomotives made by Lionel, MTH, Williams, and K-line. It can be obtained new (Lionel part number 6108274100) but the author has obtained all two dozen he has used for conversion by buying used or broken locomotives at swap meets. The vast majority have a worm that fits well on the 'Streets axle's gear, but a few do not. The worm can be pulled off the shaft on those and one that does mesh well installed. This size motor provides roughly six times the power. It weighs 5.5 ounces compared to 1.0 for the stock motor, so it provides a good deal of extra weight and traction too. With its big flywheel it provides smooth running at low speeds, and will typically "coast" a bus or tractor trailer at least half a foot after the power is shut off.

Installation of this motor in a chassis is done in a very similar way to that covered in the "Modest Motor Upgrade" and will be explained in project descriptions given in Chapters 8 and 9. Figure 19 show it installed in the Scenicruiser bus chassis from Chapter 8. Figure 20 shows it installed in a tractor trailer chassis from Chapter 9.

Figure 18: Three motors. See text for details.

Figure 19: Large direct drive motor installed in a bashed step-van chassis.

Figure 20: Another large-motor, this time in a scratch-built tractor trailer chassis (Chapter 9).

Power Unit for Big Vehicles

Figure 21 and 22 shows a step-van chassis fitted with a large motor-flywheel and a reduction gear set that multiplies the motor's torque (pushing power) while simultaneously cutting the net RPM at its drive wheels. A vehicle fitted with it will be slower at any operating voltage but able to push through much more friction.

Figure 21: Step-van plastic chassis fitted with a very large motor-flywheel and reduction gear set.

This section will discuss how to build such a power unit, which can be fitted to a plastic chassis as shown, a metal sedan chassis, or to a scratch-built chassis of a large bus or tractor trailer rig, and more. The motor to be used here is shown in Photo 9 It is similar in all important respects to the motor shown on the previous page, where it was used in direct - rather than reduction-drive applications.

Figure 22: The motor (upper left) can be found in full-size diesels from MTH, Lionel, and K-Line and other manufacturers. This one came from a broken MTH Veranda Turbine. Black casting in the front of motor is original motor mount bracket. The stock 'Streets motor is shown to in the middle back. Blue and orange gears are from Tamiya. Other parts were fabricated or purchased.

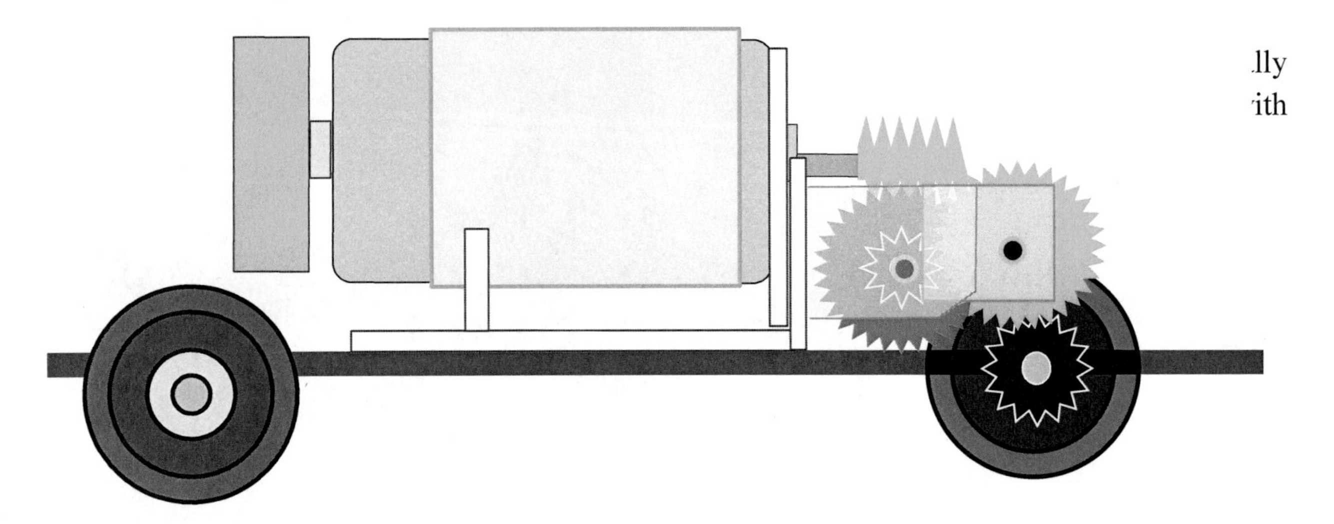

Figure 23: Overview of the concept of the power unit, assembled from the parts in Figure 18, as applied to the step-van plastic chassis. The motor unit, with gearbox, is built so its lower gear will engage the rear axle's gear.

The motor is pure overkill in terms of power, even for a vehicle weighing over a pound, but it costs little more than smaller motors, and has such a large flywheel that it runs extremely smoothly. Its size means it fits in only large vehicles (the chassis shown will barely fit back in the step-van body). As usually found, it has brass worm, which is compatible with (will fit) with 'Streets rear axle gears as well as Tamiya gears. Tamiya gears, among others, have gear sizes and spacing to fit well with 'Streets rear axles and these motor's worms. The author shops on Amazon.com and swap meets for discounts on gears and motors, and so on.

One can fit this motor without a gear reduction as discussed previously. This motor is larger and thus has an even lower RPM than that smaller upgrade, and *much* more powerful, with a very large flywheel, so it results in a vehicle that will cruise smoothly at slightly slower speeds than the motor upgrade covered earlier.

Center of gravity is a concern when building any power unit with this motor. It weights slightly more than five ounces, only slightly less than some complete 'Streets vehicles. Mounted high in a chassis, it causes a vehicle to lean in turns at high speeds to the point the outside wheels loose needed pressure and contact with the rails. Second, it can rock back and forth and exacerbate vibrations if the least unbalanced. For this reason, modelers should think "install low" when building these units.

The major challenge in fabricating a home-made gear reduction drive is arranging for good gear engagement in a mechanism build without precise machine tools. The method the author developed, after much experimentation and more than a few botched attempts that required starting over, is described in the next few steps. The entire procedure of assembly is aimed at being able to set the gear lash of each set of gear-teeth in the reduction gears engagement individually.

The steps below will build a power unit similar to that shown in Figure 21, but not that exact unit. Figure 21 is a photo of the first the author built, in 2011, shown to allay doubts readers may have about the durability of plastic gears, etc. That chassis, in a short city bus (see Chapter 6) has over 800 operating hours on it. It and two other city buses made at the same time to the same design have a total of 2100 hours. None have ever needed major repair.

Step 1: Study the figures in this section, particularly Figure 23 to develop an understanding of the basic approach and the pieces involved. The unit will be built from the motor outward, adding one gear at a time.

Step 2: Obtain a motor and strip it of all parts except the two bolts that screw into its front end (Figure 24). The motor shown is actually not part #6108274100 but is nearly identical except it has a 1/4 instead of 3/8 inch deep flywheel. It will do nicely, as will any motor of about this size with a flywheel. (One could build a power unit using the much smaller motor used in this chapter's first section. With gearing, it can power any 'Streets vehicle one might think of.)

Step 3: Fashion a faceplate as shown in Figure 25 out of 1/10-inch styrene. Use no more than 1/10 inch: the mounting screws are too short for thicker plastic. The faceplate should be big enough to cover the entire front of the motor and extend out in all four directions to at least the motor's full diameter

The piece has three holes drilled in it: one to fit around the front shaft bearing as it protrudes from the motor and two for the faceplate-motor mounting screws. It is useful if the hole that fits around the front shaft bearing fits snuggly – not tight but snuggly. (It may take two or three attempts to make a really good faceplate but it is

Figure 24: Motor used in this example: almost but not quite a dead ringer for Lionel part 6108274100, will do well enough.

Figure 25: Faceplate installed on motor.

recommended – the fit must be good and the screws, when inserted, fitted well, too. When done, screw it to the motor (Figure 25).

Step four: Find suitable gears and metal for shafts on which they turn freely but without a lot of loose play (Figure 26). One gear needs to be a reduction gear (both shown are) with about a 3:1 ratio. The other merely needs to be a single gear, not a double one for reduction (the author is just using one here because it will work as a single gear, too, and it is what he has in hand) of about the same diameter or larger. They must mesh well with the motor worm gear, each other and the 'Streets rear axle gear. Figure 26 shows the model airplane servo gears the author used. Tamiya gears will work well, too.

Step 5: Make two rectangular pieces from styrene at least 1/10 inch thick, as shown in Figures 22 to 24. Those shown are 5/8 by 1 5/16 inches long, just slightly longer than the faceplate is high. Holding one in place on the motor with one hand, place a gear so it is well-meshed with the worm and has clearance to turn, as shown, and use the other hand to mark the exact place where a shaft passing through that gear would intersect the rectangular gear enclosure piece behind it (Figure 27) Drill *both* pieces with a hole for the gear's shaft to go through them in the same exact location in each.

Assemble the two rectangular pieces, the gear, a suitable length of shaft, and spacers as shown in Figures 28. The interior distance between the two rectangular pieces must be greater than the diameter of the front motor bearing.

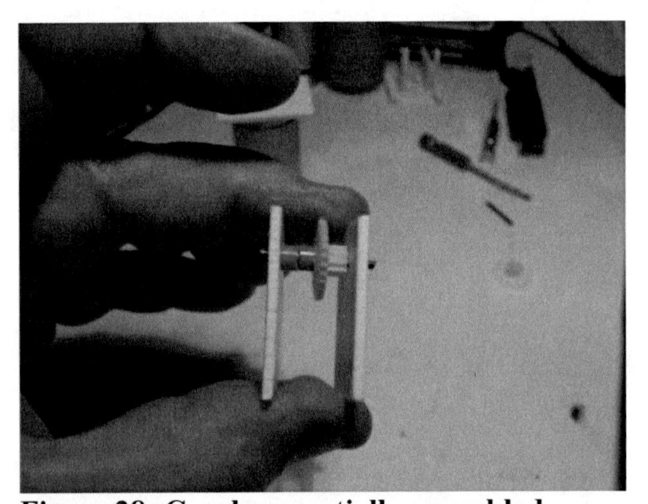

Figure 28: Gearbox partially assembled.

Figure 26: Find two gears as described in text. A thin metal rod (not shown) is needed to make gear shafts on which they can rotate.

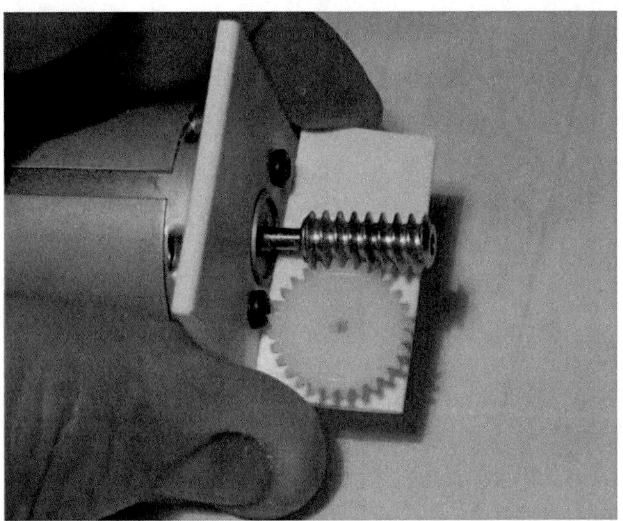

Figure 27: Find two gears as described in text, and a metal rod (not shown) to make gear shafts on which they can rotate.

Step 6: Holding the assembly consisting of the two rectangular enclosure pieces, the gear, shaft, and spacers (pieces of tubing cut to length, to limit side-to-side motion to the gear) as shown in Figure 28, position it as shown in Figure 29, so that:

The gear is centered on the worm.

The two rectangular pieces are close enough together so there is virtually no side-to-side play allowed for the gear.

The gear's teeth are firmly engaged in the worm.

Holding it there, apply Plastic Welder to fasten the two rectangular pieces to the faceplate in this exact position.

When it has begun to harden, carefully remove the gear, shaft, and shapers. Apply Plastic welder to all joint edges liberally. Let it harden. Re-assemble gear, spacers, and shaft.

Step 7: This step will trim the corners of the gearbox just built as shown in Figure 30.

Holding the shaft in place with one's fingers, carefully note a location to snip the outer lower corners so that roughly 1/8 inch of the gear will protrude past that edge, as shown in Figure 31.

One wants to see nearly but not much more than one-quarter of the gear's full circumference. Mark this position, then remove the gear, spacers and shaft. Using snipers, carefully trim off a bit at a time, working inward, until this amount of gear exposure is reached, and never getting closer than 1/8 inch from the hole for the gear shaft and the edge. The result should look about like Figure 30.

Re-assemble gear, spacers, and shaft in the enclosure. Use masking tape over the sides to cover the shaft ends so they will stay in place, but applied so as to not cover the bottom ¼ inch or so of the outer side of the enclosures sides (see Figure 31).

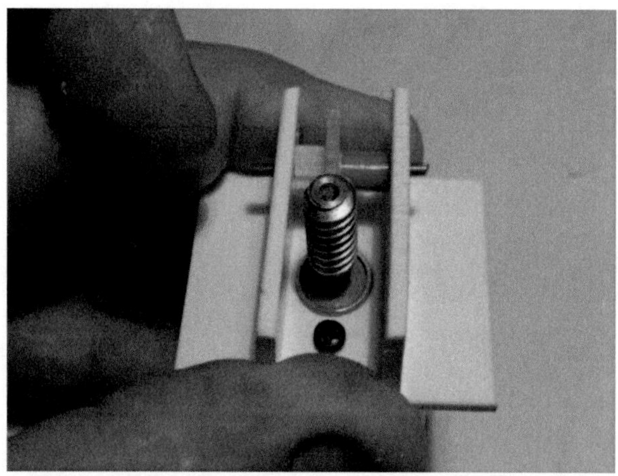

Figure 29: Find two gears as described in text, and metal rod (not shown) to make gear shafts on which they can rotate.

Figure 30: Snip corners as described in text.

Figure 31: About one-quarter of the gear's teeth are exposed.

Step 8: Make the two secondary-gear frame pieces shown in Figure 2 out of 1/10 to 1/8 inch thick styrene. Cut them so they are 3/4 inch long and 5/16 inch wide. Drill a hole for a shaft in them 7/32 inch from one end Carefully snip off and round one end as shown, leaving at least 1/8 inch of plastic from the edge of the shaft's hole, for sufficient strength to hold the shaft.

Assemble the frame pieces as shown in Figure 31. Note the small spacer (to the left of the gear) that has been made to keep the gear centered.

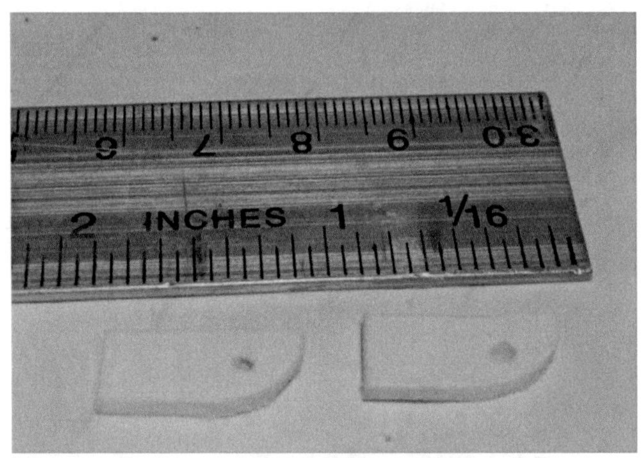

Figure 32: Two rectangular styrene pieces made for the secondary-gear frame arms.

Step 9: Position the secondary-gear assembly on the assembled motor and primary gear assembly and position it as shown in Figures 33 through 34, making sure that:

- The frame arms are on the outside of the primary-gear enclosure.
- The secondary gear's teeth are engaged fully with the teeth of the smaller diameter set of teeth on the primary gear.
- The secondary-gear frame arms do not cover the holes for the primary gear's shaft.

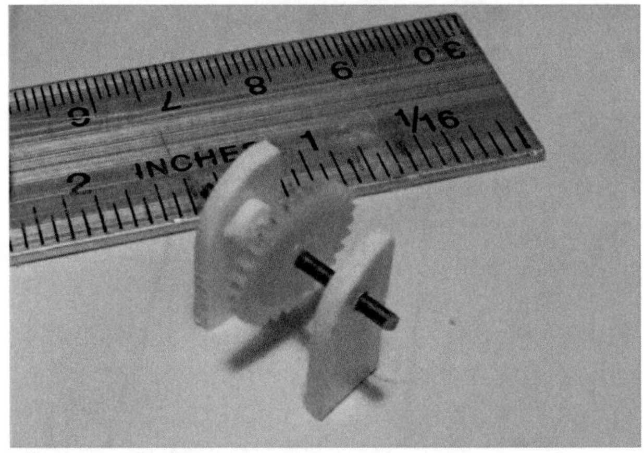

Figure 33: Two rectangular styrene pieces made for the secondary-gear frame arms.

Use brush-on plastic welder to tack-cement each arm in place. While welder and plastic are still soft, position the gear arms exactly so the shaft is parallel to the other shaft, the gears are fully engaged, and so on. Apply more welder and let it harden/ Figure 35 shows three views at this stage.

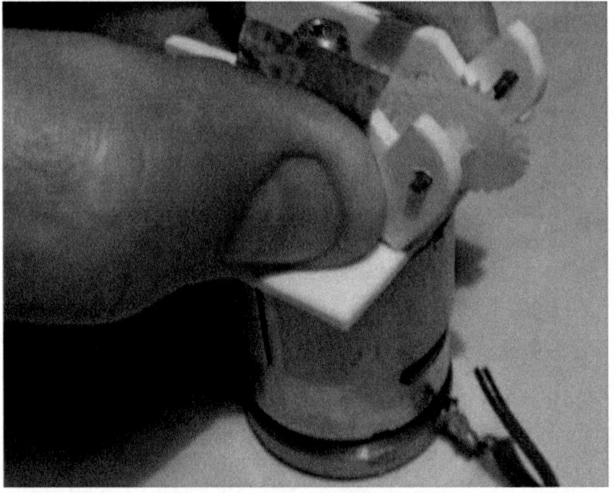
Figure 34: Two rectangular styrene pieces made for the secondary-gear frame arms.

Step 10: Cut small pieces of styrene and attach them to reinforce the power unit's structure as shown (A in Figure 36). Using thin styrene sheet, cut small tabs (B in Figure 36) and glue them as shown on both sides to prevent the gear shafts from working loose. Glue them well but

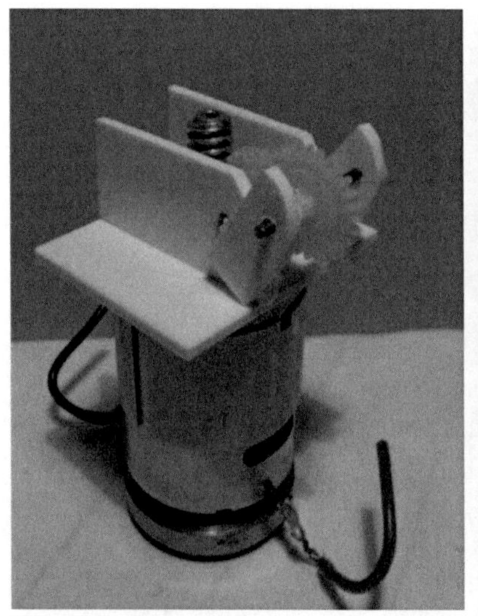
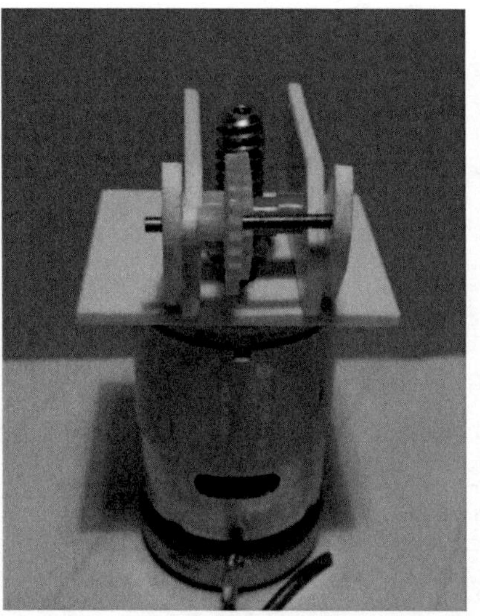
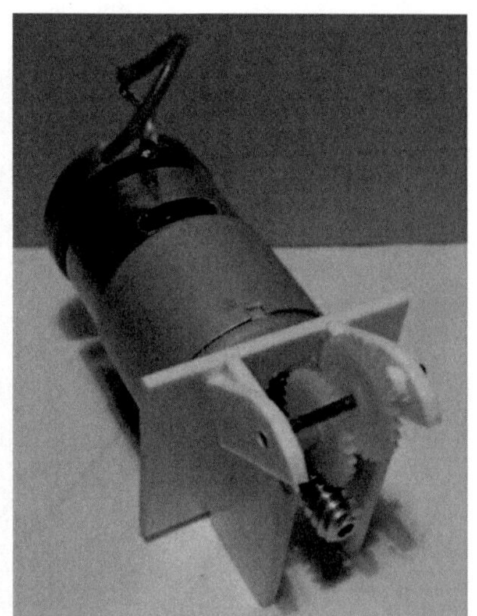

Figure 35: Three views of the nearly-completed power unit at the end of Step 9.

Step 10: The basic power unit is done. Test it to make sure it works.

The only standard 'Streets vehicle the unit will fit in is the step van. However it fits in most buses and tractor trailers. Chapters 8 and 9 will discuss its use in some of them.

Notes: This project is the most difficult project in this book and a challenge to build, particularly the first time attempted. Modelers should anticipate that getting everything right, including the gears meshing well, may take several tries.

A reduction gear is not necessary in buses or tractor trailers and modelers may wish to use a direct drive instead. Those will run well, and acceptably slow and smooth, given the large motor and its flywheel. A reduction gearbox provides *very* low cruising speed with *exceptional* smoothness, but note that, by its nature, the gear set is slightly noisy.

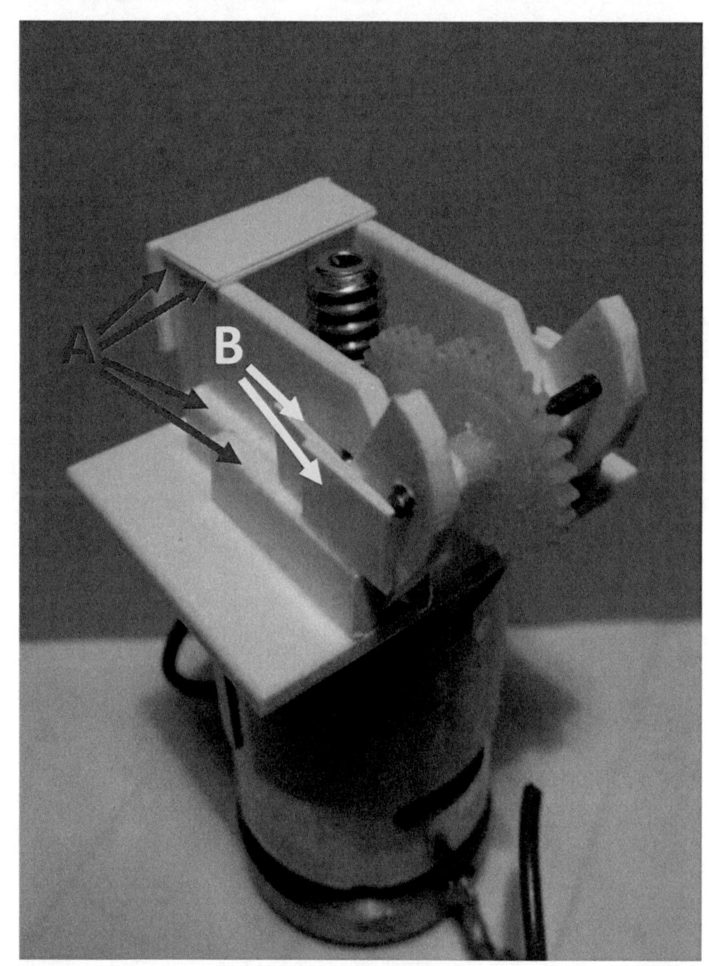

Figure 36: Reinforcement pieces (A) and shaft-movement limiter tabs (B) are attached. The power unit is complete when this is done.

Table 3 compares some of the power options covered here as installed in vehicles discussed in this book. The author has estimated the relative skill and effort required; a reduction gearbox large motor is by far the highest effort. Supercapacitors are the most costly but give the slowest smooth cruising speed other than with a reduction gearbox, and are much easier to install. While electronic flywheels provide the lowest smooth speed, the author prefers a mechanical flywheel because the vehicle can be made to back up and it slows less on curves.

Table 3: Comparison of Various Performance Characteristics of Power options for Vehicles

Performance Characteristic	Standard Motor		with E-flywheel		Modest Upgrade		Big Motor	w. gears
	WBB Sedan	Brooklin DeSoto	WBB Sedan	Wht Box '50 Ford	WBB Sedan	Wht Box '50 Ford	Scenicruiser	
Vehicle weight	7.0	15.0	7.3	9.4	7.7	9.8	25.2	25.7
Motor weight - oz	1.0		1.3		1.7		5.5	
Motor draw @ full load and voltage - W	3.0		3.0		5		19	
Slowest speed in scale mph: clean rails	34	31	19	21	23	27	17	5
at voltage of . . .	6.5	6.8	3.9	4.4	4.4	4.4	4.4	2.2
Slowest speed in scale mph: dirty rails	43	40	33	33	29	34	23	16
at voltage of . . .	8.3	8.7	6.7	7.0	5.5	5.5	6	8
Top speed @ 16 V on clean rails	88	75	86	75	105	105	72	47
Slowdown from straight to D-16 - %	30%	30%	30%	30%	20%	20%	15%	5%
Coast w.o. power - inches @ 8V	0	0	94	60	5	7	6	8
Interior installed?	Yes	Yes	Yes	No	No	No	Yes	No
Rectifier installed?	Yes	Yes	Yes	Yes	No	No	No	No
Can vehcile back up?	No	No	No	No	Yes	Yes	Yes	No
Estimated drive of power upgrade - $	0	0	$40	$40	$15	$15	$24	$32
Relative effort and skill required	0	0	2	2	4	4	5	12

Large Trucks and Streetcars 7

This chapter covers conversion of heavy trucks and streetcars – bigger, heavier and longer than cars or pickups and yet not so big as to require the power and wheelbase "tricks" needed for buses, large trolleys, and tractor trailers. It may seem strange to include streetcars here rather than with buses (Chapter 8). But while buses and streetcars perform roughly the same function in the real world, they are entirely different conversions. Unlike buses, streetcars have medium-length wheelbases, more like trucks than buses.

Conversion using a plastic chassis (Figure 1) is pretty much required for trucks due to wheel sizes needed. That is more difficult than with the metal chassis, where changing wheelbase requires only loosening two screws, realigning the chassis, and tightening the screws again. A plastic chassis must be "cut and pasted" manually as described later in this chapter: a matter of up to an hour or a bit more of work.

Any plastic chassis weighs so little that it needs the weight of a die-cast metal body – at least four additional ounces of weight – to hold it on the road. Otherwise the force of its center pickup springs is more than sufficient to lift it off the road. Usually, a die-cast metal body provides enough weight, but some lighter metal bodies such as those by Yat Ming are a bit too light. Modelers working with those light die-cast models, as well as plastic or resin models, will have to carefully add several ounces of lead shot, BBs, or other weights both to bring to vehicle weight up to a recommended minimum six ounces and to balance it front to back.

Figure 1: This plastic panel van chassis is laid out like the metal sedan chassis but weighs only a sixth as much and its wheelbase is not adjustable without modification. The step-van, vintage truck, and shorty bus have a plastic chassis, but with different wheelbases and wheel sizes.

Wheel size is usually the determining factor. As was covered in Chapter 2, the metal sedan chassis has wheels that are 26 inches high at 1:43 (the scale of most die-cast cars) or 29 inches at 1:48 – just right for cars and small trucks, and regardless, these are the smallest wheels available for 'Streets. The panel van's wheels are larger (scale 32 or 36 inches) – the size of tires on medium trucks. Thus, for most cars, a sedan chassis is recommended. For 1:43 medium trucks and 1:48 or 1:50 medium and heavy trucks, the panel van's wheels are often a very good size, so its plastic chassis is a very good choice for a conversion.

In some cases still bigger wheels are needed. The early step van, if the one or two needed for the project can be found, has very good 1:50 "big truck" wheels. And of course, the school bus has extremely big wheels, if and when needed. These two also have a plastic chassis, so that is what is used for most trucks.

Fire Dept. Rescue Truck: A More Complicated Conversion Lesson

The Signature Models 1:50 1960 Mack C Fire Department Rescue Truck in Figure 2 is a good candidate for conversion. It jas good looking, all die-cast one-piece body with plenty of room inside. It is a good example of a typically "complicated" conversion: the actual conversion – mounting the die-cast body on a 'Streets chassis – is very simple. The complexity comesin the form of many small issues related to making it a good runner *while keeping it* a good looking model.

Figure 2: Signature Models 1:50 Fire Rescue Truck.

Step 1: The die-cast model is wrapped in plastic from the beginning in this project because there are a good deal of graphic and small attached details that could be marred in all the handling. It is disassembled (Figure 3). A look inside finds nothing that would make conversion difficult. In fact quite the opposite: there appear to be no towers or metal that has to be removed at all (Figure 4).

Figure 3: Model disassembled.

Step 2: The wheelbase of the Mack Rescue truck is 3 9/16 inches, while the chassis' wheelbase is just slightly over 3 1/8 inches long. There are two possible solutions to this mismatch.

First, the truck's body could be shortened by 7/16 inch. The rear body of the die-cast truck is a box. It would be easy to cut 7/16 inch out of it so that the box would still look good, then bond the two pieces back together (this is done to a bus in an example in Chapter 6). The stock 'Streets wheelbase, with its ability to cleanly run through D-16 curves, would be preserved. The unacceptable downside, however, is that the bodywork needed to hide the seam would mean the truck had to be repainted: losing all those wonder graphics and the factory finish.

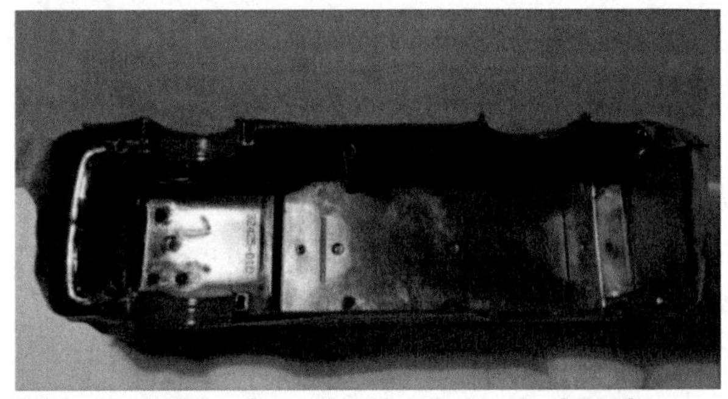

Figure 4: The interior is remarkably free of towers or metal ribs that could get in the way of the chassis.

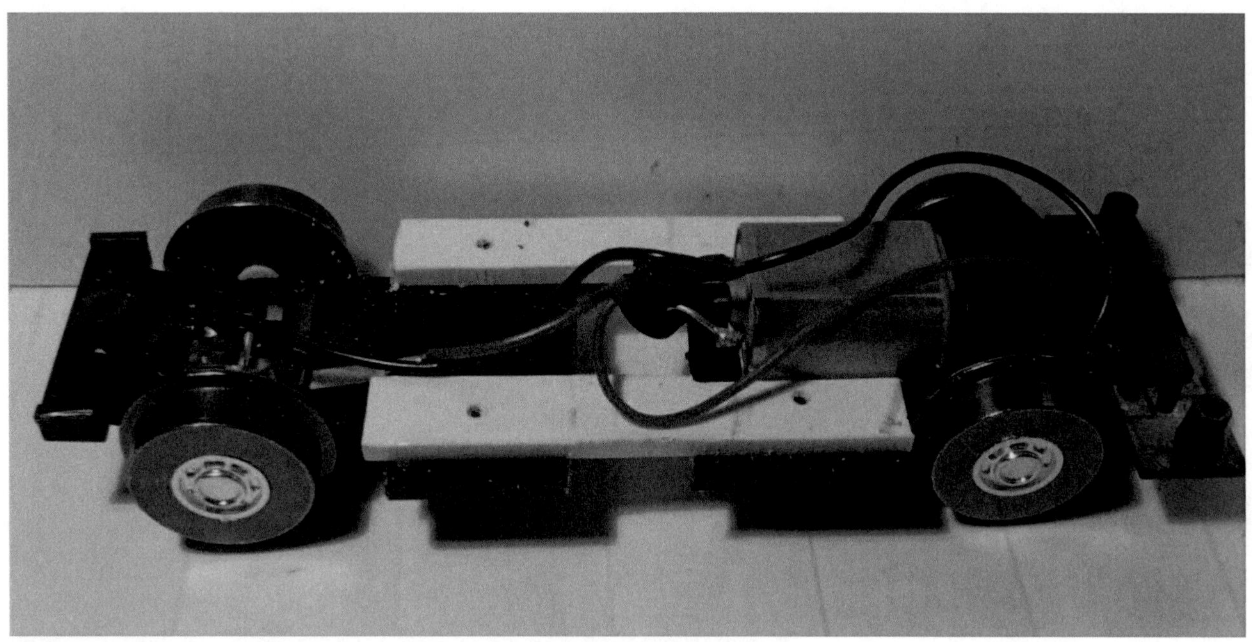

Figure 6: Step-van chassis is cut and stretched 7/16 inch.

The second option is to lengthen the chassis. This will result in a wheelbase of 3.6 inches – about the limit that a stock 'Streets motor can power through D-16 curves smoothly. An upgraded, larger motor (covered in Chapter 6) would fix that problem and would be simple to do on this chassis. However the author decided to move ahead, keeping the stock motor for the moment and adding that upgrade only if needed.

The step-van was disassembled and the chassis removed. The rectifier was pushed up and away from its cup. A band-saw would have made a cleaner cut, but the author used a razor saw by hand to cut from underneath, just ahead of the chassis motor well. Here the wires, like in most cases, had just enough slack to stretch without having to splice in longer wire. Beams of 1/8 inch thick styrene, 3/8 inch wide and 2 3/8 incesh long, were plastic-welded and then screwedin to lengthen the chassis by 7/16 inch (Figure 5). The lengthened chassis is compared to the die-cast body to check it is the correct length.

Step 3: Mounting towers as shown in Figure 6 were made of Loctite Repair Putty. First, the windows at the rear (but not the cab) were painted black on the inside.

By putting the front mounting towers to the sides, right behind the front wheels, the entire front of the die-cast body is kept clear of additions: it will be possible to re-fit at least part of the original die-cast model's cab interior.

The photo in Figure 6 shows the die-cast body with the protective tape removing after the mounting towers had been made, after the epoxy putty had hardened, and after the author had thoroughly scrubbed his hands with hot water and soap. Again, the repair putty is easy to use but *it leaves a residue on fingers that will permanently mar glossy finishes and more,* leaving fingerprints that cannot be removed without damaging the finish. Before starting on making the towers. Modelers must make sure the die-cast body and all trim is completely covered with tape so it is well protected.

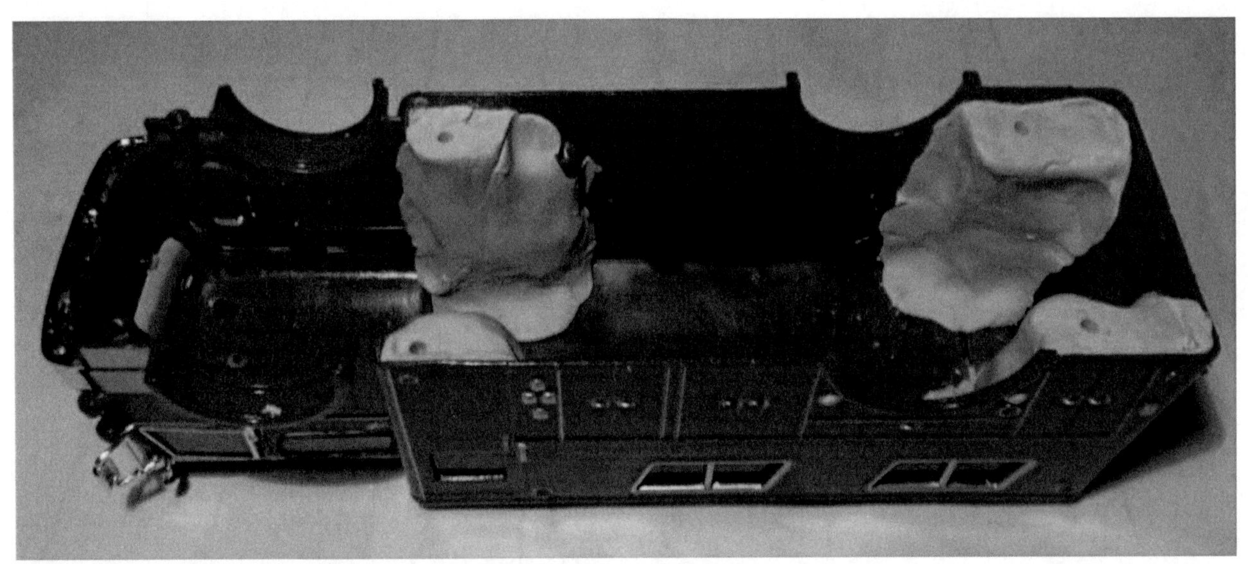

Figure 6: Truck body with towers completed and drilled.

Figure 6 shows the towers as completed and drilled. They are not pretty and it is best not to try to make them so. Think biological, not mechanical – a starfish grasping at shellfish or mollusks adhering to the side of a ship. The putty was pushed into every nock and cranny of the body and out along the sides to maximize contact area with the interior of the casting. It needs to be the right height and flat only where it will meet and support the chassis. There, it needs to be at least 1/8 inch thick around any holes to be drilled for fastening screws that hold it to the chassis.

Step 4: When the repair putty had hardened (about half an hour) and hands had been washed, the chassis was trial fit. Based on that, the top of one tower was trimmed slightly. Then, at the rear, the towers were marked and drilled through the original chassis mounting holes. At the front sides, new holes were drilled through the chassis and then used to mark the epoxy for drilling of the mounting holes.

Step 5: The chassis was mounted on the body with four screws inserted into the holes created and drilled in Step 4 (Figure 7). It is tested. It ran well enough and made its way through D-16 curves smoothly if perhaps a bit slower than stock vehicles. It was run for several minutes to make sure there were no problems.

The fire truck has been converted to 'Streets. The basic conversion is done, but the project has to deal with a number of issues.

Step 6: Ride height adjustment. Close study of Figure 7 will reveal that the truck does not sit evenly on its chassis. At the rear, it is too low by about 1/10 inch. (This is easiest to see by studying the gaps in the wheel wells).

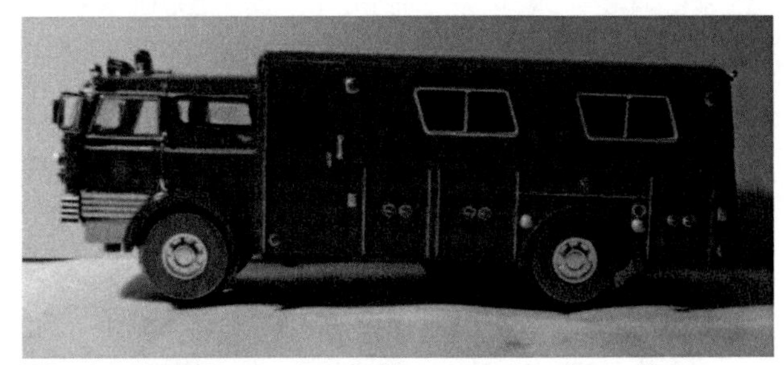

Figure 7: Converted fire truck after five-minute test run. It sits too low at the rear by nearly 1/8 inch.

The solution to the ride heigh was to drill a hole in each of two small pieces of 1/10 inch styrene and insert them between the chassis and repair-putty mounting towers at the rear. This leveled the body nicely.

Step 8: Weight adjustment. Although the vehicle runs well on straight flat roads, it does not climb as well as exected, balking at a 10% straight incline A standard step van can climb about a 20%: this vehicle has lost half its capability. It also spins is wheels a lot going around curves. Not doubt the long wheelbase contributes to the problem, but it seems clear: extra weight would help traction. Three ounces – 32 pennies in a roll placed over the motor – were added to increase traction enough to overcome addition friction of the longer wheelbase (Figure 9). With the added weight installed directly over the rear axle, the firetruck climbs a 15% grade. The weight makes it run smoother through curves, too.

Step 9: Interior. The original cab interior extended back into the rear body about half an inch. It was cut shorter so as to fit around the new chassis and motor and the inserted in the truck body. When fastened down, the chassis keeps the interior firmly in place. The author added a driver figure.

Figure 8: Front wheel wells are 5mm wider than the outer edges of the tires.

Step 10: Front wheel wells. The die-cast model had a much wider track than the 'Streets chassis as shown in Figure 8. At the rear this is not so noticeable, but at the front there is close to a quarter-inch gap between the outside of wheel well and wheel. It looks silly.

One could make wheel extensions and glue them to the wheels to widen them, as covered in chapter 2. Such wheels are easy to make but very difficult to glue on so well aligned that they do not wobble as the wheels roll.

Figure 9: A roll of thirty-two pennies (3.0 oz.) was taped above the motor: it just clears the roof of the die-cast body, but fits. This improved traction and speed through curves nicely.

Figure 10: Heavy cardboard was cut and fit around the cab for protection prior to grinding the wheel wells off. It was not needed, but it was better to waste time than regret not having done so.

Figure 10 shows the preparations made for this in order to protect the die-cast body's finish. Layers of cardboard were cut and taped on. The the die-cast body was held against a belt bench sander and carefully, gradually, the wheel wells were ground down to only 1 mm from their original 5 mm. This left shiny metal that was painted flat black to simulate the vinyl wheel-well edge on many heavy vehciles. The wheel well edge at the rear was painted to match. The overall look is quite acceptable to the author although no longer prototypically accurate.

The wheels were painted red before assembly: they looked good chrome , but the the author prefers the red look. The body, with interior, was remounted on the chassis, and the vehicle was complete (Figure 11).

Important Points About this Model. This is particularly good project that yielded one of the author's favorite models. There were several elements that made this Corgi model an ideal candidate.

Good detail: Given all the effort that goes into conversion, it is best to buy a quality model that has a particularly good, detailed look.

One piece deicast body is generally much easier to mount than a two-piece die-cast body, or a die-cast cab and plastic rear body: it can be relied on for strength, as a two-piece cannot.

Wheelbase less than 4 inches. A longer wheelbase would have meant power problems.

Interior. It was possible to preserve the cab's interior, which is a nice feature that adds a lot.

Figure 11: Completed Corgi 1960 Mack Fire Rescue Truck is a splendid conversion, good looking, solid and apparently durable, and a very good running.

Having done a really good, detailed step-by step of a plastic-chassis conversion with the Corgi Fire Rescue Truck in the preceding section, this chapter will close with a less detailed summary review. It will concentration on the problems encountered with and give a few useful lessons from a three-axle heavy truck.

The Daron die-cast NYC Sanitation truck in Figure 12 is a very good-looking model that signaled from the beginning – when being ordered off the internet – that it would be a difficult conversion. It has several characteristics that could be seen in photos on the website when ordering, that while not red flags, meant a lot of work would be needed and perhaps some compromises would have to be accepted. These were:

Figure 12: Daron die-cast garbage truck proves to be a challenging conversion.

Two-piece body. A good single-piece die-cast body can be relied upon to provide a lot of the structural strength for the vehicle – it can hold the chassis in place, not the other way around. But here:

The chassis has to provide all the structural strength for the vehicle. Wheelbase extensions, must be made strong in order to do that.

The two sections must be mounted separately. That requires more work, and much worse…

Real estate for mounting holes gets scarce. Finding room for the five to eight mounting screws that will be needed can be nearly impossible. Often there is just not a lot of room for that many mounting holes, positioning brackets, and so on, particularly when the junction between the two pieces is in the middle of the vehicle, where motor, rectifier, wiring and more need to go.

In a many cases, one can bond the two pieces together with repair putty or fasten them together with nuts and bolts, screws, or wires. This can be done even when the rear body is plastic, too - the case with many low-price "die-cast" toy trucks. But fastening the two pieces together so they are structurally one just moves the "pain point" of conversion work elsewhere. One beauty of a one-piece body, as for example the preceding Fire Rescue truck, is that it is both strong *and* has a completely open interior. On this truck, if one can fasten the cab and rear body together so it is one piece (one can), it leaves a partition at that junction, which restricts what and how one can fill the interior with motor, wiring, and so on.

Plastic rear body. The only die-cast metal part of this "die-cast" model is the cab itself. The rear body and chassis is lightweight plastic, and this means a good deal of weight will have to be added to the vehicle over its rear axle in order to provide the weight and traction a good 'Streets vehicle needs.

Short Over-Axle Cab. Very short over-axle cabs are difficult to mount to the chassis. They go *right* over the front axle with little front overhang: there is often no easy way to securely mount screws ahead of the front axle – the only space below the cab is taken by the axle frame at the sides and the center pickup in the middle. And because the cab is short mounting screws from behind the front axle won't reach, either.

The third axle is *not* a problem. In fact it can be considered an advantage, even if it means more work. The Daron truck was selected as an example here in part to show how and why.

Summary of Conversion: Despite the problems discussed above, this truck was converted to 'Streets. Selecting the chassis was easy, since only one would really do; both the sedan and the panel van's wheels are way too small to look good on this truck. The larger step-van wheels would look satisfactory, perhaps: they are slightly smaller than the model's original wheels. However, the Daron model's cab is much wider than the fire truck's. Centered under the cab, the outer edges of the step-van's wheels would fail to come out to even the inner edges of the die-cast body's wheel wells. By contrast, the larger diamcter wheels of the short school bus are as far across, outer edge to outer edge, as the cab is wide, and the garbage truck will look quite good with them: they are almost exactly the size of its original wheels.

Figure 13 shows the chassis used. In order, it was:

Lengthed ten millimeters to match the model's wheelbase from the front to the leading rear axle.

Trimmed at both ends: at the front so there would be no interference with the cab fitting in its proper palce right above the front axle. At the rear, the chassis was cut shorter so as to accommodate the third axle, when fitted.

Fitted with an oversize flywheel motor – see Chapter 6: this will be a heavy, large truck dragging a third axle. The additional power will be useful.

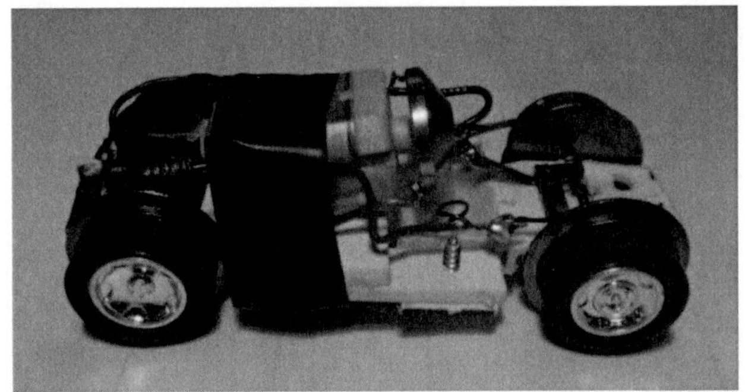

Figure 13: School bus chassis is so short that even stretched by 10 mm it still looks short. It has been upgraded with an oversize flywheel motor as described in Chapter 6.

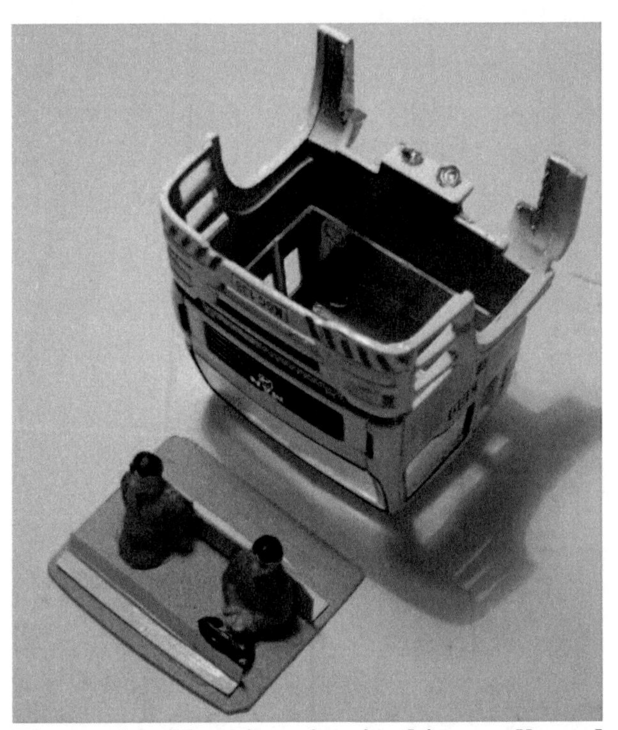

Figure 14: New interior is thin cardboard cut to fit snuggly in the cab up against the lower edge of the plastic window piece inside the cab. Cardboard dash, two figures, and a steering wheel complete the interior.

The cab was filled with epoxy and mounted to the rear section as shown in Figure 16. The epoxy fills the entire cab from the cardboard interior as shown, molded into a central platform that will sit flat on the chassis with portions cut out for the wheels on both sides.

Figure 15 also shows how the rear body and cab were permanently attached to each other. The author decided that fastening them together was the better approach as compared to mounting cab and rear sections to the chasis separately.

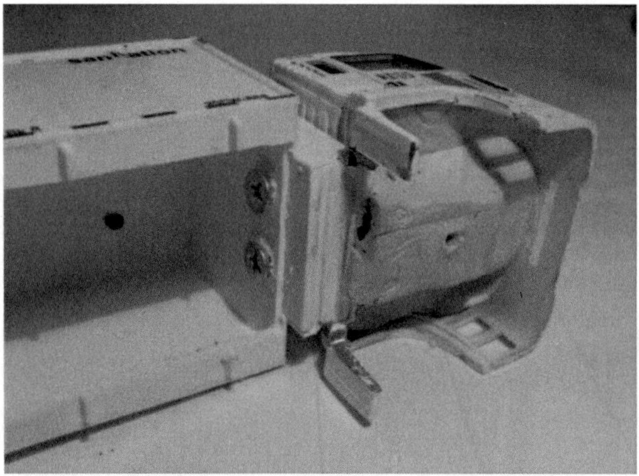

Figure 15: Once the interior was inserted, about two-thirds stick of Loctite Epoxy Repair Putty was inserted into the cab and molded as seen here. The floor of rear garbage truck section was largely cut out so it would fit over the motor, etc. Holes were drilled in the cab and plastic body and screws seated home into the epoxy to hold them together.

Figure 16 shows how the now one-piece truck body was mounted to the chassis. At the front, a small platform (A in Figure 17) was made to fit over the front axle assembly. It was not glued down but simply drilled for a screw (tip of screw visible in Figure 16, A) passing through it and attached to the putty on the underside of the cab (the hole for it can be seen in Figure 16.)

Just about halfway back on the chassis, a framework (B in Figure 16) was made of plastic rod. Screws (not visible in the photo) from the chassis underside hold it firmly in place.

Figure 16: See text for details of the front mounting platform (A) and rear mounting framework (B). The round, blue assembly atop the motor is a roll of pennies weighing four ounces: enough weight that this chassis runs without a die-cast body on it.

The body was then trial mounted by sitting it on the chassis, with the cab resting as it would on the small platform over the front axle and the inside of the roof of the rear body resting on the framework. The metal cab is so heavy compared to the plastic rear body that the center of gravity of the entire truck body is about half an inch ahead of where the framework is located at the center of the chassis. Plastic shims were cut and added to the top of the framework until the cab and body sat straight. At that point, the chassis was screwed to the cab at the front using the screw from underneath (tip visible in Figure 16), and styrene plastic welder was put along the top of the framework and it was pressed home to cement it to the inside roof of the rear body. Once the cement has hardened, the body can be removed by loosening the three screws: one at the front under the cab, and one on each side about halfway back on the underside of the chassis, which free the framework.

The third axle is a trailing bogie that can swing sideways in curves, and is shown in Figure 17. Crude as this wire framework may look, the author has found nothing that works as well. Copper wire is easy to bend into shape and adjust so the wheels roll with little friction. Visible in the photo but not recognizable is a very thin wire that has been soldered to the copper bogie framework and taken forward alongside the motor. Its other end is soldered to the copper finger of the front axle contact fingers: this vehicle has electrical contact to the outer rails through all six wheels.

Figure 17: The third axle may look a bit crude but it works *perfectly*. Thin copper wire bends easily to make the frame and assures excellent electrical conductivity to the wheels: Only their weight keeps them on the rails, but that is sufficient.

The angle of the hook through the mounting post and how it is bent relative to the rest of the framework (that actually holding the axle) has to be adjusted so that:

a) The bogie turns freely from side to side.

b) The axle rides with its weight on the rails, but no additional tension or weight from the vehicle on it.

A third center roller was added to the very back of the chassis, so the six-wheel outer-rail electrical contact is matched with a similar increase in center-rail contact (Figure 18). While a position so close behind another roller may not be ideal, in this location the roller stays in contact with the center rail even in the middle of D-16 curves.

Figure 18: A third center roller was added to the very back of the chassis.

The 50% increase in conductivity over a stock two-axle vehicle, in company with the flywheel, make this an extraordinarily smooth runner.

Small modeling details were done last. A third figure, standing on a small fold-out platform at the rear, was added. Fuel tanks, equipment, pumps, and tanks and hoses along the underside or the rear body were added on each side of the truck based on observation of several local garbage trucks.

A test run showed that the converted truck ran very smoothly at slow speeds, and certainly had a top speed as fast as one would ever see a garbage truck run. It climbs 12% straight slopes and 4% D-16 slopes, more than sufficient to handle anything on the author's layout.

Those test runs also revealed that the model is far too wide. The rear body is wide, but the real culprits are the black simulated hydraulic operating mechanisms that stick out from the rear body by about 3/16 inch. These tended to snag model cars parked alongside the road and anthing else close by.

Those black plastic pieces were trimmed back as much as possible. The truck is still quite wide, and doesn't play nice with nearby traffic or street light posts and signs on narrow roads, but it is an excellent runner and one of the author's favorites (Figure 19).

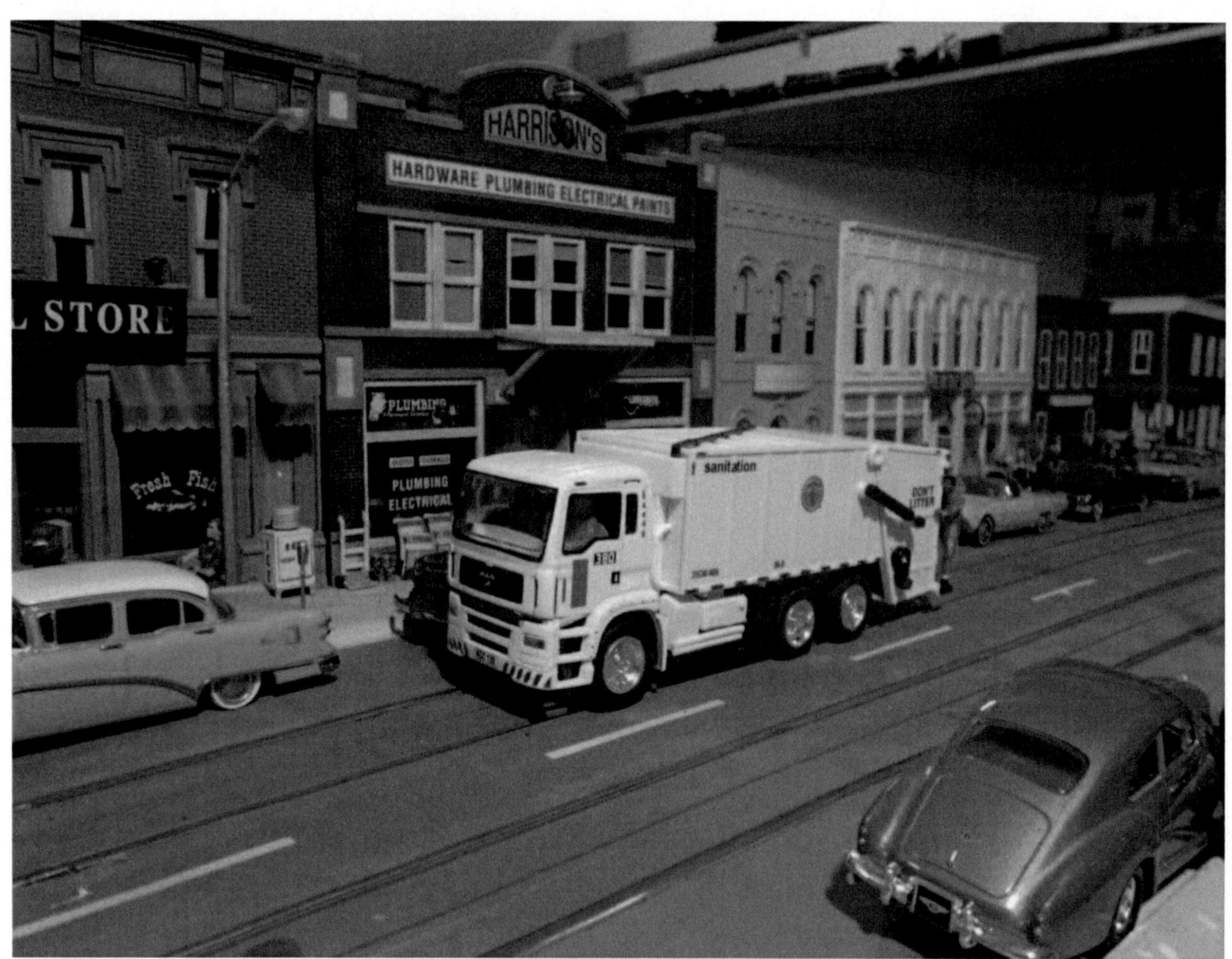

Figure 19: Although a lot of work there is no denying it was worth the trouble. This is an excellent-running, interesting-to-look-at model that is a delight to watch on the layout.

Corgi Birney Trolley

Figure 20: Corgi product #55203, a Philadelphia Birney Safety Car Trolley, is a lovely, detailed model.

Corgi's lovely 1:50 die-cast model of a Philadelphia Birney Safety Car trolley makes a nice conversion (Figure 20). While Lionel makes a Birney trolley too, this one is a fairly easy conversion and produces a slower moving trolley, with a more of a model than toy look to it. It slows much less around D-16 curves than most two-axle trolleys and has a tolerable swing-out on curves, always a concern with trolleys.

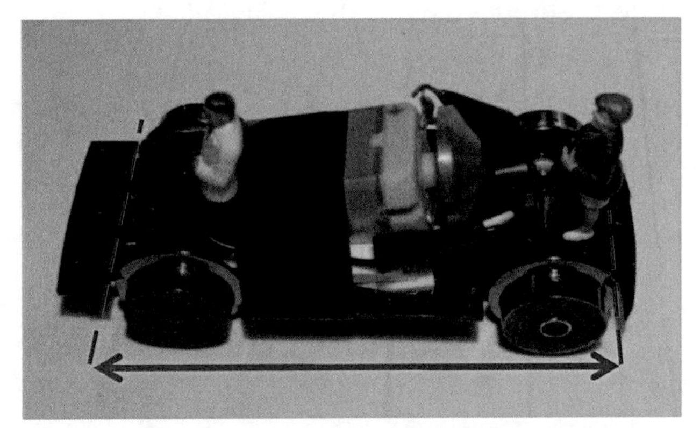

Figure 21: Chassis is unmodified. Author added figures to see through the trolley's windows, and after this photo was taken, painted everything else flat black.

The panel-van chassis that was upgraded with a larger, flywheel motor in Chapter 6 was used. It was not modified in any way, beyond addition of the two figures shown in Figure 21, which will be seen through the windows, and painting of wires and motor flat black (not shown), so they would not show as much through windows.

Step 1: The trolley's lower chassis and its wheels were removed, but no further disassembly was done: Corgi trolleys are somewhat difficult to disassemble and can sometimes be very difficult to re-align and

Figure 22: Underside of trolley was cut as shown. See text for details.

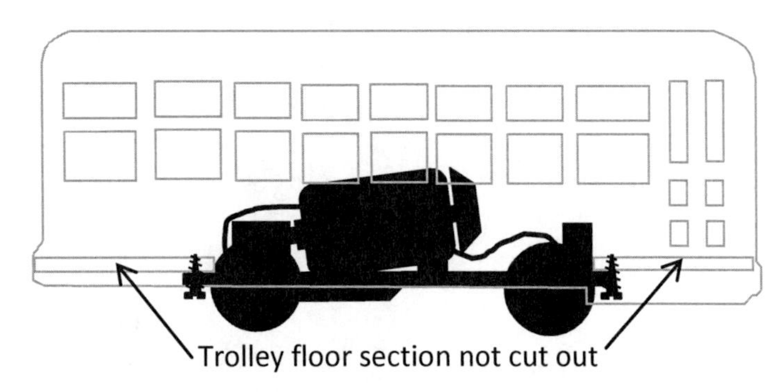

Figure 23: Panel van chassis with upgrade motor from Chapter 5 slips into the rectangle cut out of the bottom of the trolley interior.

reassemble. The author used a Dremel rotary tool with various high speed cutter bits to cut a rectangle out of the bottom of the trolley's interior, as shown in Figure 22. This rectangular cut out is halfway between the two ends of the trolley, and was initially made about ¼ inch narrower than the trolley bottom and just a bit shorter than the red arrow in Figure 3.

Step 2: The 'Streets chassis was then repeatedly trial fit – trying to place it into the position shown in Figure 23, gradually filing away plastic to widen and/or length the rectangular cut-out section until it just slips in.

That chassis was screwed to the trolley's bottom through the two original mounting holes at the rear, and one was added at the front.

A good deal of weight had to be added above the powered axle to give the trolley enough traction to run well. The author was flummoxed as to why: the chassis ran superbly with the stock panel van body (4.1 ounces), and the trolley body (9.7 ounces) weighed more. Regardless, with that extra weight added the end result is a superb, slow-running trolley (Figure 24) that looks particularly good on streets and roads with other scale model traffic.

Figure 24: The Corgi Birney trolley is a good runner and just the right size to look good.

Difficult Conversions

Although there are cars that cannot be converted to 'Streets because they are too narrow (see Chapter 2) any truck is generally large enough to convert. However some are so difficult to convert that an owner may not want to take on the challenge. Warning signs that a conversion will be difficult include:

A two-piece non-articulated body front and back. The garbage truck covered earlier had a two-piece body, as opposed to the fire truck's body which was one-piece. Any truck that has front and rear sections that must be rigidly fastened together will be more difficult to convert. Fastening the two pieces together while cutting out enough room from the junction where they meet so that clearance is made for motor, and so on, can be a challenge, as can the only alternative - mounting each separately but in the right positions relative to one another. It can be done, but it's best to carefully think through the if and how before starting.

A two-piece upper and lower body including cast chassis – is very difficult. Figure 25 shows an Ertl die-cast 1950 Chevy truck model that would make a good looking conversion. It also has a wheelbase exactly the same as the step-van, making it all the more appealing. But it has three die-cast pieces: the rear box, meaning it presents the problems discussed above, and an upper front piece consisting of cab and hood, and finally a die-cast fenders-and-chassis piece onto/ which the other two pieces fit.

Figure 25: This Ertl 1950 Chevy REA truck is among the most difficult conversions possible because of its three-piece body.

ERTL also makes this same model as a tractor for big rigs with just two pieces, not the box. Many ERTL models of trucks from the 1930s through the 1950s are made this way, with the cab and fenders-chassis as separate pieces. Most of the tractors are easy to convert by using the model's chassis for 'Streets, adding flanged wheels and center pickups to it, as will be shown in Chapter 9. But that "trick" works well only when the motor can be put in the trailer as it is in most big rig conversions. The model in Figure 25 needs its own motor. In addition, ERTL's 1950 Chevy, in tractor or truck form, requires about one cubic centimeter of metal to be ground out of the lower portion of the cab's casting so the front wheel flanges will fit inside the cab, which leaves the cab casting very delicate and difficult to attach well to the chassis. Conversion is not recommended.

A truck too wide. Chapter 2 discussed trucks so big they required considerable work widening axles so that the 'Streets "tires" would properly fill the truck's fenders side to side. This complicates a conversion, and any truck that wide is likely to be so large that it may be "too big" to fit satisfactorily on the layout as was discussed in Chapter 2's final section.

It is up to owners to decide what they will tackle. Basically it boils down to asking, "Do I want this operating model enough to do all the work required to convert it?" On some occasions, the answer may be "No."

Buses and Trolleys

8

Buses are among the most interesting vehicles one can run on a 'Streets roadway system. They are large and draw the eye in ways smaller vehicles do not. Many are attractive, even stylish. And they are romantic, recalling times when intercity travel wasn't as routine as it is today but often a multi-day adventure. Perhaps most important, they are the roadway equivalent of passenger trains, and thus seem to naturally fit into the theme of a model train layout in a way toy cars do not. Trolleys covered here are arbitrarily distinguished from streetcars (Chapter 7) on the basis of wheelbase: a streetcar has a the wheelbase no longer than a standard 'Streets vehicle; a trolley, longer.

Buses and trolleys in some ways offer the biggest conversion challenge a modeler will face. A tractor and a trailer, while longer overall, pivots with respect to one another, so the vehicle bends through curves. Buses do not. The long non-articulated wheelbase, heavy weight, and just four fixed wheels (usually) make for potential problems like those discussed in Chapter 5. Buses nearly always require additional power and traction. So there are no easy projects in this chapter: a bus, done right, is at least a somewhat involved project. But a bus is worth the effort: when a converted bus is done well – so it runs smoothly and dependably – it is a delight to run and watch.

Figure 1: An inter-city Greyhound Yellow Coach bus enters town and heads down Main Street toward the bus station while a short-wheelbase GM 4510b city bus heads out to the suburbs. Both are Corgi models converted in projects covered in this chapter

Slow Moving City Bus

A really nice-looking city bus that runs very well through D-16 curves can be made by fitting a *shortened* Corgi 1:50 die-cast bus body onto a 'Streets step-van chassis of normal length, but upgraded with a more powerful motor or a reduction-geared power unit. The step-van chassis is strongly preferred here because it has longest stock wheelbase, at 3.15 inches. If a panel-van chassis is used, it is best to lengthen its wheelbase to 3.15 to 3.25 inches first.

Figure 2: Corgi 1:50 GM 4510 bus has a wheelbase 1 9/16 inches longer than the 'Streets step van chassis

The Corgi bus body will be cut and shortened to fit the 'Streets chassis. Based on experience the author would not recommend wheelbases over about 3¼ inch for vehicles expected to negotiate D-16 curves well. A later section in this chapter will present a full-length Corgi bus conversion intended to run on nothing tighter than D-21.

Corgi makes a number of die-cast models of various buses but all are so similar that it makes little difference, from the standpoint of conversion, which is picked. Figure 2 shows the GM-type bus selected for this conversion. It has a wheelbase 1 9/16 inches longer than the chassis on which it will be mounted.

Step 1: A large-motor chassis should be used due to the weight and need to have power to push the bus through tight curves. A decision about whether to use a reduction-geared or direct-drive chassis must be made by the modeler. See Chapter 6 for a discussion of that as well as a discussion about choosing the type of chassis. Here, a reduction-geared power unit was mounted on the chassis (Figure 3).

Figure 3: Step van chassis with large-motor power unit (see last section of Chapter 6).

Step 2: The bus is disassembled, and body and windows retained. The bus will have to be shortened between its wheels by 1 9/16 inches, by making to cuts perpendicular to the long axis of the bus, that far apart. One should determine exactly where to cut in order to preserve as much as possible the even width and spacing of windows, and so on. The green tape shown in Figure 4 indicates the portion that will be cut out: it will remove two windows and a bit of post in front of the side doors, resulting in a normal look for the shortened bus. The cuts are made with a band-saw.

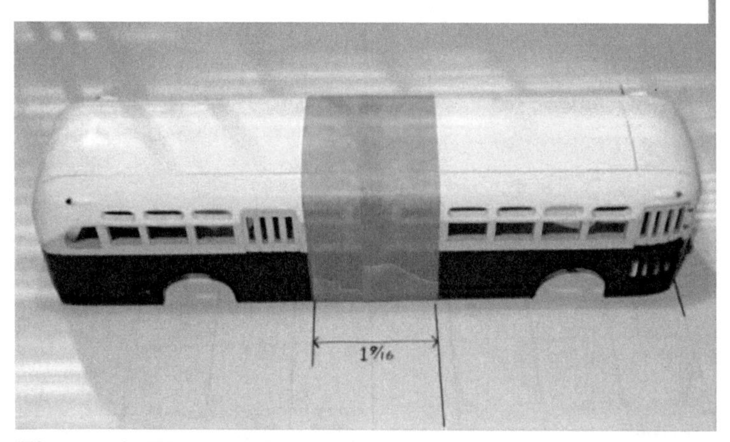

Figure 4: The portion to be removed is marked, here with green masking tape.

Step 3: The two end pieces are fitted together after filing their edges smoothed round (Figure 5). The author used Loctite Epoxy Repair Putty to bond together the two pieces of the chassis and hold them in place. The repair putty is applied, smeared across the seam between the pieces, about 5/16 inch thick along the roof and 3/16 in thick along the sides, for about 1 inch on either side of the seam (Figure 6). While the putty is still soft the pieces can be adjusted to a good fit. The repair putty must have at least an hour to harden: allowing a full twenty-four hours is recommended,

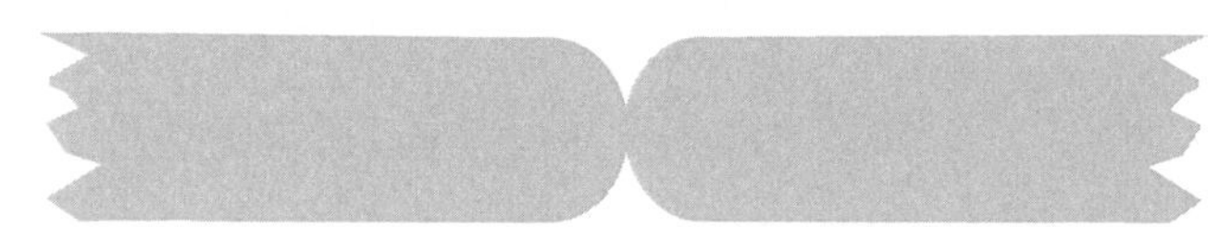

Figure 5: To the extent it does not destroy cast detail like window frames, it is best to round the edges of the two cut pieces where they meet. This helps body-filler (Step 5) adhere.

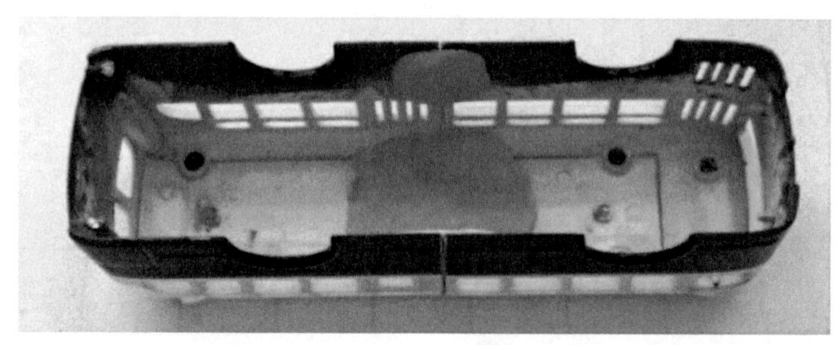

Figure 6: The two pieces are bonded together with repair putty.

Step 4: The seam where the two pieces meet is filed and sanded so it is smooth. Bondo glazing putty is applied to the seam along the top and sides (Figure 7).

Step 6: When the putty has dried at least 24 hours it can be sanded. The author uses 220, 320 and 400 grit in series. The entire body is sanded, and all graphics removed.

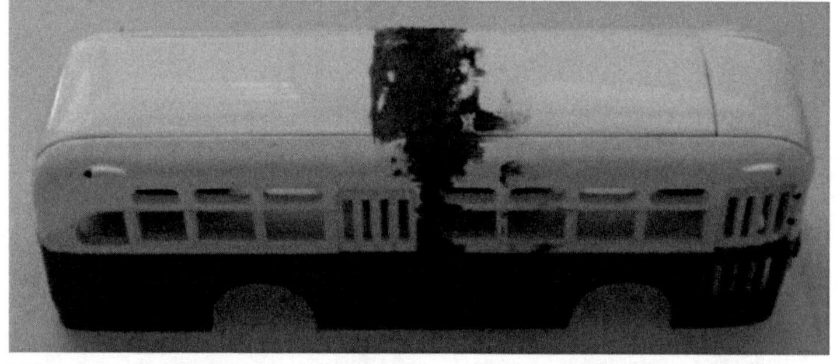

Figure 7: On the outside, Bondo glazing putty is used to fill seams, and allowed to harden. for 24

Step 6: This particular Corgi model does not have cast-in screw towers that can be used to mount the 'Streets chassis to the body. Some do, in which case one can make extensions of the plastic chassis floor to reach them, drill them, and use the original Corgi screws into those original mounting places to attach chassis to body (example in the next section).

Figure 8: Repair putty is used to make three mounting towers for the chassis,

Here, Repair Putty is used to make three mounting towers (Figure 8). Usually, trimming tower height is required, and shimming may be needed also to adjust ride height. The chassis should be mounted to the body and the vehicle tested. Then the body should be removed for completion.

Step 7: The body is primed. The author used Rust-Oleum Auto gray primer but modelers can use a primer of their preference. The author used this primer because he has had good results with it. It fills small scratches very well.

Step 8: Once the primer is dry it can be sanded and the model painted and, after that, graphics added.

Step 10: The original window piece(s) for the Corgi bus can be cut by 1 9/16 inch in the appropriate place and fitted back in the body (black Gorilla Tape was used in Figure 8, above). Body is mounted on the chassis.

The bus is complete. Figure 9 shows this bus, which currently has close to eight hundred operating hours on it.

Figure 9: Completed bus runs smoothly at "downtown city bus speeds" of 10 - 15 mph.

Easier-to-Make City Bus

The chassis in the preceding project was from a step-van, unaltered except for the addition of the reduction-geared power unit. A project involving considerably less work would be to mount the shortened body, done as described there, on an unmodified step-van chassis. The 1:50 converted Yellow Coach 743 bus in Figure 10 was done in that way. This particular model is perhaps the least aesthetically pleasing of the available Corgi models – it has less front and rear overhang than other models and is therefore noticeably "stubbier" looking. The slit-like windows look out of place when the model is shortened. But any of the more attractive buses could be done in the same way.

Figure 10a: Corgi 1:50 Yellow Coach 743 was shortened as described in the previous project. This particular model may be the least good-looking of the various Corgi buses available. The model shown looks a bit worn because it has been run about fifteen hundred hours over a five-year period.

Shortened and converted in this way, the Corgi bus is half an inch longer than the stock step van and weighs 14.7 ounces as opposed to the original 12.9. That is not so much added weight as to bog down the stock motor or cause immediate problems the vehicle pictured was converted in 2009 and has over fifteen hundred hours on it. Motor and chassis seem to be in excellent shape. (Not so the paint and graphics, which show signs of handling the past four to five years). The vehicle runs through curves as well as it did with the original body on it – that is, acceptably, but slowing noticeably in D-16 curves. With the added weight makes it slightly less prone to stuttering and stalling due to electrical connectivity issues at low speeds that if still had the original body.

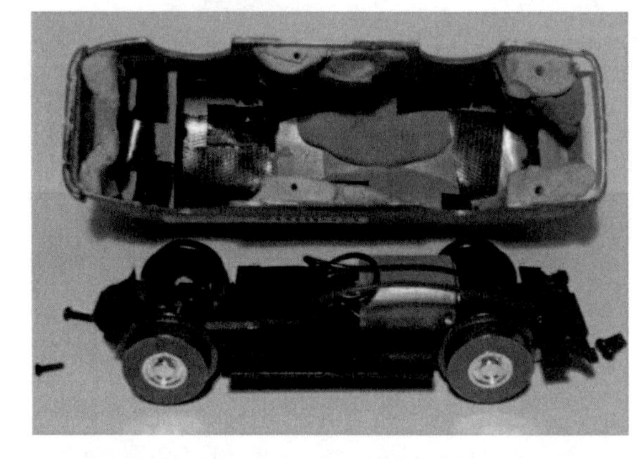

Figure 10b: Repair putty was used both to bond the two cut ends of the shorter bus, and to provide mounting towers for the chassis, which was unmodified except for some trimming of the front and rear corners to fit within the rounded body ends.

An alternative variation would be to upgrade to a larger geared or geared motor as described in Chapter 6. The added power would not make as much of an improvement as the inertia provided by the flywheel would, which would make the bus run *much* smoother at low speeds

Cross Country Greyhound Bus

Conversion of the Corgi 1:50 GMC PD-3751 Greyhound bus shown in Figure 1 earlier in this chapter was done without any shortening of the Corgi die-cast body: in fact, that metal body was not modified in any way. No repair putty was needed for new mounting towers because the 'Streets chassis was mounted on the bus's original mounting holes using the original Corgi mounting screws.

The wheels of the early K-Line 'Streets step-van are the best match and one of those chassis was used. A large motor-flywheel power unit as made in Chapter 6 was used as the reduction geared drivetrain. The motor from it, removed from the gearbox, could have been used without reduction gearing instead: the bus would run faster and quieter at highway speeds, but not run as smoothly at slow city-traffic speeds.

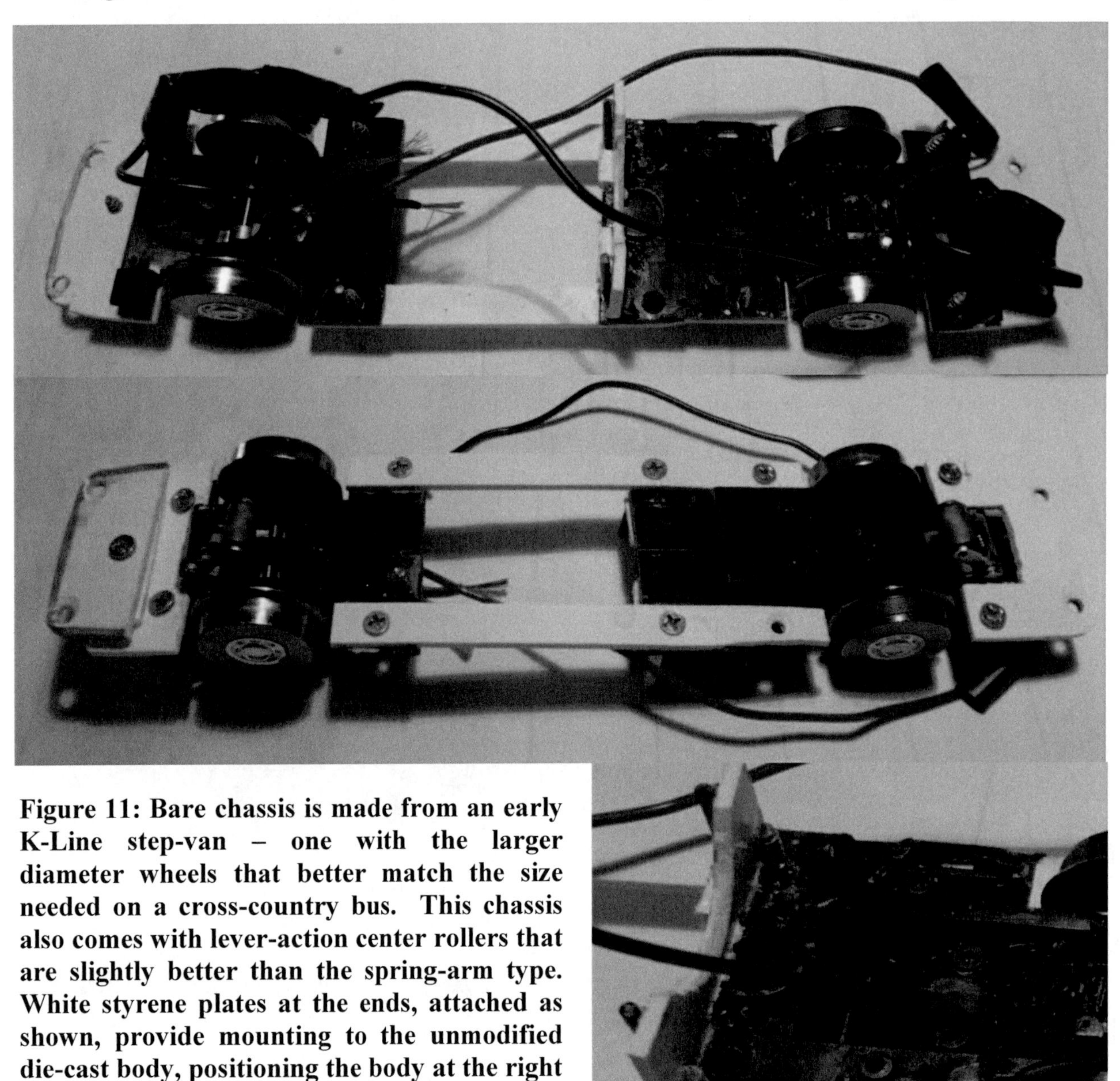

Figure 11: Bare chassis is made from an early K-Line step-van – one with the larger diameter wheels that better match the size needed on a cross-country bus. This chassis also comes with lever-action center rollers that are slightly better than the spring-arm type. White styrene plates at the ends, attached as shown, provide mounting to the unmodified die-cast body, positioning the body at the right ride height to look realistic.

Figure 12: Completed chassis with the power unit installed and wired.

Step 1: Disassemble the body. Paint the windows inside the bus black: the motor will be visible otherwise.

Step 2: Previous examples here and in Chapter 5 and 6 have shown how to prepare and build a lengthened plastic chassis: Build a chassis lengthened to the wheelbase of the die-cast model bus (Figures 11 and 12). In this case it is 122 mm (4.8 in.), an increase of 42 mm (1 21/32 in.). This particular Corgi model has mounting holes for screws cast into the body at the front and rear. Plastic pieces are made as shown. When attached to the underside of the 'Streets chassis with a 1 mm shim in between them and the plastic chassis, they position the wheels at the right ride height. The pieces were shaped to fit into the body snuggly, put in place, and then drilled so they match the screw-mounting holes in the die-cast body.

Step 3a (reduction gearing): the power unit is mounted and taped in place with electrical tape applied with a bit of tension so the secondary gear teeth engage the rear axle's gear fully. It is centered and made upright (Figure 13); then positioning rods (Figure 14) are made and plastic-welded in place. The welder is allowed

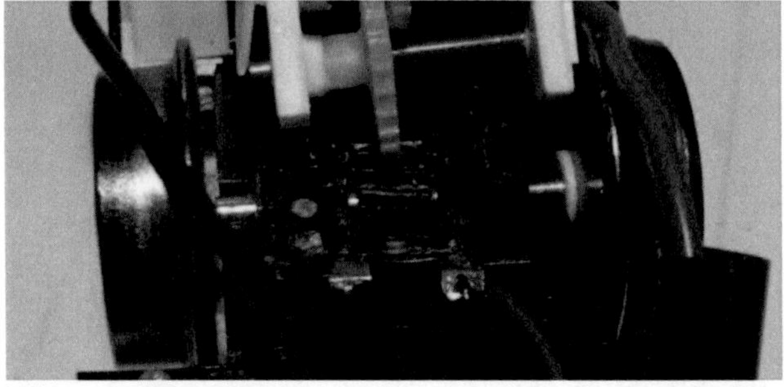

Figure 13: Power unit positioned properly: the secondary gear is centered on the rear axle gear and perpendicular to it.

Figure 14: Once the power unit is properly positioned, positioning rods (A) are cemented in place. After cement has thoroughly hardened, tape is removed, paper shim (B) is inserted, and unit is re-taped.

to harden. Then, the electrical tape is removed. A thin shim – the author uses three of four thickness of printer paper – is placed under the positioning rod on each side so as to lift and provide a small amount of gear play and the motor is again centered and taped down with a bit of tension in the tape. The chassis is done.

Step 3ba (normal gearing): The motor will sit, when completed, as shown in Figure 15. First, prepare a faceplate as shown in Figure 16. It is narrower than tall and its width must be made so it will fit down into the chassis well where the original motor sat but without side-to-side play. The lower image in Figure 17 shows the rear motor mount, a piece of 1/10th inch or thicker styrene cut to the diameter of the motor. This should be built and attached 1 13/16 inches ahead of the centerline of the rear axle, so that the lowest point of the motor when resting in the motor-mount is ¼ inch above the floor of the chassis.

The plastic piece shown in the center of Figure 18 drops into the motor well to prevent the motor, when installed, from moving so far back that the worm would have clearance problems by reaching beyond the gearbox. This piece is 1/10 inch or more thick and about 3/8 inch front to rear, but must be made to precisely fit each case: when assembled the worm should engage all the teeth of the axle gear but not go beyond it to the rear. Worm-gear engagement can be controlled with shims between the rear motor mount and motor (pushes the worm farther down on the gear) or under the front mount and the chassis floor (raises the worm from the gear). When gear engagement is correct, tape the motor in place with electrical tape.

Step 4: Solder the leads from the chassis to the motor. Test the unit. Then mount the body on the chassis. **The conversion is now complete.**

Figure 15: Motor positioned correctly and installed in bus chassis.

Figure 16: Motor faceplate, installed.

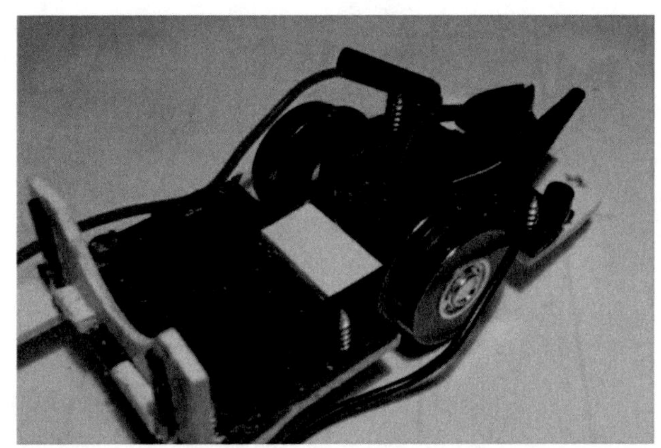

Figure 17: Plastic piece just drops in but must be just the right length front-to-back.

Greyhound Scenicruiser

Figure 18 shows a Corgi 1:50 model of a Greyhound Scenicruiser, perhaps *the* iconic bus of the '50s and '60s. A scale 5 feet longer than most other Corgi full-size cross-country buses, it has two rear axles and so can be given a swiveling rear truck, greatly reducing friction through curves. In addition, the extra axle's mounting was used as an opportunity to add an extra center pickup. With its swiveling axles and six-wheel, three-center pickup electrical connectivity, this is an extremely good runner in addition to being very good looking.

Figure 18: This Corgi 1:50 Greyhound Scenicruiser is a handsome model of this most iconic 1950s cross-country bus, and makes a wonderful conversion. The dual rear axle permits the use of a swiveling truck at the back which makes the bus run well through curves.

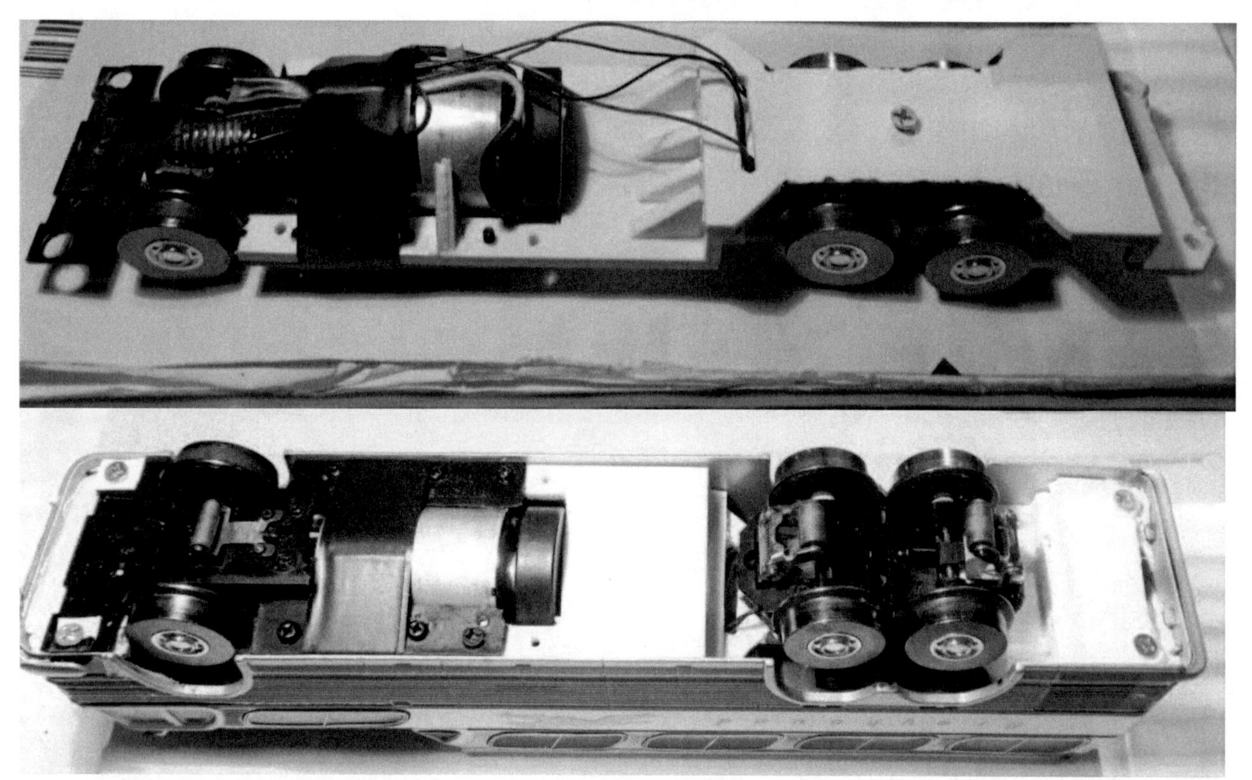

Figure 19: Chassis of the converted Scenicruiser. The bus is front-wheel drive using a full-size can motor.

Figure 20: Swiveling truck was made from two step-van front ends, each cut at a point where the saw blade would pass just behind the edge of the wheels: front center pickup, front axle, copper axel contract brush, and wiring were all brought with each piece. They were connected with the styrene framework seen at the left, ontop of which was glued a styrene plate on which the bus chassis pivoted underneath.

Figure 19 shows the chassis. Key points of its design are that:

- The bus body was not cut or modified in any way: it is completely original.
- Two K-Line step-van chassis – the original version with the larger wheels (they best match the model's original size) were used for the chassis. A bit more than half of one chassis was left over for future projects.
- This bus has front-wheel drive. As discussed in Chapters 5 and 6, it runs well enough, although it does not climb as well as rear-wheel drive buses.
- No reduction gearbox is used, the motor is mounted direct drive, so as to be as low as possible to leave room for the original interior above it. A gearbox would have raised the height and made that impossible.

Figure 21: This Scenicruiser is one of the most photogenic vehicles on the author's layout.

Two Motors - All Wheel Drive

The Corgi 1:50 GM 4515 in Figure 22 is an easy project, but expensive because it requires two "donor vehicles." This bus model is one of several Corgi buses that are riveted, not screwed together: two metal rivets at the rear had to be drilled out. At the front the chassis was held to the body by the front bumper and headlight assembly, which was pried loose.

Figure 22: Corgi 1:50 model of GM 4515 city bus was converted at its full length (4.8 in wheelbase).

The front axles were cut off two panel van chassis just to the rear of the front wheel wells. They were bolted together with 1/8 inch styrene (Figure 23).[1] Rectifiers were removed, leads to one motor switched, and pickup leads from both ends connected. New mounting towers in the body were made using repair putty (Figure 24). The original mounting holes and screws were used to mount the chassis to the body.

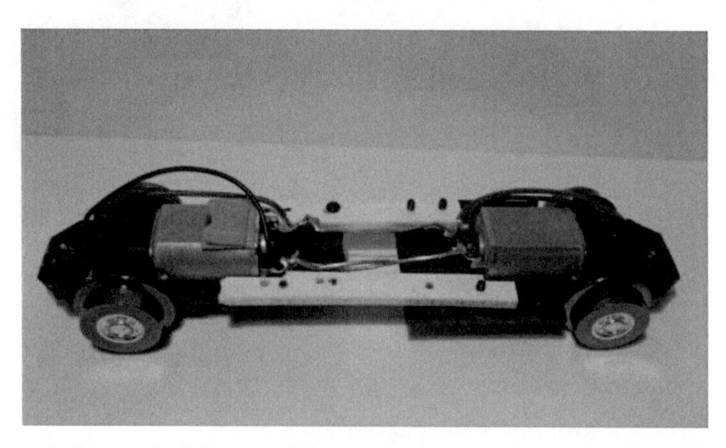

Figure 23: Chassis is made from two panel-van chassis with the front ends cut off, connected together to the correct wheelbase for the bus body.

This bus has one traction tire on each axle, so electrical connectivity suffers noticeably. It runs poorly, stuttering badly at speeds below 55 scale mph and stalling on occasion. A 2-amp bridge rectifier feeding both motors was installed to protect an electronic flywheel (*two* sets of three 1.5F 5.5 V supercapacitors in series – see Chapter 5). With this expensive ($60) addition, the bus, with its two motors, two traction tires and all-wheel-drive, runs well through D-16 curves in spite of its rather long wheelbase.

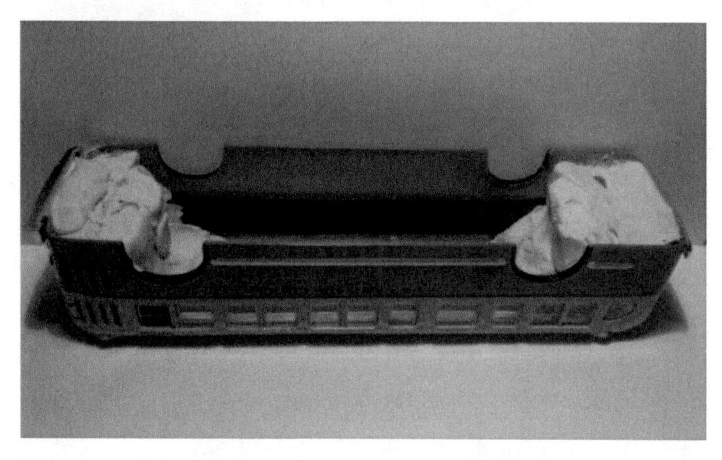

Figure 24: Windows were blacked out with electrical tape. Repair putty was used to make mounting towers and add "road hugging weight" at both ends.

---

[1] One of the chassis shown was used in a previous project in which it had its sides trimmed to fit within a smaller, narrower die-cast body. That is irrelevant to this project.

Two-Motor, Four-Wheel-Drive PCC Trolley

This PCC trolley in Figure 25 makes it a clean sweep for Corgi in this chapter. It was shortened to just ten inches long by removing 1 3/16 inch (two full side windows) just ahead of the side doors, in the same way the GM 4505 and Yellow Coach 743 bus models were shortened. Reducing length this much cut front and rear overhang below that of what it would have been otherwise, and *far* below that of the available O-gauge PCC and Peter Witt trolleys

The rear halves of two sedan chassis were bolted together end-to-end to make rigid a two-motor chassis (Figure 26). The front portions left over were cut as short as possible and, with their center pick-ups intact, were made into "trailing" one-axle trucks (see garbage truck example, Chapter 7). The front one, a *leading* truck, behaves itself well – much better than the author feared it might.

With a 3 $^{1}/_{8}$ inch wheelbase, two motors, and two traction tires, it "negotiates curves" on its own terms. Electrical pickup from eight wheels and four center pickups means it runs very smoothly.

Shortened as it is, it will make it around the author's downtown Main Street loop, but it demands a good deal of room at both ends as it rounds the one D-16 curve (Figure 27).

Figure 25: Converted, shortened Corgi PCC Trolley.

Figure 26: Two-motor sedan-derived center chassis has rigidly fixed axles – both driven. It was strapped to the original interior shortened by the same amount as the body (figures added by author).

Figure 27: The lady in a pink dress to the right is safe. The rear of the bus will miss her by more than two scale feet. But any traffic in the lane coming from the left will by knocked aside as this trolley rounds the corner.

Tractor-Trailers

9

No type of roadway vehicle fits into the spirit of a model train layout more than a tractor trailer. Big rigs haul freight, just like trains. They are big, complicated, and powerful looking, just like trains. Many a kid dreamed of driving a big rid someday, just like trains. And they are fun to put on a layout, just like trains.

Making a good-looking and good-running 'Streets tractor trailer is not inherently more difficult than making an operating car, truck or bus, but it is more complicated simply because so much more must be made. There are the tractor *and* the trailer to make, and they must be made so they not only run, but run well when connected together.

Like buses, tractor trailers are heavy, which means power and traction are often issues. Also like buses, they are long, and so wheelbase problems can create challenges. But unlike buses, tractor-trailers are articulated, which helps with length- and wheelbase-related issues, but creates additional stability issues to be kept in mind when handling all that weight.

Don't Just Follow the Directions

This chapter includes three step-by-step projects for making tractor trailers that when followed will yield good results: the author built each as he was photographing and writing, one step at a time, exactly as described. All three tractor-trailers worked well when completed.

But the intent of this chapter, and this book, is that readers *learn*, either by building or just studying the examples, so that they can set out on their own, to either slightly or greatly modify

Figure 1: These tractor-trailer rigs running on 'Streets roadways look big and powerful, and increase the operating fun and "things to watch" factor of a layout a lot.

the methods, concepts, and models covered here. Readers will hopefully convert *their* favorite model tractor-trailers – not just the author's as covered here. And an important part of the message is: to use the spare parts on hand, or those that one can buy inexpensively. Don't always go buy exactly what the author used. As an example, this chapter's third project uses parts taken from a broken Atlas trolley to modify a New Ray 1:43 Mack big-rig model so it runs on 'Streets roadway. Parts taken from just about any small four-axle diesel, trolley, or subway car would probably have worked just as well. A modeler would have to innovate and change a few minor details to do so. The author's hope is that many readers will.

Cost: Not Trivial by Any Means

The cost of materials needed for some projects covered here can be quite high. As Table 1 shows, at the extreme a good 'Streets tractor-trailer will cost as much as a new Lionchief Plus locomotive. The project produces something that is unique, and quite different from anything available from manufacturers, but still, that is a lot of money.

The author has made attempts to include projects that cut the cost as much as possible. The "Easy and Inexpensive Tractor-Trailer" project is mostly aimed at being easy to do, but it keeps price below one hundred dollars. Particularly if a modeler already has a spare pickup truck to use (many will), cost can be kept below seventy-five dollars, not much more than a new WBB vehicle costs. The Bargain Mack can be built for less than the list price of standard 'Streets vehicles, and perhaps even less if one scrounges for used parts.

Table 1: Materials Cost for Various Projects Covered in this Chapter

Item	Cost
Easy and Inexpensive Tractor-Trailer	
Road Sign. Ford F-1 pickup + shipping	$22.00
WBB Panel Van + shipping	$65.51
Glue, paint, epoxy, scrap parts, etc.	$5.00
	$92.51
Chilly Mack Ten-Wheeler	
Corgi Mack B-60 Carolina big rig + shipping	$84.99
Two WMM panel vans +shipping	$130.51
Large can-motor (see Chapter 5)	$22.00
1/3 sheet Evergreen styrene & shipping	$4.83
Glue, paint, epoxy, scrap parts, etc.	$4.00
	$246.33
Chilly Mack – Eighteen-Wheel Version	
Add another WBB panel van - total of	$306.51
Big Mack Fourteen Wheel Big Rig	
New Ray Mack B-61 big rig + shipping	$22.50
Two Lionel buses +shipping	$109.00
Large can-motor (see Chapter 5)	$22.00
1/2 sheet of Evergreen styrene & shipping	$7.25
Glue, paint, epoxy, scrap parts, etc.	$4.00
	$164.75
Big Mack – Eighteen-Wheel Big Rig	
Add another K-LbL bus - total of	$219.25
Bargain Mack Fourteen Wheel Big Rig	
New Ray Mack B-61 big rig & shipping	$22.50
Atlas trolley - non-runner, cracked body	$20.00
Two center pickups, axle bought used	$4.00
1/2 sheet of Plastruk styrene	$3.00
A dozen or so 3/4 inch washers	$1.50
Glue, paint, wire, etc., as used, say . . .	$4.00
	$55.00
Eighteen-wheeler version	
Add another axle bought used	$56.33
SpecCast International Eighteen-Wheeler	
SpecCast UP Intern. big rig + shipping	$47.19
Two and a half panel vans +shipping	$161.00
Large can-motor (see Chapter 5)	$22.00
1/2 sheet of Evergreen styrene & shipping	$5.50
Glue, paint, epoxy, scrap parts, etc.	$4.00
	$239.69

Inexpensive and Easy Tractor-Trailer

A stock chassis and motor is used for the tractor and a lightweight trailer made for it to pull.

Step 1: A panel-van chassis is needed. Disassemble a panel van and set aside the body.

Step 2: Cut away the areas outlined in red dashed lines in Figure 2 from the chassis sides, and cut off flush at the chassis floor all posts and projections.

Step 3: Drill a 3/32 to 1/8 inch hole in the center of the chassis, ahead of the motor, as shown. Keep this hole is ahead of the end of the motor shaft by at least 1/32 inch (Figure 3).

Step 4: A Road Signature brand 1:43 Ford F-1 pickup was used; it can have a big truck look when fitted on the panel van's wheels (see Chapter 2, Figure 5). As shown in the pickup examples in Chapter 4, it mounts to the panel van chassis using the original front mounting tower and front mounting hole in the chassis, simplifying conversion. It costs only about $14 including shipping. (Note: any of numerous other 1:43 pickups, such as the Matchbox '56 Chevy or the Gearbox Chevy pickup cab discussed in Chapter 4 fit as easily and could have been used instead).

Disassemble the model and set aside all the parts except the cab, interior, and front bumper. Cut the pickup bed off the cab (Figure 5).

Step 5: If desired, remove the interior and put a driver and passenger in the seats and detail the interior with paint, etc. Once done, install that. The interior *must* be retained and must be kept in its original position – the interior floor will help brace and mount the cab: Make certain driver and passenger figures are not so tall they don't let the interior fit up and into the cab fully.

Figure 2: All posts and projections from the chassis are cut flush at chassis floor. Sides should be cut away at the red lines.

Figure 3: A hole is drilled just ahead of the motor. See text for details.

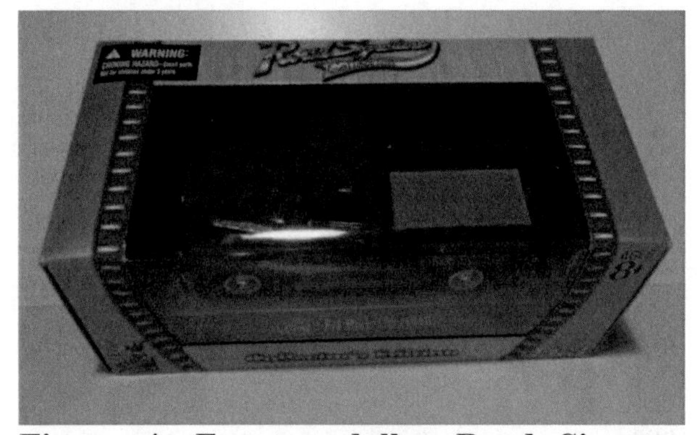

Figure 4: Fourteen-dollar Road Signature 1:43 Ford F-1 will provide the tractor's cab.

Figure 5: The cab is cut from the pickup bed.

Note: eventually, a shim will be used underneath the rear of the interior, and the tower ground down or shimmed so that it has a ride height similar to the lowest photo in Chapter 4's Figure 2: one wants a good deal of fender clearance over the front wheels to simulate a big truck. Keep this in mind.

Step 6: Cover the outside of the cab with painters tape – the epoxy putty used in the next step puts an invisible residue on fingers that *will* leave permanent fingerprints on glossy surfaces.

Step 7: With the windows, dashboard, interior and a driver (if desired) located properly in the cab, press Loctite Repair Putty around the front of it and into the crevices at the rear of the interior to lock the interior in place. This does not have to be too neat (see Figure 6).

Now use repair putty to extend the floor of the interior rearward 1/8-5/32 inch as indicated by the red arrow in Figure 6. Edges do not have to be neatly precise. Trim and shape it flat with the floor, and with a ninety-degree edge at the rear, etc. as much and as well as possible while it is soft – it is much easier to work at that time.

Step 8: Place a small pin, just less than half an inch long, temporarily in the cab's mounting tower hole (yellow arrow in Figure 6). Turn the chassis over and fit the cab and chassis together with the pin inserted into the mounting tower hole in the chassis. (This pin is to aligning cab and chassis correctly).

Center the back of the cab on the chassis so the cab is correctly aligned side to side on the chassis. Using a pin vise drill or similar, put a drill bit through the hole in the chassis (Step 3, Figure 6) and start a hole aligned with it in the bottom of the interior floor. Once that is done, separate the cab from the chassis and drill out the hole (black arrow in Figure 6).

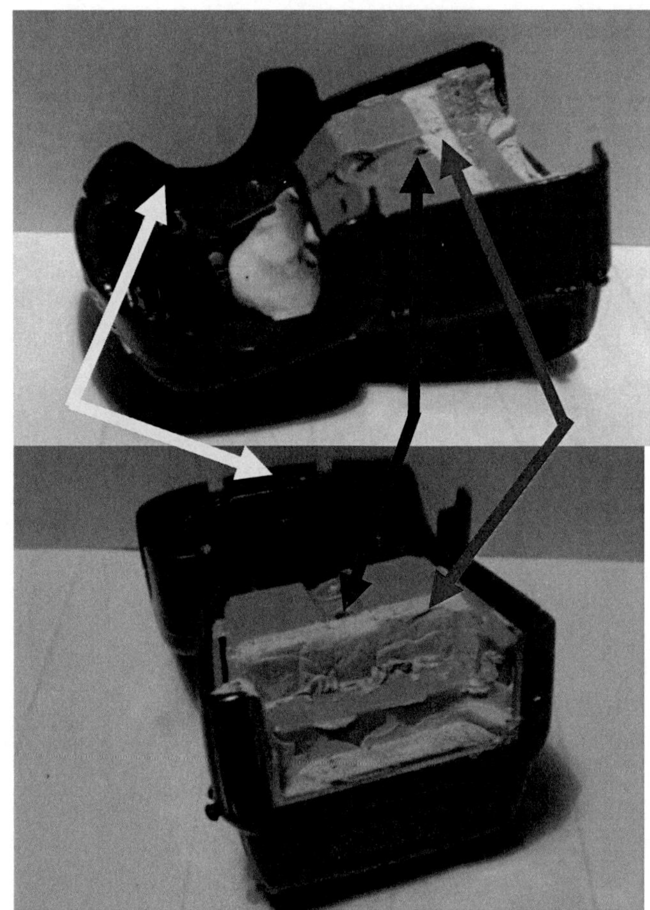

Figure 6: Two views of the cab after Steps 8, 9 and 10. See text for explanation of arrows.

Step 9: *This step is informational only.* The cab will be mounted using the pin already made to align the chassis' original front mounting tower with the cab's original mounting tower – they align *perfectly* – and a single screw inserted through the hole drilled in the chassis in Step 3 into the hole drilled in the cab floor.

As was explained in Chapter 2, Figure 5, the ride height of a cab above its wheels determines how 'big" a truck looks. Here, exactly how far above the chassis and its wheels the cab sits – and thus how "big" it looks, is controlled by: 1) trimming off a tiny bit of the top of the chassis mounting tower and 2) the thickness of a shim placed between the top of the motor and the bottom of the interior at the back of the cab.

Step 10: Place the cab and chassis together (the pin – yellow arrow in Figure 9 - helps get the correct alignment) and look at the ride height – the gap between fender and wheels tells this tale. (Check that the pin is not so long that it is keeping the two mounting towers from meeting firmly. If so trim a tiny bit off it.)

Trim or shim the top of the front mounting tower on the chassis a bit lower or shim to raise the ride height– it is a matter of personal preference. Make a shim, if needed, to place between the top of the motor and the underside of the cab interior to adjust that height there so the cab is level(the author adjusted the front so that no shim is needed at the rear). Finally, trim the front extension of the mounting tower off (Figure 7).

Figure 7: Detail of the front mounting tower with the pin in it and some of its top trimmed away. Portion of that tower forward of the red line has to be removed so the back of the bumper piece will fit.

Step 11: Put the bumper on the cab – the piece slips on with the hole in its back end around the cab's front mounting tower. It is best to glue it in place (Duco Cement works well) in place with the cab upside down and let the cement harden for fifteen minutes or so first). Now position the cab on the chassis, with the bumper on, the pin in place in both mounting towers, and the back of the cab centered side to side. Run a screw through the hole in the bottom of the chassis and into that on the cab interior floor and gently tighten it (Figure 8).

Figure 8: Cab mounted on chassis. The author has trimmed the portion of the chassis behind the rear wheels narrower (compare to Figures 5 and 6).

Step 12: Build the small piece shown in Figure 9a out of styrene at least 1/10 inch thick, and mount it as shown on the rear of the chassis, using the original screw mounting holes in the bottom of the chassis. Once mounted, add the mounting platform atop it as shown in Step 9b.

The basic tractor is done. Modeling details to complete its appearance will be added later. Check that it runs – it may need weight added temporarily to it to provide enough to test it.

Figure 9: Scratch-built styrene trailer mounting platform is screwed on from beneath.

Step 13. Make the trailer frame shown in Figure 10 out of styrene at least 16th inch thick. Width is 13/16 inch, length can be as desired, but around 4 ½ inches is recommended.

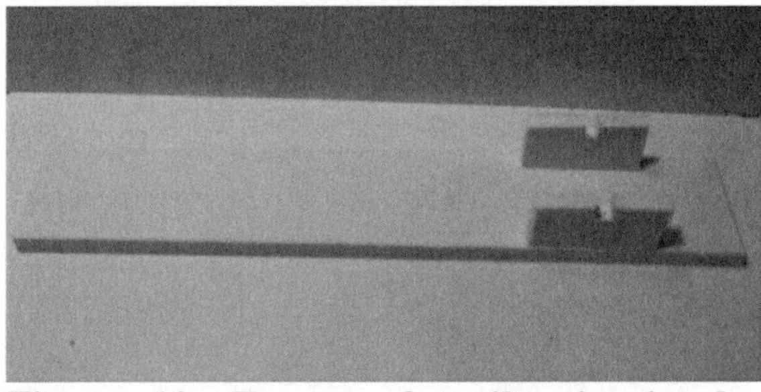

Figure 10: Frame of trailer is simple: three styrene parts all scratch built.

Find a flanged wheel and axle to use for the trailer. The author had a spare panel-van axle, which is ideal since it matches the look of the wheels used on the cab. The axle shown has a gear and bearings but they are unimportant here. It is mounted on the trailer, held in by thin styrene plates glued on as shown in Figure 11. About ¼ inch back from the front, drill a hole and insert a screw that protrudes about ¼ inch out on the bottom side: it hooks into the tractor.

Figure 11: Trailer is completed as described in text.

Step 14: Test the tractor-trailer as shown in Figure 12. Again, more weight may be needed.

Figure 12: Completed basic tractor trailer is tested. Trailer should track well.

Step 15: From here, this tractor-trailer is a modeling project to complete as the owner wishes. The tractor can be detailed and the trailer completed as a freight box, tanker, dump or whatever. This page is only a guideline.

Tractor: The author made gas tanks for both sides, attached step plates made from scrap chrome parts salvaged from other models, etc. A chrome exhaust was added.

Trailer. The trailer shown in Figure 13 (left) was made by cutting a plastic display case that contained a 1:43 die-cast car to a scale 7 feet wide, scribing some panel seams and then mounting in on trailer frame. It was primed and painted. A rear bumper and spare tires under the frame and similar equipment were added.

Flat black paint was used to paint the tractor and the trailer's lower frame, etc., to make irrelevant details less noticeable.

The author scratch built a second, tanker, trailer as shown in Figure 13, right. It was *not* an easy to build and is not detailed here, but left as "an exercise for the reader."

The model is complete.

Length, weight and complexity of the trailer were kept minimal here so as to avoid problems. Despite that it is near several limits for a stock motor-chassis. It is not *at* them – but close. The model can be "enhanced" by:

a) Adding electrical pickup to the trailer's wheels and a center pickup there, or

b) Making the trailer longer, heavier, or both

Either, and certainly both together, would complicate the build enough that the author would not consider it an easy project any more.

The author expected this rig to have wheel spin problems in D-16 curves, but it has only a trace. And it is common for the front wheels on lightweight tractors (this is, relatively) pulling a significant trailer (this is not) to sometimes jump the rails on tight curves.

The solution to those problems if they occur is to add weight as low as possible over and just ahead of the tractor's rear axle, putting it in the tractor and/or the trailer. (The stock motor can pull up to another six ounces of weight).

Figure 13: Finished model with two different trailers made for it. The Texaco trailer was a difficult a diffuclt built but worth the trouble. Note the painted wheels and rims.

Successful Die-Cast 'Streets Big Rigs: Put a Big Motor in the Trailer

The design of the "semi-big-rig" covered in the previous section is *not* something that can be successfully scaled up to handle most die-cast model tractor trailers. Reasons why are, in order of importance, are:

- Weight. The tractor and trailer in the previous example together weighed 8.5 ounces – only slightly more than the stock panel van. A stock motor and chassis can pull up to 13 ounces without problems. Much beyond that and the motor begins to bog down. But 1:50 die-cast model tractor-trailers typically weigh 20 to 24 ounces, and 1:43 may weigh up to 32 ounces.
- Wheelbase (distance from the tractor's fixed rear axle to the trailer's) was 4 1/8 inches. By contrast most die-cast O-gauge big rigs will require a wheelbase that is from around five inches (for 1:50 tractor trailers) to six inches long (for larger 1:43 models). Wheel-to-rail friction increases drastically over wheelbase lengths of four and one half inches. However, long-wheelbase friction is less severe in a tractor and trailer than a bus, because the tractor and the trailer are articulated. This means that usually only one axle – the leading axle at the rear of the trailer, is running at a sharp angle to the rails due to the long wheelbase, as compared to both front and rear axles on a bus. Still, the additional friction can be substantial, particularly when a lot of weight is on the wheels.
- More wheels. A tractor-trailer will have from 50% to 150% more wheels to pull – so fiction is increased by that amount. This increases burden on the motor.

For all these reasons, a stock motor and chassis cannot pull a converted a *die-cast* model tractor trailer. Something else is needed. A good deal of experimentation and testing revealed the best method is to put the motor in the trailer, where the trailer's weight helps traction, with the motor driving the lead axle if there is more than one, and with it pushing a motor-less tractor. Figure 14 shows the author's preferred configuration for the layout of an 18 wheeler.

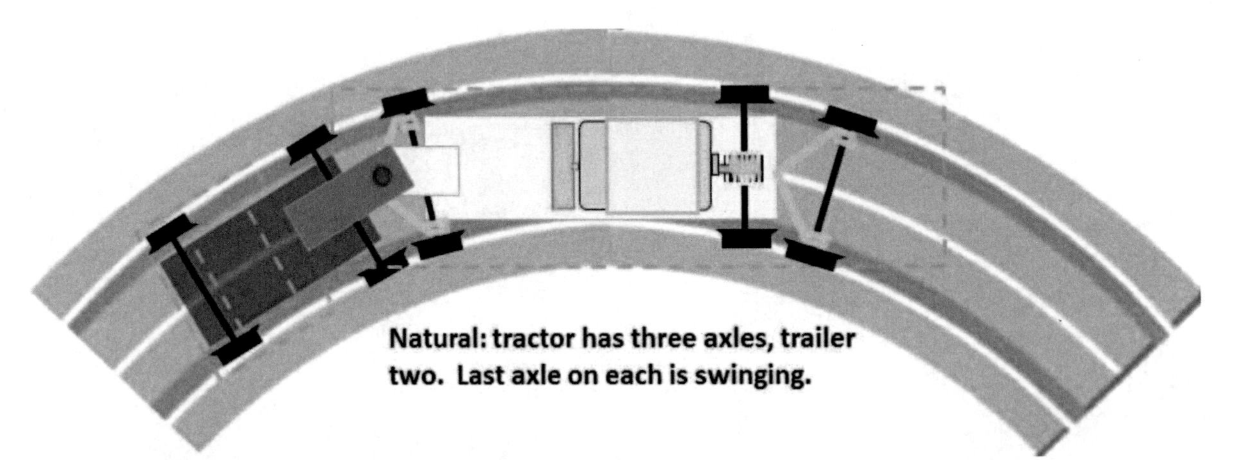

Figure 14: Recommended way to convert a die-cast tractor-trailer: a large motor in the trailer, ahead of and driving its lead axle. Tractor has no motor and is pushed by the trailer. Second axles in pairs, if they exist, are made single-axle pivoting trailing trucks.

Motor-less Tractors: A Great Idea

Figure 15: Motor-less conversion of a 1:50 SpecCast International KB tractor allowed a prototypically correct trailer mount height and retention of the original model's cab un-modified, including its opening doors and hood and model engine.

With the motor no longer on the tractor's chassis, much more modeling detail can be accommodated in a conversion, and the work is also easier to do. Figure 15 shows two views of a converted SpecCast International KB tractor that is a good example. With no motor at the rear, the trailer mounting plate can be located at a prototypically correct height. Furthermore, normally the motor intrudes into the rear of the cab, meaning its back wall has to be trimmed at the bottom, and the interior or cab assembly may have to be removed. Here, the model's cab is moved over with full interior, working doors and hoot, etc. – no modifications at all. Various hardware like fuel tanks and exhausts were also moved over – the result is a very good *model.*

Some die-cast model tractors, particularly many Ertl trucks from the 1930s through the 1950s, have two-piece die-cast body-chassis combinations (Figure 16). It is nearly impossible to mount their cabs neatly on a 'Streets chassis. However, when there is no motor involved, it proves easy to simply mount 'Streets axles and center pickups on the original ERTL chassis and use that. Some modification is required, but it is fairly straightforward.

Figure 16: Three 1:43 tractors by Ertl. All three have internal ribbing and two-piece cab-chassis castings that make it very difficult to mount the model's cab on a 'Streets chassis. However, as long as a motor is not involved, it's easier to convert the model – cab *and* chassis – directly to 'Streets (the green Diamond T on the right already has been).

The Diamond T in Figure 16 was disassembled, and a driver put in the interior, then the interior was re-installed (Figure 16).

Figures 17 through 19 show how a "chassis insert" was made using only the wheel-axle assemblies and the center pickups from a panel van. Here, the axles are contained in and ride on plastic. The friction is greater than that of metal bearings, but the motor in the trailer will have two to three times the power needed and easily overcome the added rolling friction.

In this case, the author used two front axles (no gear on either). Geared axles are saved for use in trailers, as powered axles. The center pickups are held in place by plastic sheet cut and glued in place to hold them firmly: Should they ever need to be removed the plastic will be cut off.

Single-strand 18-gauge copper "picture hanging wire" was used to make electrical pickups on both axles and both center pickups, simply twisted in one loop around each. Wires were brought to the rear for eventual connection to the trailer.

Details like marker lights, trim, running board rubber mats, and so on., were painted, mirrors and such added, and details like floorboards and so forth on the truck painted (Figure 20).

Figure 17: A simple plastic insert is made for the Ertl chassis with plastic used to retain both axles in their proper place.

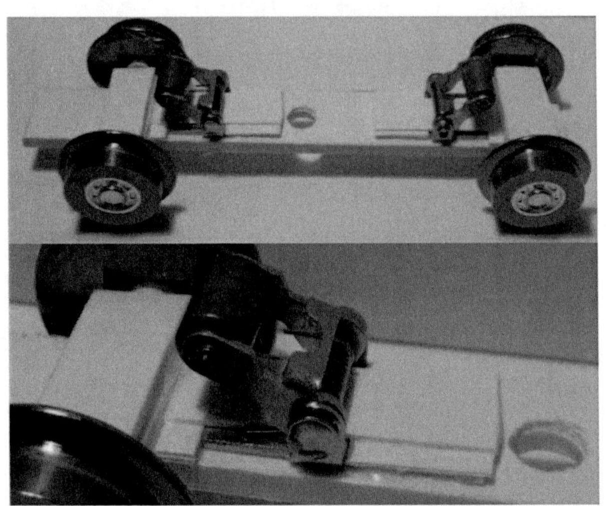

Figure 18: Front and rear center pickups are attached (without wire leads) being held in by plastic sheet plastic welded in place.

Figure 20: Completed Diamond T tractor.

Figure 19: Copper wire is used to make "pickup fingers" for axles and center pickups and wires soldered to them.

Chilly Mack

Figure 21: Corgi die-cast 1:50 model for this project.

The Corgi 1:50 Carolina Freight lines Mack Truck B-60 series tractor and trailer in Figure 21 will be converted to a 'Streets reefer truck in this project.

The Tractor

This tractor will be converted in the same way as the Diamond T on the previous pages: 'Streets wheels and pickups will be added to its chassis, except here, the axles will ride in the original chassis mounting locations. The chassis will provide electrical connectivity to the wheels and hence to the outer rails.

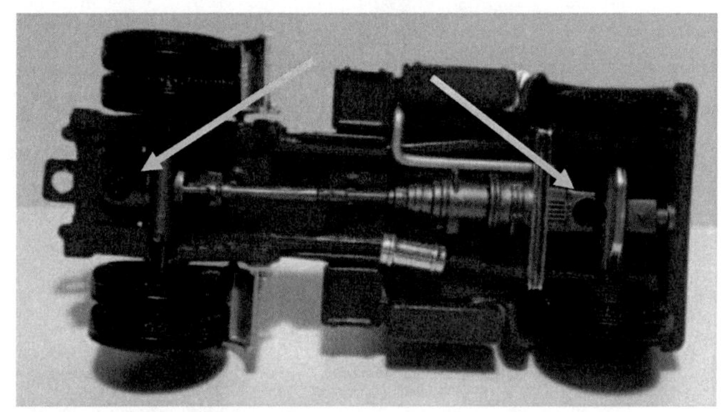

Figure 22: Tractor comes apart once two screws are removed

Step 1: Two screws are removed to disassemble the tractor (arrows, Figure 22). Even after removal, some tugging of the plastic drivetrain parts is needed to unseat them from the chassis. *Save the original screws.*

Figure 23: Axles and center pickups from one WBB panel van.

Step 2: Disassemble two WBB panel vans – the big rig will need at least three axles - and remove the front axles and center pickups from both (Figure 23). If two panel vans are too expensive, any O-gauge axles with wheels around 3/4 inch diameter can be substituted but if they don't look too train-like. Other center pickups could be used, too, but 'Streets pickups have a very light spring pressure (since the vehicles weight so much less than a loco). Some pickups from locos have such high spring tension they will push a 'Streets vehicles clear up off the rails. Caboose pickups often work well here if 'Streets pickups aren't available.

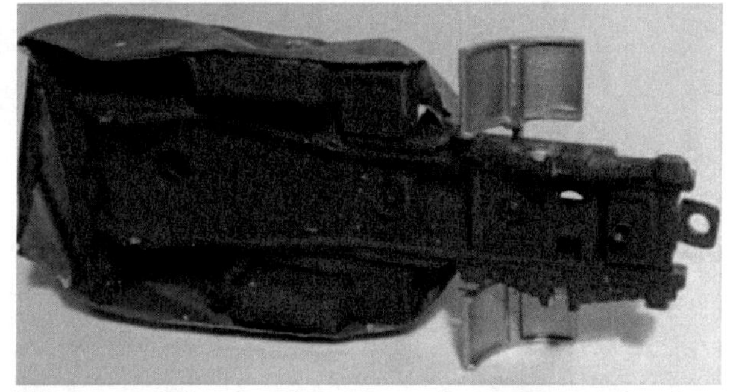

Figure 24: Tractor is wrapped in protective tape. Axle mounts are filed down to shiny metal and so axles fit well.

Step 3: Wrap the tractor in painters tape (Figure 24). Trial fit the axles in the Corgi chassis' axle mounting slots. All four slots will need to be carefully filed out a bit wider and deeper – to expose unpainted metal so as to assure to electrical contact. Make sure the axles fit completely in and roll with no binding.

Step 4. A "chassis insert" is made out of 1/10 to 1/8 inch thick styrene so as to fit within the chassis' frame rail recess as shown in Figure 25. (A thin sheet of paper can be pressed inside the chassis and up against all the side frames to impress a pattern on it that can then be used as a guide to cut the plastic piece to the correct shape.) Mounting screws holes are drilled as shown, and it is mounted to the chassis with the original screws.

Step 5: Axle mounting retainer blocks are made that will keep the axles in their mounting slots. These are straightforward to make but require some intricacy in position and size. Study of Figures 26 and 27 and their details will help

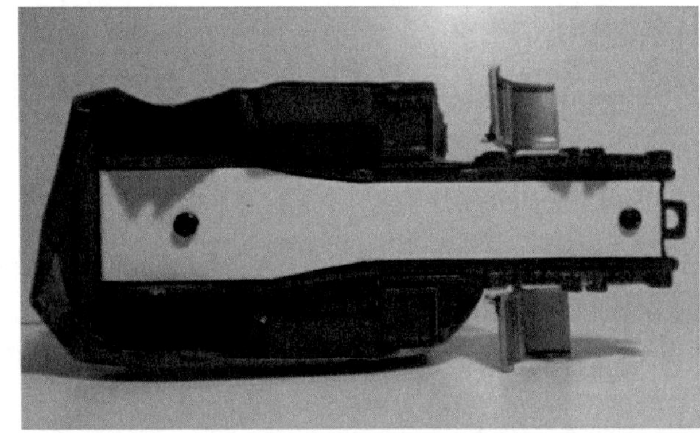

Figure 25: Plastic chassis insert is made.

readers make theirs. The mounting towers are built up a section at a time: the author used 1/10-inch styrene. When complete and installed, they allow the axles to roller free in their slots, but keep them from working loose from the chassis: the axles should be able to "flop around" by about ½ mm. The front tower must be ahead of the front axle and the rear tower to the rear of the rear axle. They are

Figure 26: Chassis insert is built up to make the front and rear axle retainer towers.

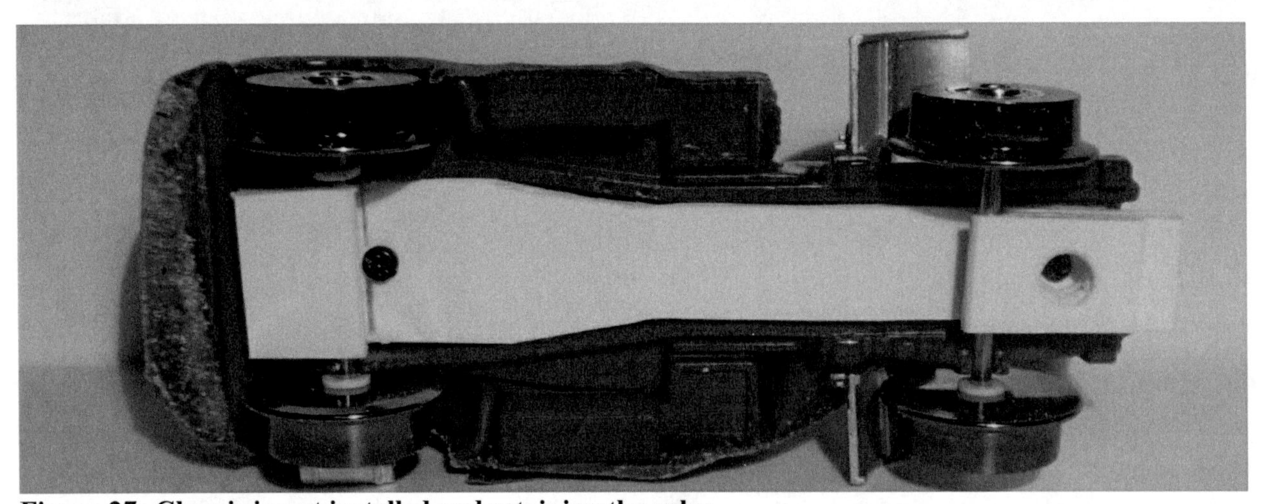

Figure 27: Chassis insert installed and retaining the axles.

made so that the two mounting screws for the chassis insert are accessible. Figure 28 shows the insert installed and holding the axles and wheels in place. It is a good idea to check that they roll freely.

Step 6: The center pickups are mounted in much the same way as for the Diamond T example given earlier. They must be mounted at a correct level, so that they are about halfway levered out by their springs when the wheels are on the rails. On the author's example, that meant being atop a 1/8-inch spacer shown glued on, so that the mounting screws are still accessible, in Figure 29. (Readers should measure their model, particularly if making a similar model but not exactly this one, to determine if 1/10-inch, or 1/8-inch, or 3/16-inch is best for theirs, and make the piece that thick. It simply glues on.

Step 7: Center pickups can just be glued in place with plastic retainers in a way similar to as done on the Diamond T. In order to demonstrate another method, here they are mounted to the plastic using the mounting screws that originally held them in place on the 'Streets chassis. They were each held in place by and a hole started for the screw. *One must make certain that both have room to move fully up and down without interference and without touching the axle.* The hole for the screw was drilled out, they were put in place and screwed on. (It is best to start the screw and "tap" the hole first, seating it all the way in, then withdrawing it and mounting the pickup). A .08-inch plate was placed between keep them from pivoting or working sideways (green arrow, Figure 30)

Step 8: A hole is drilled at mid-chassis and a screw partially inserted. Make certain the screw does not go in so far as to make electrical

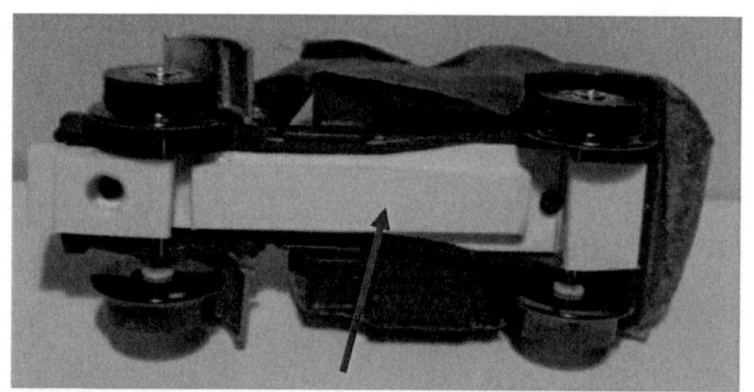

Figure 28: Spacer to hold the two center pickups in place is cut and glued in place.

Figure 29: The two center pickups have been installed (Step 6). Copper "picture hanging wire" is used for pickup fingers for both. That on the right has been pulled through but on the driver's side is about to be.

Figure 30: Close up view of center pickups when complete. A hole was drilled at mid chassis and a screw inserted as a center pickup electrical mounting lug. See text for explanation of the colored arrows.

contact with the metal chassis. Both copper pickup leads were wrapped around it and a soldering lead left (yellow arrow in Figure 30).

Step 9: Use a multi-meter or similar to test that the wheels are electrically connected to the chassis and that the center pickups are not.

Making the Powered Trailer

Step 1: The trailer disassembles after removing four screws near the corners of the chassis, from underneath. Set the chassis aside for now.

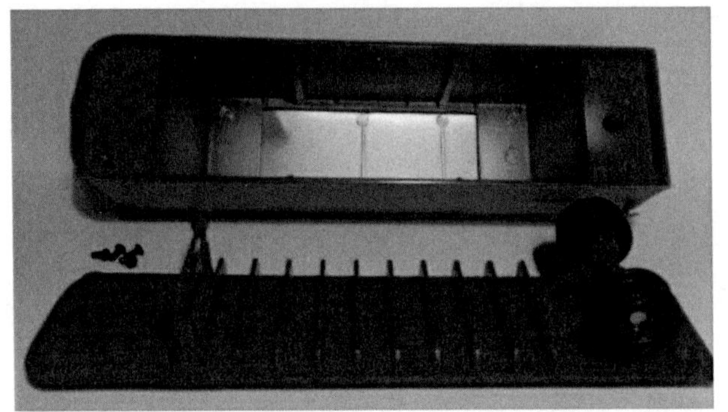

Figure 31: Trailer disassembles by removing four screws for underneath.

Step 2: Take one of the panel-van chassis and cut it in shape as shown in Figure 32 (black plastic). Note the shape exactly: the front has been cut off the central well for the motor cut out to make it a pronged shape, with narrower fingers near the front. Cut off the top of the gearbox, being careful not to damage the gear.

Step 3 makes a "motor cradle" as shown in Figure 32 (white styrene) and detailed below. Modelers new to this type of work should not be frustrated if their first attempt only leads to a realization of how to do it well the second time.

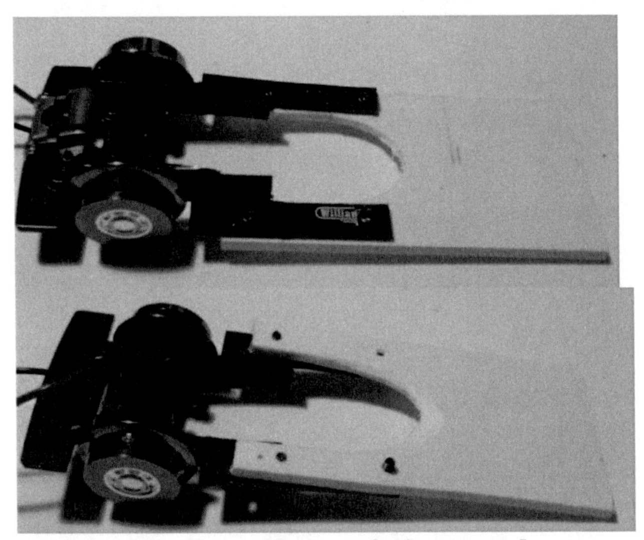

Figure 32: Two views of the panel-van chassis with its rear axle, as cut and trimmed, and the "motor cradle" screwed to it. Note the parabola's edge is filed at an angle to maximize contact space/support.

- The motor cradle should be made out of fairly thick plastic (for strength), made the width of the panel van chassis, and have a parabola cut out of it as shown. Dimensions will vary depending on the shaft length and diameter of the motor: it must be custom measured and made.) That shown is 3 1/16 inches long, 1 5/8 wide, and the parabola is 7/8 inches at its widest and 1 ½ inches long.
- The edge and back (tip of the parabola) are filed to an angle (see Figure 32) to best hold and support the motor body.
- The motor should sit naturally within the cradle, with the worm engaged onto the axle's gear, meshing with it fully, and with

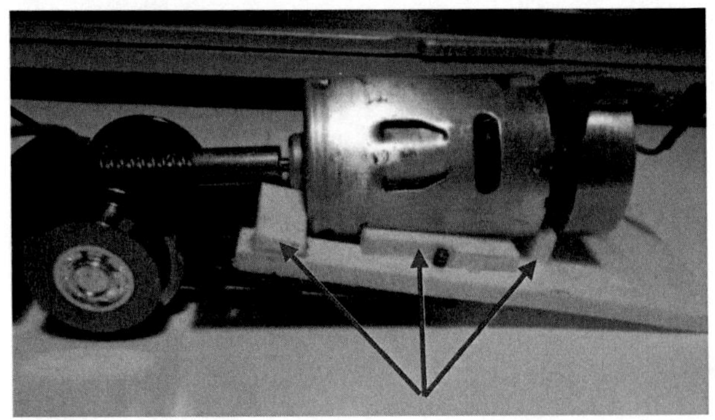

Figure 33: The motor in position but not taped or bolted down on the motor cradle.

the end of the worm just missing the back wall of the gearbox.

- Retainers – red arrows in Figure 33 – are glued on to keep the motor in its position.

Step 4: The motor is mounted to the chassis using electrical tape in tension to hold it firmly in place. Two or three layers should be sufficient. As discussed in other chapters, this works better than any other method the author has found to mount a motor.(Figure 34).

Figure 34: Motor mounted in cradle.

Step 5: Test the motor at eight volts. It should turn the rear wheels even when the wheels are lightly held. If the worm slips on the gear, the back of the motor can be shimmed slightly by inserting a thin shim from underneath the motor, through the parabola, at its apex.

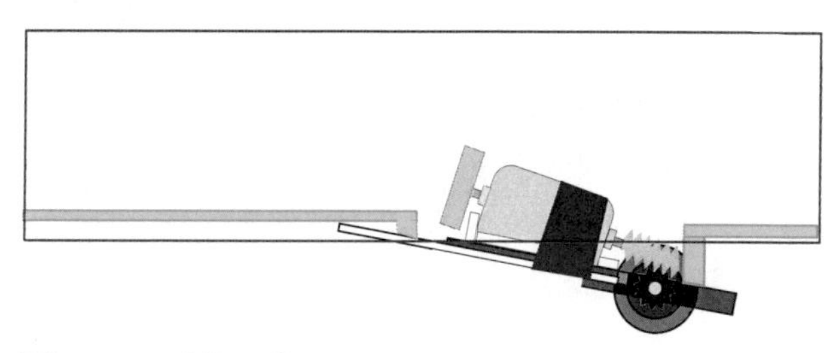

Figure 35: Overall concept of how a powered trailer is built – see text for details.

Step 6: The motor used is larger than shown in Figure 35, but otherwise that diagram shows how the motor platform in Figure 34 will be mounted. The motor will be mounted at an angle so that not too much of it shows below the trailer. The additions shown in green are made for 1/8-nch styrene (for strength):

a) End pieces are made (the green pieces in Figure 35) and screwed in place (Figure 36).
b) The rear tower (yellow arrow, Figures 35 and 36) requires some tailoring to fit but must be made to fit tightly and glued on well.
c) Motor platform should fit well (Figure 37). When it does, it is centered in place and plastic welded to the front. Working through its original rear mounting holes, holes are drilling into the tower and the motor and cradle attached with screws.
d) When the glue has hardened the chassis is unscrewed from the trailer body (Figure 37). The basic chassis is done.

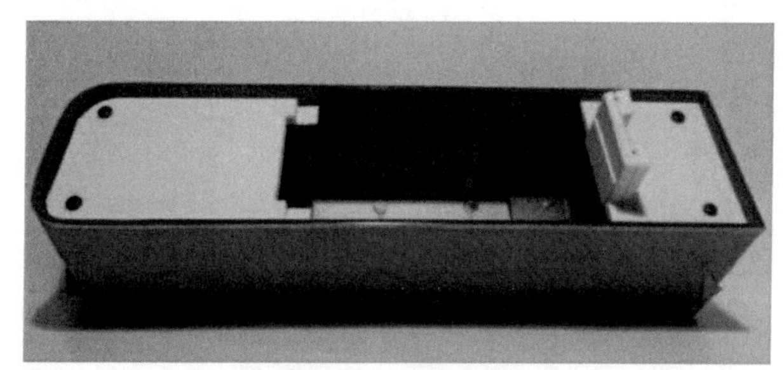

Figure 36: Trailer with front and rear sections of chassis screwed on, showing the mounting tower (arrow).

Figure 37: Motor platform on chassis with electrical post bolts (arrow) installed.

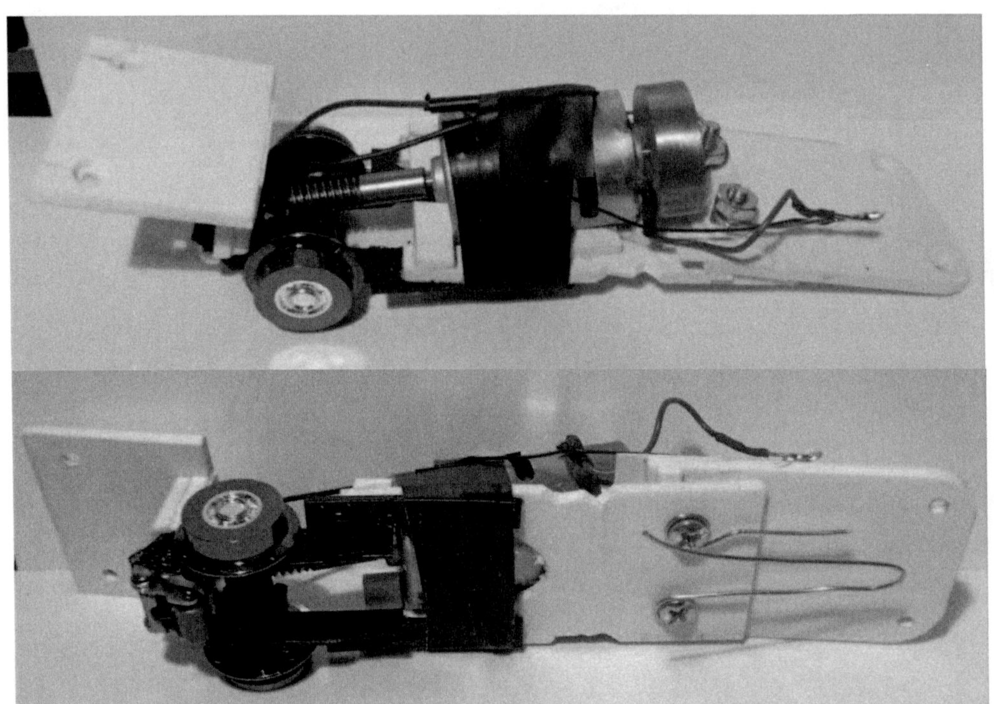

Figure 38: Rear leads are brought forward, one each to one of the bolts installed in Step 7. Motor leads are brought out, too, and soldered to each copper lead.

On the underside, other copper leads are screwed under each bolt head, with that for post connected to the outer rail made very long, as shown.

Step 7: Holes are drilled. Two bolts are inserted both to hold the motor platform to the front and to act as electrical posts (Figures 37 and 38).

Step 8: Leads from the axles and center pickup are brought forward and connected to those two electrical posts. The wires from the motor are connected too. Figure 38 gives views of the chassis from above and below. On the underside, copper wire is used to make a soldering lug lead on the negative (outer-rail) terminal and a particularly long lead for the center-rail (positive) leads on the other (in the figure it is bent forward and then around toward the rear).

The chassis should be tested when all this is done by holding it to powered rails at about seven or eight volts. When all checks out, the chassis is remounted into the trailer.

Step 9: The front chassis platform is drilled and a plastic pin inserted and glued to attach to the tractor. Figure 93 shows it in its place. (It also shows a small shim put there to level the trailer front to rear when mounted on the tractor). The copper wire from the center-rail post is led to it and wound spiral-like around it as shown: the electrical connection of trailer and tractor the out-rail connectivity will be through the metal-to-metal contact.

Figure 39: Trailer is finished. Black paint has been applied to the visible white plastic.

Step 10: The paint is removed from the top of the trailer mounting tongue (Figure 40).

Figure 40: Tractor's trailer mounting tongue is cleaned of paint to improve electrical connectivity through it.

Step 11: The trailer is mounted on the trailer. The center pickup lead – the single wire from the truck is connected to the other lead on the bottom of the trailer. Test run the tractor trailer at this point. It should run smoothly and at fairly low speeds, without too much gear whine and no perceptible vibration or stutter.

Completing the Model

Step 12: Modeling details were addressed last. Any exposed white styrene underneath tractor and trailer was painted flat black. Wheels were painted: an owner has the option to leave them chrome, but the author preferred to original painted-hub look. Mirrors and a spare tire were added. The Carolina logo on the front of the trailer was removed (Goo Gone) and a scratch-built chiller unit mounted there. A driver was installed (through the window in this case).

The completed model (Figure 41) weighs nearly two pounds (7.1 ounces for the tractor, 22.7 for the trailer). It runs smoothly backwards and forwards with no strain or wheel-spin through curves and attains speeds from a scale 20 mph (4.5 volts) up to an estimated 65 mph at 14 volts (the author has not run it over a scale 65 mph).

Figure 41: The Chilly Mack, completed.

Big Mack

The 1:43-scale New Ray Mack B-61 tractor and thirty foot trailer shown in Figure 42 is among the most widely available die-cast big-rig models and among the lowest cost. That shown cost twenty dollars including shipping. In spite of its bargain basement price it is a fairly good model. Only the cab is while metal, but tractor and trailer are nicely detailed and rendered very close to scale.

Figure 42: New Ray 1:43 model of a 1953 Mack B-61 is a nice model, and inexpensive. It is available with several different trailers, including the thirty-foot box shown here.

1:43 Means Really Big Wheels

As discussed in Chapter 2, 1:43 models of big vehicles need big wheels: among 'Streets vehicles, *only* the school bus wheels really do well on the Big Mack tractor, for two reasons. First, among all 'Streets vehicles, only the early K-Line step vans and the school bus have wheels that are big enough to look like they belong under the fenders of the Mack tractor. Many toy-train wheels are the right size, too, if more train-like and less road-like in appearance.

But beyond wheels size, as Figure 43 shows, only the school bus wheels are *wide enough* to fit well. Any other 'Streets wheels, and any toy train wheels, will have to be widened which is difficult work to get done well.

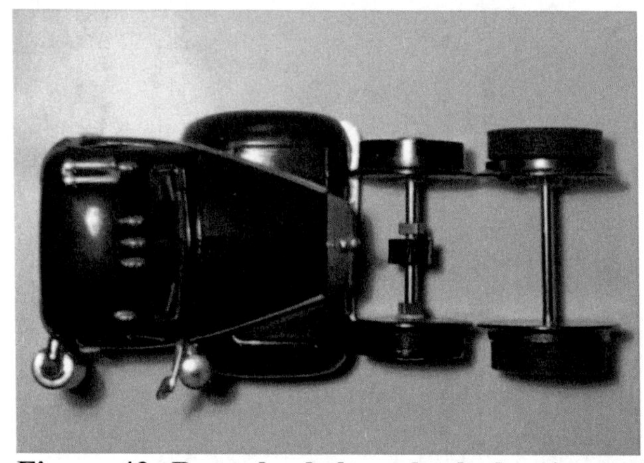

Figure 43: Bus wheels have both the size and width suitable to look good on the New Ray Mack. Most others are too narrow.

Two Example Conversions Done Here

Two different conversions are covered here.

1) The first follows the author's preferred, and recommended, way of converting a tractor trailer, basically the same approach as taken with Chilly Mack covered in the preceding section, scaled up to 1:43 and with some changes needed to address the bigger but much lighter plastic trailer and its unique needs. This results in a very good looking, smooth-running and durable model costing about $165 in parts and materials.

2) The second method is an attempt to keep total cost as low as possible, and also to demonstrate two additional useful modeling methods. By using salvaged and used parts and making some innovative use of them, it produces a durable model that is nearly as good looking and that runs quite satisfactorily. Total cost for this project, which is meant to be an example of how to keep costs *very* low, can be under $60.

Big Mack with Everything

The recommended approach uses 'Streets school bus wheels, a large flywheel motor, and a methodology very similar to that used in the Chilly Mack example given earlier in this chapter and in the truck and bus examples in Chapters 7 and 8. It requires two or three (if one wants a true eighteen wheeler) school buses as donors of chassis and wheels. Since its conversion is very similar to those earlier examples, it will be summarized here, not given in detail.

Figure 44: Tractor converted to a school bus chassis.

Tractor

Figure 44 shows the completed tractor. The New Ray model's cab was mounted on a school bus chassis lengthened 5/8 inch and trimmed so the New Ray cab would fit on it (Figure 45) using the methods covered in Chapter 4: no more than *very* small changes to anything covered there was needed.

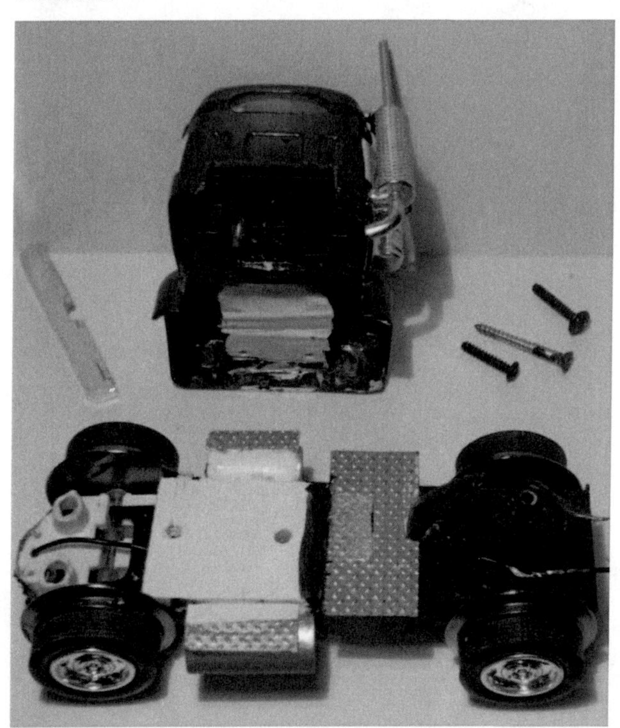

Figure 45: Tractor in Figure 44 disassembled.

The New Ray tractor was then mounted on that chassis. To do so, the model was disassembled, the cab removed, and the rest of the model's parts put aside as they are not needed for this project. The interior was removed from the cab, a driver glued in, and the interior reinserted. Repair putty was used, and the cab was mounted on the chassis as detailed step-by-step in Chapter 3's Mack Delivery truck example. Again, only tiny details differed from what was done in those earlier examples.

Another satisfactory way to make the tractor is to use the method covered in the Chilly Mack example, except using school bus wheels rather than panel-van wheels (Figure 46). Since the Mack chassis is plastic it cannot be used to conduct the outer-rail power as on Chilly Mack; electrical pickup identical to that used on the Diamond T discussed earlier is used instead.

Figure 46: Tractor made from New Ray chassis (back) is equivalent in all important ways to that from Figure 44's (front).

Trailer

The trailer is made in a manner almost identical to that in the Chilly Mack example earlier, except a school-bus chassis is used because it has the larger wheels. The difference in work that has to be done is quite minor.

The second trailer axle (Figure 47) is made as a swinging axle in a manner *identical* to that used on the garbage truck in Chapter 7, Figure 18.

The plastic New Ray trailer is a pound lighter than most Corgi die-cast trailers. With the motor and metal axles added it still weighs only 12.6 ounces compared to 22.7 for the Chilly Mack trailer: this rig runs well but does not have outstanding traction. Tubes of BBs are particularly good for adding substantial weight (Figure 48) and two were used here.

As always, after the conversion is done and the vehicle is tested, modeling details were added and paint applied to finish the model's appearance (Figure 49).

Figure 47: Second axle is a swinging trailer-axle that was simply hooked into a small hole drilled in the back of the school bus chassis.

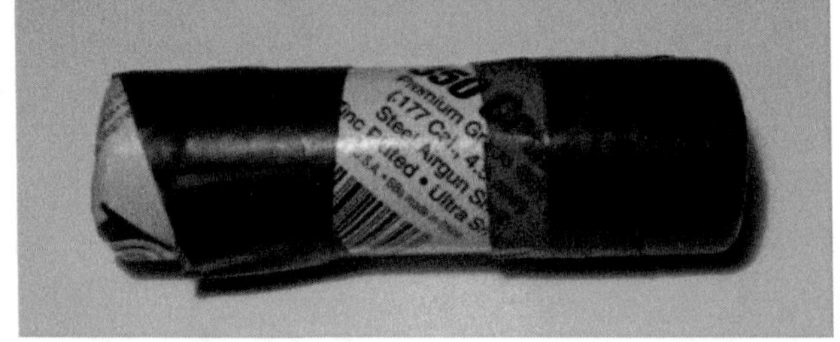

Figure 48: Tube of 350 BBs, unopened, weighs just under 5 ounces. Two tubes fit snuggly side by side in the trailer just ahead of the motor, and bring its weight up to 22 ounces.

Figure 49: First version of Big Mack, completed.

Bargain Basement Big Mack

This project builds a Big Mack on a budget aimed at keeping total cost below $60. How well that succeeds depends on a modeler's success at finding used parts for the project, as the author did. A broken Atlas trolley (Figure 50) was found at a TCA meeting for twenty dollars. It did not run and had a badly cracked body on one side, but as expected, the motors, axles, wheels and pickups were fine: it was the electronics that were damaged.

An Atlas trolley does not have to be the "donor unit" in this project. What is needed is *any O-gauge unit* with:

- Swiveling trucks with two axles each, with the ideal wheelbase = 1.25 – 1.5 inches.
- Wheels 3/4 to 7/8 inch in diameter at the flange where they roll on the rail.
- At least one truck powered, preferably by a motor mounted low.

The Atlas trolley shown in Figure 50 met all these criteria. So did several non-running diesel switchers found at the same meeting, but they cost from two to ten dollars more.

The trolley's four axles will provide all four axles of the converted Big Mack.

The trolley was disassembled and everything but its chassis and the powered truck (it had just one) set aside. The swivel truck's wires were cut and was removed from the chassis. The four wires from it were tested with a multi-meter to determine which was which: center-pickup lead, outer-rail pickup lead, and the two leads to the motor. The motor was tested with eight volts of DC power to it, and ran well, as expected. (the author's experience is that very few non-running locos with can motors have a bad motor.).

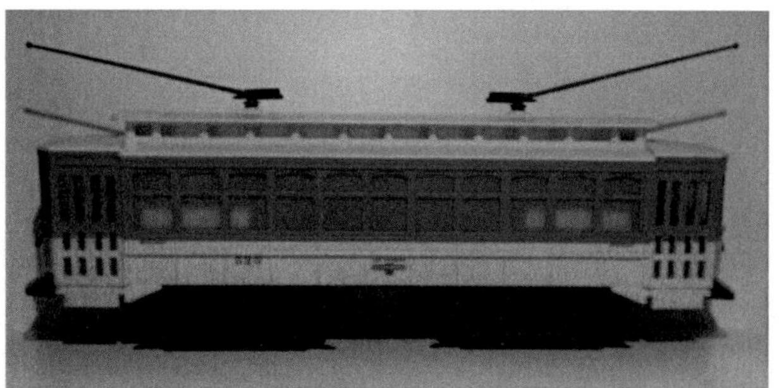

Figure 50: Atlas trolley parts donor looks good in this photo, but was a non-runner, with a large crack in the body and broken windows on the other side.

Figure 51: The truck from the trolley was removed and tested. The chassis was trimmed as described in text shown here.

The chassis was trimmed of all projections above its floor and cut so it was a mere platform projecting a bit over the edges of the truck (Figure 51): the truck swivels under this remaining piece of the trolley chassis. This "power platform" will be mounted in the trailer and will drive the entire truck. Whatever it lacks in power compared to the much larger motor used in the previous Big Mack, it will make up in having, a) two powered axles, and b) a swiveling truck under the rear of the trailer, which will drastically cut rolling friction through curves. It will run nearly as well.

The other, non-powered truck is disassembled and its two axles taken to be used in the tractor.

Tractor is made first . . .

The New Ray tractor can be converted in the same way that tractor in Chilly Mack was: new, flanged wheels and center pickups can be mounted on the original model's chassis, *if and only if those wheels are at least 7/8 inch in diameter* – that is, the size of the 'Streets school bus wheels. If an owner chooses to use wheels and axles of that size, a conversion using the New Ray chassis can be done. Again, since the chassis is plastic, outer-rail connectors and wiring have to be installed but the conversion is otherwise like that covered earlier.

But the trolley's wheels are only ¾ inch diameter, and that 1/16 inch difference in radius makes a big difference in what fits and what doesn't. If mounted in the New Ray plastic chassis, even if everything possible is done to make proper clearances, the chassis sits too close to the road. There is not enough room underneath the chassis for the center pickups to completely travel through their range: they bind or hold the tractor's wheels up off the rails. A new, scratch-build chassis has to be made, as shown in Figure 52 and described below.

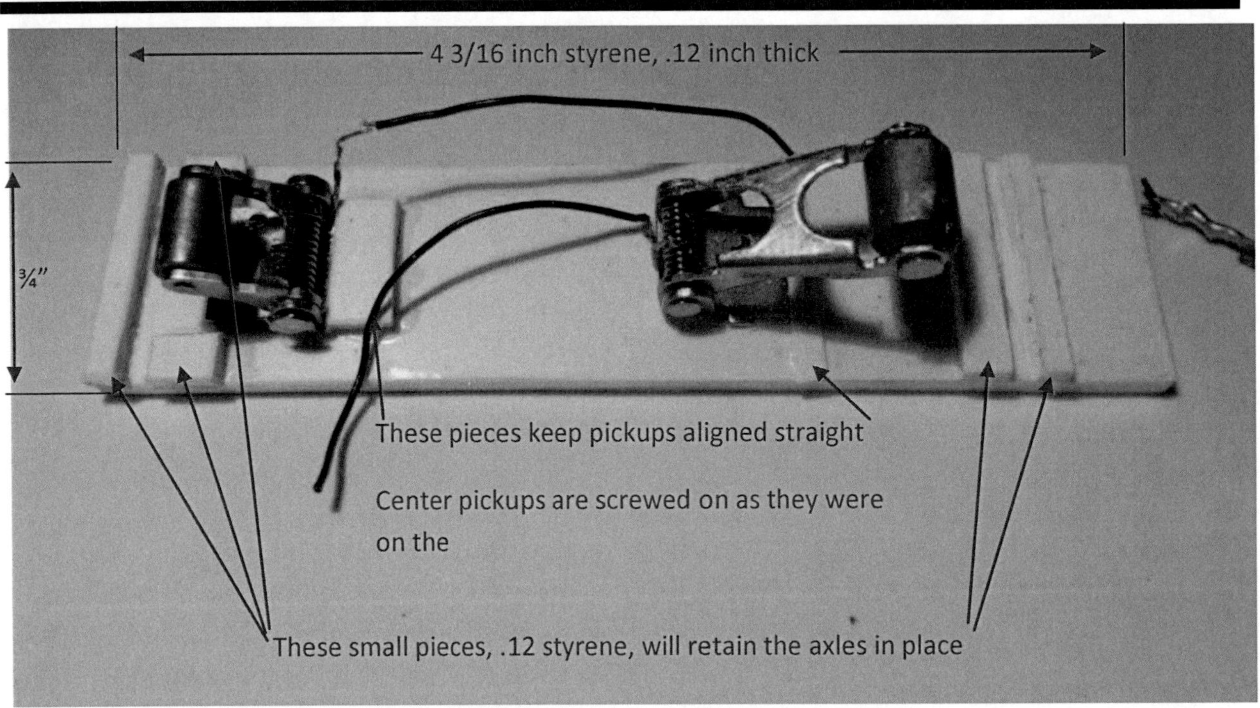

Figure 52: New chassis must be built for the tractor if using the trolley's wheels.

Step 1: The new chassis is made of styrene sheet that is .125 (1/8 inch) thick, beginning with a rectangle 4 3/16 by 3.4 inch thick. Figure 52 shows the underside of this chassis while under construction. In order for the center pickups to have sufficient room to operate, the axles must be mounted on the *underside* of the chassis. The figure shows small pieces glued in place to hold the axles. Wheelbase here is 3 3/8 inches.

Two center pickups are mounted on the underside of the chassis, so that their rollers are as close to the axles as possible without contacting them. These were in the author's spare parts box and came from cabooses, a Each is mounted with one screw (as they were originally on whatever they were on). Thus they could twist in place: small pieces of styrene are glued alongside their frame to prevent that.

Figure 53: New chassis from underside when more complete. See text for details.

Step 2: Figure 53 shows the chassis from the underside with the wheels in place. The wheels and axles used are from the trolley. The front axle has have been widened using two fiber washers per wheel in order to fill the front fenders sufficiently side to side – see Chapter 2 for details on how that is done. The rear axle has been widened with one metal washer added per side.

Thin copper wire is wrapped twice around each axle and soldered as shown in Figure 54 to make power leads from these axles. The figure shows the lead in the middle of the axle, but once done it is pushed fully to one side. In the figure one can see the leads coming out from between the inside edge of the wheels and the edge of the chassis.

Both axles are held in place with pieces of plastic cemented in place. Should they ever need to be removed the plastic is just cut off and can be replaced.

Figure 54: Homemade outer-rail pickup from the axle works very well.

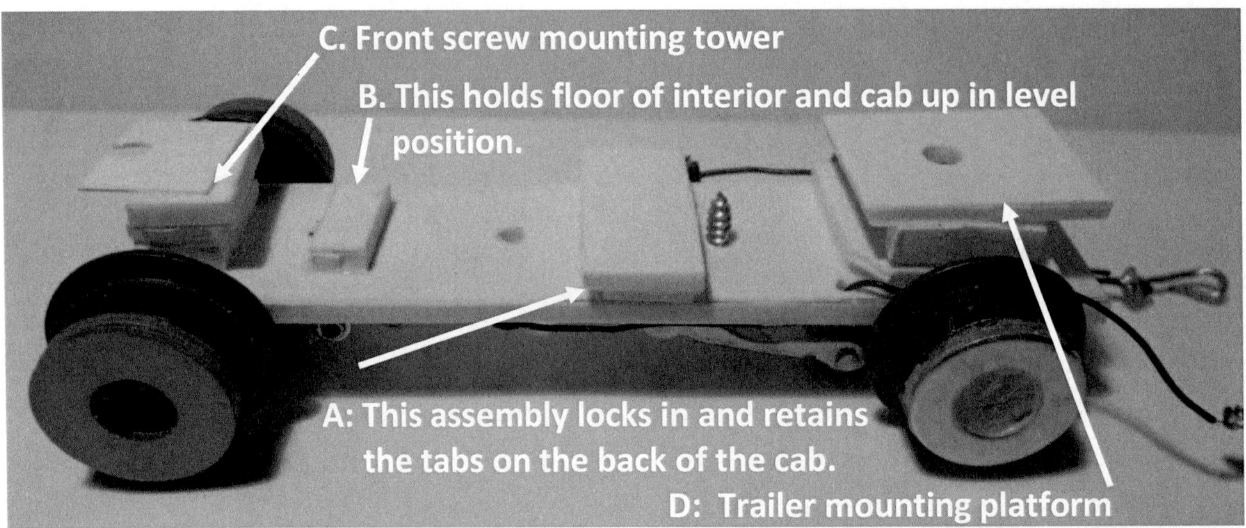

Figure 55: New chassis from topside when done.

Step 3: The cab is held by hand on the chassis with its front wheels at the right point, front to back, in the fenders, to determine the location for the retaining lip assembly, item A in the figure, that will hold the tabs on the back of cab (see Figure 55). With that in place, piece B is made and glued in place, so the cab sites level when its tabs are held by piece A. The front mounting tower, B, is then made so that it can grasp a screw in the cab's front mounting hole (Figure 55). The cab is held on with two screws (Figure 56) and the result looks like Figure 57.

Figure 56: Cab mounting screws.

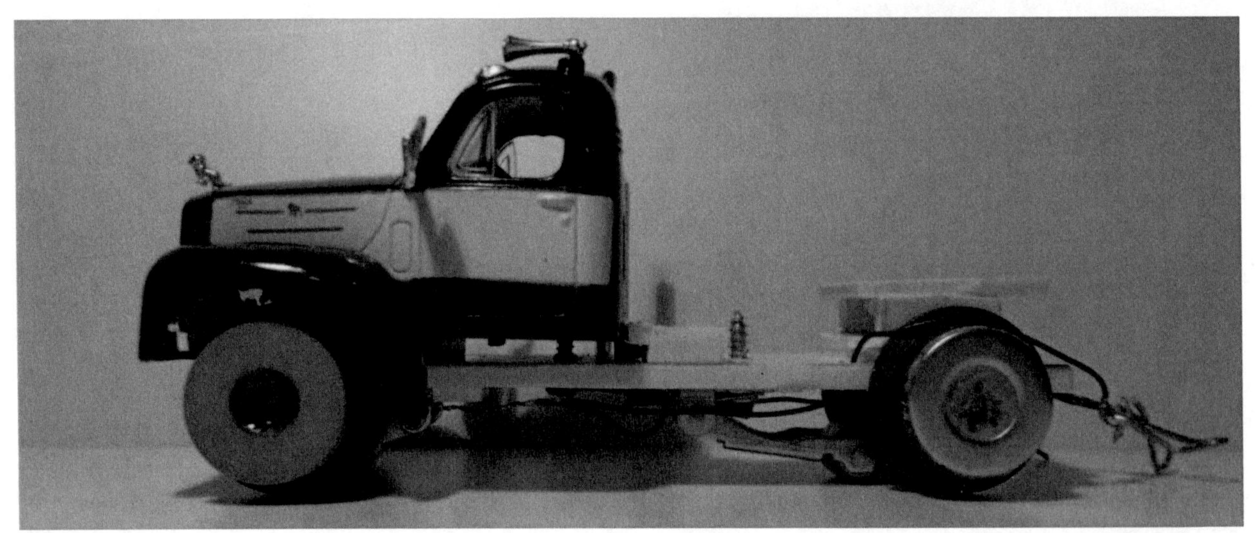

Figure 57: Chassis is done, with cab mounted, but before modeling details are completed.

Figure 57 shows the tractor before detailing and modeling details are completed, but with all elements of the conversion complete. It was tested: this tractor is unpowered but it was put on a 'Streets road and checked to make sure it rolled well and that the electrical pickup on both axles and both center pickups worked properly. Once tested, it was put aside until later.

Powered Trailer

The New Ray trailer was wrapped in painter's tape to protect it and to keep its doors in place during work on it. It was disassembled and all parts except the trailer body put aside. A new chassis was made out of flat .10 styrene sheet (Figure 58). The area shown in red outline was cut out of it, and the power platform mounted. (Figure 59). For that, the flat portion of the original trolley chassis was mounted on the upper (inside) side of the chassis and screwed on. The two-axle truck is then inserted (while

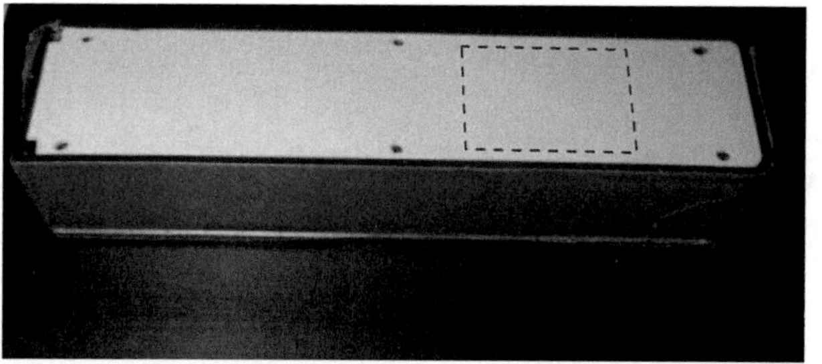

Figure 58: Trailer body is used as a template to size a new chassis to fit it.

sideways) into its mounting slotted hole from underneath and turned 90° to hold it in place (as it was on the original trolley). Its wires were brought forward to two power posts made as described earlier (see Chilly Mack project). See Figure 59.

Finessing Overhang: Modelers have a choice of exactly where they mount the truck in the chassis. Just as in the real world, one can move the axles of the trailer forward or toward the back to adjust how it behaves in turns. If farther back, the trailer has a relatively small rear

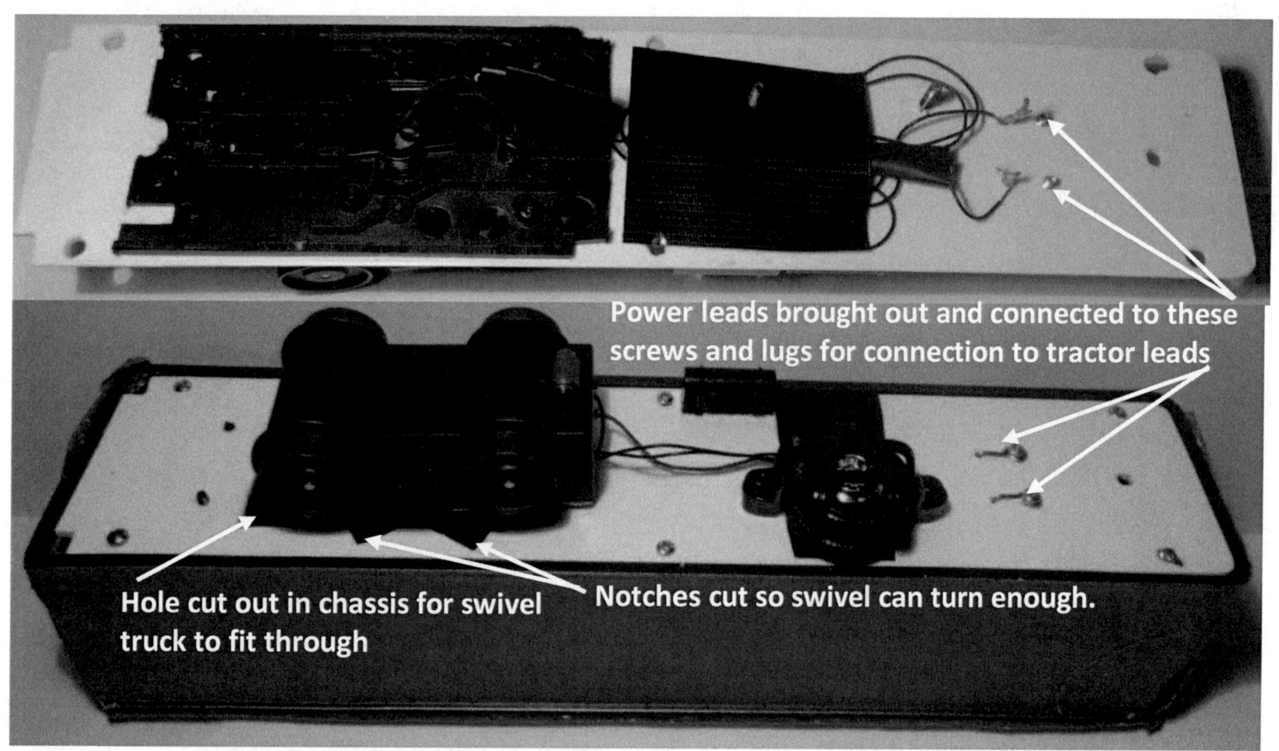

Figure 59: Big Mack Trailer converted with trolley swivel truck.

overhang on curves, but a lot of intrusion into the inside of its lane at the middle or a curve. If positioned farther forward, there is more rear overhang and less lane-intrusion (Figure 60).

The tractor and trailer are joined by placing the trailer's peg – just a bolt inserted through the hole that can be seen in Figure 59, into the tractor's mounting platform hole and attaching the two power leads to the lugs on the bottom of the trailer.

The entire rig was tested on the layout and it ran well. The basic fourteen-wheel conversion is done.

Modeling details are completed by painting all exposed styrene sheet flat black, painting and detailed the wheels, adding fuel tanks, etc., (all parts taken from the New Ray model when disassembled) and painting marker lights, etc. (Figure 61).

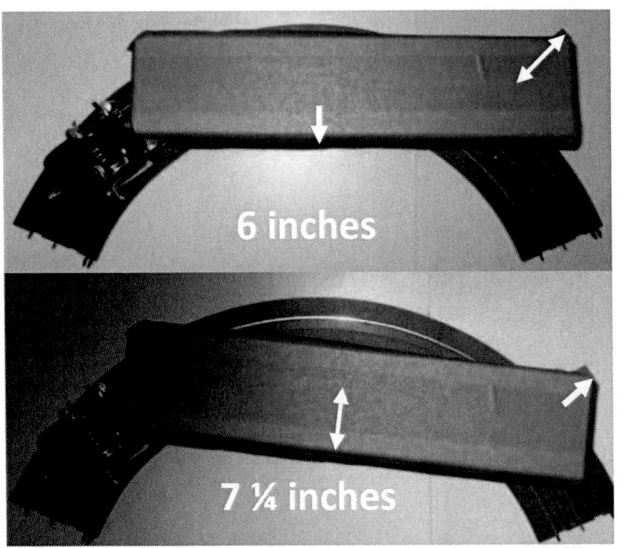

Figure 60: A lot of "stick out" on curves is unavoidable with this trailer, shown here on D-16 curves, but the positioning of the rear axles determines *where* it occurs. Top, distance from tractor's rear axle to swivel point is 6.0 inches. Bottom, distance is 7 ¼ inches. It is up to the modeler to determine how they want the trailer set up.

Figure 61: Bargain Big Mack 14-wheeler on the road. Yes, it has wheels that look slightly too small, but a small change about to made (next page) will help – a lot.

18-Wheel Variation

Given the slightly small tire size on the model, a third axle does give the whole rig a more impressive and balanced appearance. Besides, if 10 or 14 wheels are good, 18 must be better!

A trailing axle as shown in Chapter 7, Figure 18 could have been easily added to the tractor. However, that type of axle has to trail far enough back so it can swing in curves, and allowing it room to do so means creating a small gap – an additional scale foot or more – between it and axle ahead of it. The method used here allows more realistic, closer spacing. The tractor holds its third axle rather loosely in a small plastic projection glued to the rear of its frame. This keeps it parallel to the tractor's other axles but allows it to slide sideways in curves (Figure 62). This does look bizarre as the tractor-trailer rounds a sharp curve, but *any* solution that works well will.

Figure 62: The tractor's third axle stays perpendicular to the chassis axis but can slide sideway in curves. It looks a bit strange as it does, but works well and allows tight back-to-back spacing of the two axles.

Figure 62 shows how the bracket is shaped and attached. It constrains the axle to stay parallel to the other two axles, but allows it up-and-down room so that the axle can rest its entire weight on the rails. As can be seen, it does not need to be fancy or precision-made: that shown works perfectly. It was painted flat black to "disappear" it, like the rest of the plastic chassis, after the photo was taken.

Figure 63: Bargain Big Mack 18-wheeler on the road. With the added axle it looks good.

Other Tractor Trailers

Figures 64 through 66 show three more big rigs that have been converted to 'Streets. In company with the Chilly Mack shown earlier they are the author's four favorites and run on the layout most every day. All are 1:50 scale in keeping with the recommendations given at the end of Chapter 5. In all cases the motor is in the trailer and driving its leading axle.

The silver and black corgi International cab-over is one of a pair of Corgi tractors bought as a set – the other is the Kenworth shown in Chapter 5's Figure 15. It is towing a scratch-built plastic trailer.

The die-cast SpecCast UP big model shown in Figure 64 was a bargain at $47.19. Its trailer is also scratch-built but of wood with printed card-stock sides. Note the wheels and their trim: they contribute a lot to the truck's look.

The Corgi Greyhound Van Lines rig is a lovely and very heavy model converted in a fashion *identical* to that used on the Corgi Carolina ten-wheeler covered earlier. The author left it with just three axles, as it and the Chilly Mack are a good contrast to the eighteen wheelers.

Figure 64: Corgi 1:50 International cab-over tractor with sleeper is pulling a plastic scratch-built trailer.

Figure 65: This SpecCast UP eighteen-wheeler is the author's favorite, not just because it is Union Pacific, but because the cab doors open and close and the model still has its model diesel motor under the opening hood.

Figure 66: Corgi 1:50 Greyhound ten-wheeler is handsome, very heavy (26 oz.) and runs extremely well.

Index